SUCCEED IN...

Maths

SUCCEED IN...
Maths

Tony Fisher

ARCTURUS

This edition published in 2012 by Arcturus Publishing Limited
26/27 Bickels Yard, 151–153 Bermondsey Street,
London SE1 3HA

ISBN: 978-1-84193-180-7
CH000728EN
Supplier 16, Date 0312, Print run 1784

Printed in Singapore

CONTENTS

CONTENTS

CONTENTS

CONTENTS

ABOUT THIS BOOK

This revision guide covers content that you would expect to find in **Foundation** and **Higher** tier GCSE Mathematics examinations and also the Scottish Standard and Intermediate level examinations.

The guide is divided into four main areas:
- Number
- Algebra
- Shape, Space and Measures
- Handling Data

Each area is divided into topics that are subdivided into small sections. Each section contains facts, examples and explanations designed to refresh your memory, together with examiners' tips to help you do better in your exam.

At the end of each topic there is a test that you should try in order to check your understanding. Answers to the tests are at the back of the book.

UNDERSTANDING THE LEVELS
Sections in the guide are labelled to help you measure your progress.

Section labels

4	Level 4 is basic level. Everybody sitting the examination will be expected to know this information.
3	Level 3 is competent level. Candidates at this level can display an understanding of the principles in question and are able to complete simple tasks based on these principles.
2	Level 2 is intermediate level. At this level, candidates are able to perform competent mathematics at a standard that would be expected on the higher level examination paper.
1	Level 1 is high level. At this standard, candidates demonstrate an excellent use and understanding of mathematics and they would expect to score well on a higher level examination paper.

CALCULATORS

As the GCSE examination contains both a calculator and a non-calculator paper, both kinds of questions are covered in this book.

You will require a **scientific calculator** for use in the calculator paper.
There are many sorts of these; the best thing to do is to get your own and become familiar with the way it works. The calculator sequences given in this guide are based on those using direct algebraic logic or visually perfect algebraic logic. If you don't have a calculator like this, you will need to look at the instruction booklet for your calculator.

To prepare properly for your exam, you will need to practise both calculator and non-calculator methods. To help do this, use a calculator only for those questions that are accompanied by a calculator symbol in the book.

Two sorts of algebra are tested and feature in the book:
- Manipulative algebra: this involves using and manipulating letter symbols
- Non-manipulative algebra: this mainly involves graphs

It is important to remember that during your exam, you will be tested on your key maths skills. These will not have been topics that you have specifically covered in class. They are the skills that you are supposed to develop throughout the course by doing all the work in the syllabus.

These skills are:
- Representing: this means understanding a situation or a problem and selecting the maths to solve it.
- Analysing: this means to use mathematical reasoning and appropriate mathematical procedures.
- Interpreting and evaluating: this means being able to justify your results, to be able to critique findings and to spot patterns in data.

Keep these skills in mind when you are looking at the questions.

MAKING THE MOST OF YOUR KNOWLEDGE

Very few people come out of an exam without making a silly error that might have been avoided with better exam technique; this might mean the difference between one grade and the next.

Here are a few tips that might help you to avoid losing marks in this way:
- Take your time. There is enough time to read the whole of the exam paper and plan your approach before you start answering questions
- As soon as the exam starts, write down all the formulae you have learnt
- Read questions as many times as it takes to understand them
- Follow instructions in the question fully. For example, if the question says, 'You **must** show your method', you will get no marks if you don't – even if you get the answer right!
- You do not have to answer the questions in order. Start with questions **you** find easiest
- Don't get bogged down on a question you can't do. Leave it and come back to it
- Check your answers. Possible ways of doing this are:
  - Doing the question again!
  - Working from your answer back to what is given in the question – this is particularly useful for some algebra topics
  - Making sure that the answer is sensible
- You are told how many marks a question is worth on the answer line. You will get method marks for most questions that are worth more than 1 mark (even if you get the wrong answer). So make sure you **show your method**. This means writing down all the calculations that you do to get your final answer. Try and show these logically and neatly
- Make sure your calculator is in degrees!
- Always make sure you add the units (if necessary) to your answer
- Be as accurate as you can and take a moment to think things through if you aren't sure
- Crossed out work will be marked **if it can be read**. So cross out work neatly and **don't use Tipp-Ex!**

REVISION

Revision is about looking back at work you already understand and making sure it is fresh in your mind. It is about making sure that:

- You can recall maths you could do easily in class ten or so weeks ago
- You remember formulae like $A = \pi r^2$, or facts like how many pounds there are in a kilogram or what special maths words like 'reciprocal' and terms like 'product of prime factors' mean

This guide will help you revise, but you might need more help – perhaps from a maths textbook, a teacher or a friend – if you are trying to understand and learn something that is new to you.

DOING REVISION

- To revise maths you need to do maths, so using a pencil and paper when you are working through this guide is essential. Using this guide you can do maths in several ways:
  - When you are sure you understand the worked examples, cover them up and try to do them yourself. Don't forget to show the method and check how well you did
  - Do the test questions trying to produce model examination answers, including method. Don't forget to check your answers
  - Repeat questions (a few days later) and try to produce better examination answers. This will help keep things fresh in your mind and is a good tactic to help check understanding
  - Get hold of as many past exam papers as you can and work on them alongside this guide
- Keep your revision work safe and secure. Use it for your final revision closer to the exam
- Do revision between the non-calculator and the calculator paper, focusing on those topics that did not appear on the non-calculator paper
- Do your revision in a planned way and in short bursts of no more than between 20 to 30 minutes at a time. Do this at least 5 or 6 times a week for at least 5 or 6 weeks before the exam
- Do not spend a long time on stuff you know really well. Just refresh your memory and move on
- Don't panic if you find it hard to understand something. Spend no more than 5 minutes on trying to sort it out by yourself. If you still have a problem put it aside and get help from a teacher or a friend
- Revision will make a difference – the more you do the greater the difference it will make!

Good luck and good practising!

Section 1: Number
1. CALCULATING WITH WHOLE NUMBERS AND DECIMALS

4

Multiplying and dividing whole numbers

To find the product of two numbers multiply them together.

e.g.1   Find the product of 528 and 43

METHOD   The Box Method $528 \times 43 = (500 + 20 + 8) \times (40 + 3)$

×	500	20	8
40	500 × 40 20 000	20 × 40 800	8 × 40 320
3	500 × 3 1 500	20 × 3 60	8 × 3 24

$528 \times 40 = 21\ 120$ $20\ 000 + 800 + 320$
$528 \times 3 = \underline{\ \ 1\ 584}\ +$ $1\ 500 + 60 + 24$
$\underline{22\ 704}$ $21\ 120 + 1584$

ANSWER   22 704

METHOD   Long Multiplication Method $528 \times 43 = 528 \times (40 + 3)$
$= 528 \times 40 + 528 \times 3$

$$\begin{array}{r} 528 \\ \underline{43} \times \\ 21\ 120 \\ \underline{1\ 584} + \\ \underline{22\ 704} \end{array}$$
528×40
528×3
$21\ 120 + 1584$

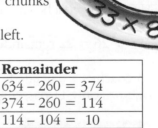

ANSWER   22 704

e.g.2   Work out $634 \div 26$

METHOD   The 'Chunking' Method – Take off 'chunks' of 10×26 until none remain.
Then work out the number of 26s left.

26s		Remainder
10	10 × 26 = 260	634 − 260 = 374
10	10 × 26 = 260	374 − 260 = 114
4	4 × 26 = 104	114 − 104 = 10
Total 24		10

ANSWER   24 remainder 10

You can speed up the method by taking off larger 'chunks'.

26s		Remainder
20	20 × 26 = 520	634 − 520 = 114
4	4 × 26 = 104	114 − 104 = 10
Total 24		10

METHOD   Long Division Method

$$26\overline{)634}$$

600 ÷ 26 = 20 remainder 80
Put 2 in the 10s column

$$26\overline{)6\overset{2}{3}4}$$

80 + 34 (634 − 600) = 114

$$26\overline{)6\ 3\ ^{11}4}\quad\overset{2\quad4}{}\ \text{remainder 10}$$

114 ÷ 26 = 4 remainder 10
Put 4 in the units column

ANSWER   24 remainder 10

4 *Solving problems*

e.g.1   A theatre contains 45 rows of 36 seats.
There are 1233 people seated in the theatre.
How many seats are empty?

METHOD   Total number of seats = 1620   45 × 36

ANSWER   So 387 seats are empty.   1620 − 1233

e.g.2   A shelf is 583 mm wide and videos are 26 mm wide.
How many videos fit on a shelf?

METHOD   583 ÷ 26 = 22 remainder 11

ANSWER   22 videos fit on the shelf with an 11 mm space.

e.g.3   583 people go on a trip in coaches each carrying 26 passengers.
How many coaches are needed?

METHOD   583 ÷ 26 = 22 remainder 11

ANSWER   23 coaches are needed;
one has only 11 passengers.

> **Examiner's tips**
> - *Show your method by writing
> down what calculations you do.*
> - *Think carefully about how you
> interpret the remainder in a
> division problem.*

4

More than one operation

When doing sums involving more than one operation remember the following rules:

- Do calculations inside brackets (or separated by a division line) first.
- Do multiplication and division before addition and subtraction.
- Otherwise, calculate from left to right.

Calculations with brackets can be done on a scientific calculator, using the keys.

> **Remember**
> Do × and ÷
> before + and –

e.g.1 $2 + 10 \div 2$
$= 2 + 5$ do $10 \div 2$ first
$= 7$

e.g.2 $(2 + 10) \div 2$
$= 12 \div 2$ do calculation in brackets first
$= 6$

e.g.3 $(6 + 3 \times 4) \div 2$
$= (6 + 12) \div 2$ do calculations in brackets
first and 3×4 before
adding the 6
$= 9$ $18 \div 2$

Calculator

e.g.4 $6 + \dfrac{7 + 5}{2 + 1}$
$= 6 + {}^{12}/_3$ do $7 + 5$ <u>and</u> $2 + 1$ first; then do ${}^{12}/_3$ before adding 6
$= 6 + 4$
$= 10$

Calculator

DO THIS
Check each of the results in this table.

Calculation	Scientific calculator	Basic calculator
$2 - 5 + 7$	4 ✓	4 ✓
$3 \times 10 \div 2$	15 ✓	15 ✓
$8 \times 5 - 10$	30 ✓	30 ✓
$8 \times 5 - 3 \times 5$	25 ✓	185 ✗
$15 + 10 \div 5$	17 ✓	5 ✗
$5 \times (4 + 3)$	35 ✓	–

Make sure you can work out the correct answer without a calculator.

Try to use the memory buttons to get **all** answers correct with a basic calculator.

CALCULATING WITH WHOLE NUMBERS AND DECIMALS

4

Adding and subtracting decimals

When adding and subtracting decimals:

- Write numbers in columns with the decimal points lined up.
- Put in zeros to give each number the same number of decimal places.

e.g.1 $54.67 + 147.9$

METHOD
$$
\begin{array}{r}
54.67 \\
147.90 + \\
\hline
202.57 \\
\hline
\end{array}
$$

> **Remember**
> The number of decimal places is the number of digits after the decimal point.

e.g.2 $18.3 - 3.78$

METHOD
$$
\begin{array}{r}
18.30 \\
3.78 - \\
\hline
14.52 \\
\hline
\end{array}
$$

DO THIS
Check the answer to $18.3 - 3.78$ by working out $14.52 + 3.78$

4

Multiplying and dividing decimals by 10, 100, 1000, …

To multiply by 10, 100, 1000, … move the digits one, two, three, … places to the left.
To divide by 10, 100, 1000, … move the digits one, two, three, … places to the right.

e.g.1 $14.2 \times 10 = 142$ digits move 1 place left

e.g.2 $0.0142 \times 100 = 1.42$ digits move 2 places left

e.g.3 $1.42 \times 1000 = 1420$ digits move 3 places left

e.g.4 $12 \div 10 = 1.2$ digits move 1 place right

e.g.5 $0.12 \div 100 = 0.0012$ digits move 2 places right

e.g.6 $120 \div 1000 = 0.12$ digits move 3 places right

> **Remember**
> The decimal point comes after the units digit so, for example, 142 is the same as 142.0

4 *Multiplying and dividing by multiples of 10*

e.g.1
14.2×20
$= 14.2 \times 10 \times 2$
$= 142 \times 2$
$= 284$ to $\times$ by 20, first $\times$ by 10 then $\times$ by 2

e.g.2
$14.2 \div 20$
$= 14.2 \div 10 \div 2$
$= 1.42 \div 2$
$= 0.71$ to $\div$ by 20, first $\div$ by 10 then $\div$ by 2

e.g.3
0.12×400
$= 0.12 \times 100 \times 4$
$= 12 \times 4$
$= 48$ to $\times$ by 400, first $\times$ by 100 then $\times$ by 4

e.g.4
$1.2 \div 400$
$= 1.2 \div 100 \div 4$
$= 0.012 \div 4$
$= 0.003$ to $\div$ by 400, first $\div$ by 100 then $\div$ by 4

4 *Multiplying and dividing by a number between 0 and 1*

When multiplying and dividing by a number between 0 and 1 try to change the calculation to one where you multiply or divide by a whole number.

$a \times b$ (where b is between 0 and 1)

If b has 1 decimal place change the calculation to $(a \div 10) \times (b \times 10)$
If b has 2 decimal places change the calculation to $(a \div 100) \times (b \times 100)$
If b has 3 decimal places change the calculation to $(a \div 1000) \times (b \times 1000)$
So $\div$ the first number by 10, 100, 1000, … and $\times$ the second number by 10, 100, 1000, …

e.g.1
23×0.2 $\div$ 1st number by 10 and $\times$ 2nd number by 10 to give
$2.3 \times 2 = 4.6$

e.g.2
400×0.08 $\div$ 1st number by 100 and $\times$ 2nd number by 100 to give
$4 \times 8 = 32$

$a \div b$ (where b is between 0 and 1)

If b has 1 decimal place change the calculation to $(a \div 10) \times (b \times 10)$
If b has 2 decimal places change the calculation to $(a \div 100) \times (b \times 100)$
If b has 3 decimal places change the calculation to $(a \div 1000) \times (b \times 1000)$
So $\times$ the first and the second number by 10, 100, 1000, …

e.g.3
$120 \div 0.3$ $\times$ both numbers by 10 to give
$1200 \div 3 = 400$

e.g.4
$200 \div 0.04$ $\times$ both numbers by 100 to give
$20\,000 \div 4 = 5000$

Use a calculator for questions 5 and 11 only.

1. Work out the value of:
   (a) 324×37 (b) 459×38
   (c) $525 \div 24$ (d) $763 \div 31$

2. Ben has 16 boxes each containing 40 marbles and 14 boxes each containing 25 marbles.
How many marbles does Ben have?

3. A roll of paper is 850 cm long.
How many strips of paper of length 32 cm can be cut from the roll?

4. Work out:
   (a) $3 + 4 \times 7$ (b) $(3 + 4) \times 7$
   (c) $9 \div 3 + 3 \times 5$ (d) $16 \times 12 - 6 \times 12$
   (e) $\dfrac{3 + 8 \times 9}{8 + 7}$ (f) $\dfrac{125}{7 + 6 \times 3}$

5. Use your calculator to check your answers to question 4.

6. Tom, Sam and Matthew put their money together to buy a football.
Tom contributes £3.70, Sam £2.95 and Matthew 143 p.
The football costs £9.99.
How much more do they need?

7. Work out:
   (a) 0.23×100 (b) 0.037×10
   (c) 1000×0.3 (d) 6.2×100
   (e) $324 \div 100$ (f) $7.53 \div 10$
   (g) $725 \div 1000$ (h) $7.6 \div 100$

8. Work out the value of:
   (a) 0.04×200 (b) $12 \div 300$
   (c) $2.5 \div 500$ (d) 0.6×200
   (e) $60 \div 0.3$ (f) 120×0.02
   (g) $0.4 \div 0.008$ (h) 4000×0.03
   (i) $25 \div 0.2$ (j) 0.4×0.2
   (k) 25×0.2 (l) $0.04 \div 0.2$

9. (a) Explain why $24 \div 0.06$ has the same value as $2400 \div 6$.
   (b) Explain why 20×0.3 has the same value as 2×3.

10. Work out the value of:
   (a) $\dfrac{40 \times 0.2}{0.04}$ (b) $\dfrac{360 \times 0.04}{0.18 + 0.12}$

11. Use your calculator to check your answers to question 10.

12. You are told that $213 \times 58 = 12\,354$.
Write down the values of:
(a) 2.13×58 **(b)** 0.213×5.8
(c) 0.213×580 **(d)** $123.54 \div 213$
(e) $12\,354 \div 2.13$ **(f)** $12.354 \div 0.58$

13. (a) Comics are stacked in piles 80 cm high.
Each comic is 0.4 cm thick.
How many comics are in 12 piles?
(b) A magazine is 0.6 cm thick.
There are 3200 magazines stacked in 40 equal piles.
How high is one pile?

2. APPROXIMATING AND ESTIMATING

4 Rounding

143.702 may be rounded to different levels of accuracy …

143.70	the nearest hundredth
143.7	the nearest tenth
144	the nearest unit
140	the nearest ten
100	the nearest hundred

Remember
Rounded values are approximations
of accurate values.
143.7 is more accurate than 144 and
143.70 is more accurate
than 143.7

Examiner's tip
*In an exam, you might be asked to write an answer to a certain level
of accuracy, so make sure you do it.*

APPROXIMATING AND ESTIMATING

4

Rounding a number to a given number of decimal places (d.p.)

Rounding to 1 decimal place is the same as rounding to the nearest tenth
Rounding to 2 decimal places is the same as rounding to the nearest hundredth

EXAMPLES

Accurate value	Level of accuracy	Rounded value	
2.764	1 d.p.	2.8	2.8 is closer to 2.764 than 2.7
0.62345	2 d.p.	0.62	0.62 is closer to 0.62345 than 0.63
3.65	1 d.p.	3.7	**round up** to the higher value

Remember
3.65 is exactly halfway between 3.6 and 3.7.
The rule in situations like this is to round up
to the higher value.

2

Rounding a number to a given number of significant figures (s.f.)

Numbers can also be rounded using significant figures.
The first significant figure in a number is the digit with the greatest place value.
The second significant digit is the digit with the next greatest place value and so on.

These numbers all have **1** significant figure   3, 3000, 3 000 000, 0.003, 0.000 000 3, …
These numbers all have **2** significant figures   32, 32 000, 0.032, …
These numbers all have **3** significant figures   324, 324 000, 0.00324, …

EXAMPLES

Accurate value	Level of accuracy	Rounded value	
2.815	1 s.f.	3	nearest unit
0.07634	1 s.f.	0.08	nearest hundredth
3650	1 s.f.	4000	nearest thousand
2.815	3 s.f.	2.82	nearest hundredth
0.076 34	3 s.f.	0.0763	nearest ten thousandth
3676	3 s.f.	3680	nearest ten

4

Suitable degrees of accuracy

In **one** exam question you will be told to write your answer to a suitable degree of accuracy.
Do this by choosing the degree of accuracy used for the values given in the question.

e.g.1   Find the area of the trapezium shown in the diagram.

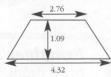

Area = 3.8586 cm²   ½ × (2.76 + 4.32) × 1.09

The lengths on the trapezium are given to an accuracy of 3 s.f.

To a suitable degree of accuracy the area = 3.86 cm²

3

Approximating to make estimates of calculations

To estimate the value of a calculation:

- Round the numbers in the calculation to 1 significant figure.
- Calculate the estimate using the rounded numbers.

The phrase 'the right order of magnitude' means 'about the right value'.

e.g.1

$$\frac{9.89 \times 284.3}{21.3}$$

$$\frac{10 \times 300}{20}$$ Round all numbers to 1 s.f.

$3000 \div 20 = 150$

So the estimate is 150

e.g.2

$$\frac{18.5 \times 5.3^2}{0.197}$$

$$\frac{20 \times 5^2}{0.2}$$ Round all numbers to 1 s.f.

$20 \times 25 \div 0.2$

$500 \div 0.2$

$5000 \div 2 = 2500$ Multiply both numbers by 10

So the estimate is 2500

e.g.3

$$\sqrt{\frac{2.07}{0.039}}$$

$$\sqrt{\frac{2}{0.04}}$$ Round all numbers to 1 s.f.

$\sqrt{(2 \div 0.04)}$

$\sqrt{(200 \div 4)}$ Multiply both numbers by 100

$\sqrt{50}$

So the estimate is 7

Examiner's tips
Make sure you do the rounding before you do the calculation. It's easier that way round!

APPROXIMATING AND ESTIMATING

Upper and lower bounds

When a quantity is rounded then its accurate value lies between two limits. These limits are called the upper and lower bounds.

If a quantity, v, is rounded to the nearest x, then:

- The lower bound of v is $v - \frac{1}{2}x$
- The upper bound of v is $v + \frac{1}{2}x$

So the accurate value of v lies between $v - \frac{1}{2}x$ and $v + \frac{1}{2}x$

e.g.1

Tom is 150 cm tall to the nearest 10 cm.

The lower bound = 145 cm $150 - \frac{1}{2}$ of 10
This is the smallest value that when rounded to the nearest 10 cm
= 150 cm.

The upper bound = 155 cm $150 + \frac{1}{2}$ of 10
155 cm is called the upper bound even though the largest value that rounds to 150 cm is 154.999 999 9… cm.

The number line shows **all possible** values of Tom's accurate height.

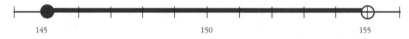

The hollow circle shows that the upper bound is **not** a possible value for Tom's accurate height. All possible values of Tom's height can also be written as $145 \leq$ Tom's height < 155.

e.g.2

Sam beat Ben in a 100 m race.
Both Sam and Ben were timed at 14.52 seconds to the nearest 0.01 seconds.

Lower bound of 14.52 seconds = 14.515 seconds $14.52 - \frac{1}{2}$ of 0.01
Upper bound of 14.52 seconds = 14.525 seconds $14.52 + \frac{1}{2}$ of 0.01

So Sam ran **closer** to the lower bound than Ben.

Calculating with bounds

e.g.1

$p = 7.5$ to 2 significant figures and $q = 3$ to 1 significant figure

	Lower bound (LB)	**Upper bound (UB)**
p	7.45	7.55
q	2.5	3.5
$p + q$	7.45 + 2.5	7.55 + 3.5
	LB + LB	UB + UB
$p - q$	7.45 − 3.5	7.55 − 2.5
	LB − UB	UB − LB
$p \times q$	7.45 × 2.5	7.55 × 3.5
	LB × LB	UB × UB
$p \div q$	7.45 ÷ 3.5	7.55 ÷ 2.5
	LB ÷ UB	UB ÷ LB

e.g.2 The length and width of a room to the nearest cm are 4.55 m and 3.12 m.

	Lower bound (LB)	Upper bound (UB)
Length	4.545	4.555
Width	3.115	3.125

Lower bound of area = $4.545 \times 3.115 = 14.157\ 675$ LB × LB
Upper bound of area = $4.555 \times 3.125 = 14.234\ 375$ UB × UB

Examiner's tip
Show the bounds you are using clearly and do not round your answers.

Test 2

Use a calculator for questions 7 and 8.

1. Round these numbers to an accuracy of 1 decimal place.
    (a) 2.67 **(b)** 13.432 **(c)** 0.681
    (d) 3.651 **(e)** 123.55 **(f)** 0.734

Write down the number of significant figures in each rounded number.

2. Round these numbers to an accuracy of 2 decimal places.
    (a) 13.543 **(b)** 2.7465 **(c)** 123.561
    (d) 0.6753 **(e)** 12.6451 **(f)** 0.5555

Write down the number of significant figures in each rounded number.

3. **(a)** Round the numbers in question 1 to 1 significant figure.
    (b) Round the numbers in question 2 to 3 significant figures.

4. Use approximations to estimate the value of:
    (a) $\dfrac{4.9 \times 38.7}{21.2}$ **(b)** $\dfrac{7974 \times 21}{407}$

Show **all** your working.

5. Work out an approximate value of:
    (a) $\dfrac{21.076}{0.19 \times 2.1}$ **(b)** $\dfrac{0.39 \times 89.2}{0.58}$
    (c) $\dfrac{9.1 \times 10.2^2}{5.8^2 - 6.4}$ **(d)** $\dfrac{8.982}{0.042}$

Show **all** your working.

2 6. (a) A burger weighs 120 g to the nearest gram.
What is the lowest possible weight of the burger?
(b) Dan lives 400 metres from school correct to the nearest 10 metres.
What is the shortest possible distance that Dan walks to **and** from school in a
5-day week?

1 7. $p = 3.6$ and $q = 0.72$ both to an accuracy of 2 significant figures.
Calculate the lower and upper bounds of:
(a) $p + q$ **(b)** $p - q$
(c) $p \times q$ **(d)** $p \div q$

1 8. A square tile has a blue border surrounding a pink square.
The tile has length 500 mm to the nearest mm.
The pink square has length 400 mm to the nearest mm.

Calculate the lower and upper bounds of the area of the blue border.

CALCULATING WITH NEGATIVE NUMBERS

4

Adding and subtracting integers

An integer is a positive or negative whole number.
For example: 1, 2, 3, 4, … and ⁻1, ⁻2, ⁻3, ⁻4, … are integers.

Adding and subtracting integers can be thought of as movement on a number line.

-6 -5 -4 -3 -2 -1 0 1 2 3 4 5 6

EXAMPLES

Calculation	Start at	Move	Answer
$4 + 2$	4	2 right	6
⁻4 + 2	⁻4	2 right	⁻2
$4 - $⁻2	4	2 right	6
⁻4 − ⁻2	⁻4	2 right	⁻2
$4 + $⁻2	4	2 left	2
⁻4 + ⁻2	⁻4	2 left	⁻6
$4 - 2$	4	2 left	2
⁻4 − 2	⁻4	2 left	⁻6

> **Examiner's tip**
> *If you have to add
> or subtract integers
> draw a number
> line to help you.*

Remember
Move right for adding a positive (+) or subtracting a negative (–⁻)
Move left for subtracting a positive (–) or adding a negative (+⁻)

3 *Multiplying and dividing integers*

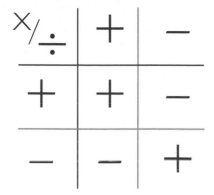

To multiply or divide integers:

- Multiply or divide the numbers.
- Use the rules in the table to decide whether the answer is positive or negative.

e.g.1	$2 \times {}^-3 = {}^-6$	$2 \times 3 = 6$	positive × negative is **negative**
e.g.2	${}^-2 \times {}^-3 = 6$	$2 \times 3 = 6$	negative × negative is **positive**
e.g.3	${}^-12 \div 4 = {}^-3$	$12 \div 4 = 3$	negative ÷ positive is **negative**
e.g.4	${}^-12 \div {}^-4 = 3$	$12 \div 4 = 3$	negative ÷ negative is **positive**

3 *Negative numbers and your calculator*

e.g.1 ${}^-7 - 2$

Calculator

${}^-7 - 2 = {}^-9$

FACTS ABOUT NUMBERS

Test 3

Use your calculator for question 4 only.

1. Work out:
   (a) $^-2 + 5$ **(b)** $^-2 - 5$
   (c) $2 + ^-5$ **(d)** $^-2 - ^-5$
   (e) $^-12 - 13$ **(f)** $22 - ^-13$
   (g) $23 - 39$ **(h)** $^-15 + 50$

2. Work out:
   (a) $^-2 \times 5$ **(b)** $^-2 \times ^-5$
   (c) $2 \times ^-5$ **(d)** $^-12 \times ^-3$
   (e) $^-12 \div 2$ **(f)** $12 \div ^-3$
   (g) $^-12 \div ^-2$ **(h)** $^-15 \div 5$

3. Work out:
   (a) $^-2 + 4 \times ^-5$
   (b) $(^-2 + 4) \times ^-5$
   (c) $^-12 \div 2 + ^-12 \times ^-2$
   (d) $^-12 \div (8 + ^-12) \times ^-2$
   (e) $(^-12 - ^-6) \div (8 + ^-10)$
   (f) $(20 - ^-5) \times (^-14 - ^-10)$

4. Use your calculator to check your answers to question 3.

---

4. FACTS ABOUT NUMBERS

Multiples

The multiples of 3 are 3, 6, 9, 12, 15, …
The multiples of 7 are 7, 14, 21, 28, …
The 5th multiple of 7 = the 7th multiple of 5 = 35

20 is the …   1st multiple of 20 and the 20th multiple of 1
                2nd multiple of 10 and the 10th multiple of 2
                4th multiple of 5 and the 5th multiple of 4

Factors

You can find the factors of a number from the
multiplication or division facts that give the number.

e.g.1

$1 \times 20 = 20$	or	$20 \div 1 = 20$	1 and 20 are factors
$2 \times 10 = 20$	or	$20 \div 2 = 10$	2 and 10 are factors
$4 \times 5 = 20$	or	$20 \div 4 = 5$	4 and 5 are factors

ANSWER   So 1, 2, 4, 5, 10 and 20 are the factors of 20.

2 Lowest common multiple (LCM) and highest common factor (HCF)

The LCM of two numbers is the lowest number that is a multiple of them both.
The HCF of two numbers is the highest factor that is common to both numbers.

e.g.1   The multiples of 24 are 24, 48, **72**, 96, …
The multiples of 18 are 18, 36, 54, **72**, …

ANSWER   The LCM of 24 and 18 is **72**

e.g.2   The factors of 18 are 1, 2, 3, **6**, 9 and 18
The factors of 24 are 1, 2, 3, 4, **6**, 8, 12 and 24

ANSWER   The HCF of 18 and 24 is **6**.

4 Prime numbers

A prime number has only two factors, 1 and the number itself.

e.g.1   Percy Proof says that the sum of two prime
numbers is always an even number.
Give an example to show he is wrong.

You need a **counter example** to show that
the sum of two prime numbers can be odd.

> **Examiner's tip**
> Learn the first few
> prime numbers: 2,
> 3, 5, 7, 11, 13, 17,
> 19, …

ANSWER   Any two prime numbers that include 2 will do.
For example: $2 + 3 = 5$, $2 + 13 = 15$, …

3 Prime factors

All numbers can be written as the product of their prime factors.

e.g.1   The factors of 20 are 1, 2, 4, 5, 10 and 20.
The prime factors of 20 are 2 and 5.

> **Remember**
> Prime factors are factors that are
> prime numbers.

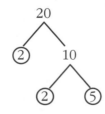

$20 = 2 \times 10$

$20 = 2 \times 2 \times 5$

ANSWER   20 as the product of its prime factors $= 2^2 \times 5$

FACTS ABOUT NUMBERS

e.g.2

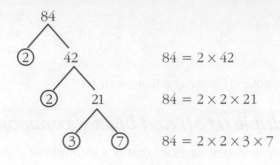

$84 = 2 \times 42$

$84 = 2 \times 2 \times 21$

$84 = 2 \times 2 \times 3 \times 7$

ANSWER   84 as the product of its prime factors $= 2^2 \times 3 \times 7$

Examiner's tip
Remember what 'product of prime factors' means.

Test 4

Do not use a calculator.

1. Here is a list of numbers:
2   6   12   15   17   24
Which of these numbers are:
(a) Multiples of 3?
(b) Factors of 72?
(c) Prime numbers?

2. **(a)** Find **all** the factors of 3000.
(b) What is the smallest number with prime factors 2, 3 and 7?

3. **(a)** Explain why 2 is the only even prime number.
(b) Ben says 221 is a prime number.
Is he right?
Explain your answer.

4. Write these numbers as the products of their prime factors.
(a) 24
(b) 72
(c) 108
(d) 60

5. **(a)** Find the prime factors of 80.
  (b) Find the prime factors of 120.
  (c) Write 80 as the product of its prime factors.
  (d) Write 120 as the product of its prime factors.
  (e) Find the LCM of 80 and 120.
  (f) Find the HCF of 80 and 120.

6. Find the LCM and HCF of:
  (a) 12 and 18
  (b) 54 and 72

7. Percy Proof says:
  'The sum of a multiple of 3 and a multiple of 2 is always an odd number.'
  Give a counter example to show he is wrong.

5. INDICES OR POWERS

Raising a number to a power

2^4 (2 raised to the power 4) is a shorthand way of writing $2 \times 2 \times 2 \times 2$.
2 is the base number and 4 is the power (or index).
The power tells you how many times to multiply the base number.

DO THIS
Show that the value of 2^4 is 16 and that the value of 3^5 is 243.

Squaring and cubing

To **square** a number raise it to the power 2.
4 squared means 4^2.
$4^2 = 4 \times 4 = 16$
Whole numbers squared are called square numbers.
All numbers squared are positive.

To **cube** a number raise it to the power 3.
4 cubed means 4^3.
$4^3 = 4 \times 4 \times 4 = 64$
Whole numbers cubed are called cube numbers.

EXAMPLES

Percy Proof says: 'The sum of the cube of an odd number and the square of an odd number always gives an even number'.

Show that Percy is right.

$1 + 1 = 2$	$1^3 + 1^2$
$1 + 9 = 10$	$1^3 + 3^2$
$1 + 25 = 26$	$1^3 + 5^2$
$27 + 1 = 28$	$3^3 + 1^2$
$27 + 9 = 36$	$3^3 + 3^2$
$27 + 25 = 52$	$3^3 + 5^2$
$125 + 1 = 126$	$5^3 + 1^2$
$125 + 9 = 134$	$5^3 + 3^2$
$125 + 25 = 150$	$5^3 + 5^2$

> **Examiner's tip**
> Learn the square numbers up to 15^2 and the cube numbers up to 5^3.

Both the cubes of odd numbers and squares of odd numbers are always odd numbers. The sum of two odd numbers is always even. So Percy must be right.

Square roots and cube roots

The inverse of squaring a number is finding its square root.
$\sqrt{}$ is a special symbol for square root.
The square root of a number has both a positive and negative value.
The inverse of cubing a number is finding its cube root.
$\sqrt[3]{}$ is a special symbol for cube root.

e.g.1 $9^2 = (^-9)^2 = 81$
so $\sqrt{81} = \pm 9$ ± 9 means 9 or $^-9$

e.g.2 $10^3 = 1000$
so $\sqrt[3]{1000}$ is 10

> **Examiner's tip**
> If you are asked for $\sqrt{81}$ in an exam either 9 or $^-9$ is an acceptable answer.

Reciprocals

To find the reciprocal of a number divide the number into 1.
This can be done by changing the number to a fraction and then turning it upside down.
The product of a number and its reciprocal is 1.

e.g.1   The reciprocal of 2 is $\frac{1}{2}$ $2 \times \frac{1}{2} = 1$

e.g.2   The reciprocal of $\frac{5}{4}$ is $\frac{4}{5}$ $\frac{5}{4} \times \frac{4}{5} = 1$

e.g.3   The reciprocal of 1.3 is $\frac{10}{13}$ $1.3 = \frac{13}{10}$ $\frac{13}{10} \times \frac{10}{13} = 1$

2

Multiplying and dividing powers of numbers with the same base

To multiply powers of numbers with the same base add the powers. $\quad a^m \times a^n = a^{m+n}$
To divide powers of numbers with the same base subtract the powers. $\quad a^m \div a^n = a^{m-n}$

e.g.1 $\qquad 2^3 \times 2^5 = 2^8 \qquad\qquad\qquad 2^{3+5}$

e.g.2 $\qquad 2^5 \div 2^3 = 2^2 \qquad\qquad\qquad 2^{5-3}$

e.g.3 $\qquad 2^5 \times 2^6 \div 2^4 = 2^7 \qquad\qquad 2^{5+6-4}$

2

Raising a power to a power

To raise a power to a power multiply the powers. $\qquad\qquad (a^m)^n = a^{m \times n}$

e.g.1 $\qquad (3^2)^3 = 3^{2 \times 3} = 3^6 \qquad$ or $\qquad (3^2)^3 = 3^2 \times 3^2 \times 3^2 = 3^{2+2+2} = 3^6$

2

Numbers raised to the power zero and 1

Any number raised to the power zero = 1 $\qquad\qquad\qquad\qquad a^0 = 1$
Any number raised to the power 1 is the number itself. $\qquad\qquad a^1 = a$

2

The power and root buttons on your calculator

Calculator button	What the button does
x^y	raises the number, x, to the power, y
$x^{1/y}$	finds the yth root of the number, x
x^2	squares a number
$\sqrt{}$	finds the square root of a number
$\sqrt[3]{}$	finds the cube root of a number
$1/x$	finds the reciprocal of a number

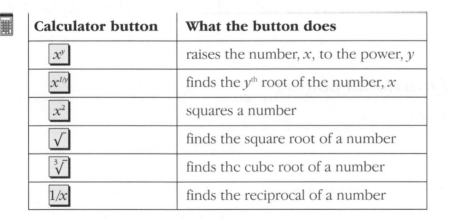

Calculate 2^4 by pressing $\qquad\qquad\qquad$ 2 $\;\;x^y\;\;$ 4 $\;\;=$

Calculate 2^{-3} by pressing $\qquad\qquad\qquad$ 2 $\;\;x^y\;\;$ 3 $\;\;+\!\!/\!\!-\;\;$ $=$

Calculate $\sqrt[3]{8}$ by pressing $\qquad\qquad\qquad$ 8 $\;\;\sqrt[3]{}\;\;$ $=$

Calculate $\sqrt[5]{32}$ by pressing $\qquad\qquad\qquad$ 32 $\;\;x^{1/y}\;\;$ 5 $\;\;=$

Calculate the reciprocal of 5 by pressing $\qquad$ 5 $\;\;1/x\;\;$ $=$

Calculate the reciprocal of 5^3 by pressing $\qquad$ 5 $\;\;x^y\;\;$ 3 $\;\;1/x\;\;$ $=$

INDICES OR POWERS

1 *Negative powers*

x^{-n} is the reciprocal of x^n $\qquad\qquad x^{-n} = 1/x^n$

e.g.1
$$3^{-2} = 1/3^2 = 1/9$$
$1/9$ is the reciprocal of 3^2

e.g.2
$$5^{-3} = 1/5^3 = 1/125$$
$1/125$ is the reciprocal of 5^3

e.g.3
$$2^{-5} = 1/2^5 = 1/32$$
$1/32$ is the reciprocal of 2^5

1 *Fractional powers*

To work out $x^{1/n}$ find the nth root of x. $\qquad\qquad x^{1/n} = \sqrt[n]{x}$
The nth root of x is the inverse of raising x to the power n.

To work out $x^{m/n}$ find the nth root of x then raise to the power m. $\quad x^{m/n} = (x^{1/n})^m = (\sqrt[n]{x})^m$

e.g.1 $\quad 4^{1/2} = \sqrt{4} = 2$ $\qquad\qquad\qquad$ because $2^2 = 4$

e.g.2 $\quad 27^{1/3} = \sqrt[3]{27} = 3$ $\qquad\qquad$ because $3^3 = 27$

e.g.3 $\quad 27^{2/3} = (27^{1/3})^2 = (\sqrt[3]{27})^2 = 3^2 = 9$ $\quad$ Find the cube root of 27 and then square

e.g.4 $\quad 32^{3/5} = (32^{1/5})^3 = (\sqrt[5]{32})^3 = 2^3 = 8$ $\quad$ Find the 5th root of 32 and then cube

1 *Negative <u>and</u> fractional powers*

$x^{-m/n}$ is the reciprocal of $x^{m/n}$.

e.g.1
$$27^{2/3} = 9 \qquad\qquad\qquad \text{find } \sqrt[3]{27} \text{ and then square}$$
$27^{-2/3}$ is the reciprocal of $27^{2/3}$
So $27^{-2/3} = 1/9$

e.g.2
$$4^{3/2} = 2^3 = 8 \qquad\qquad\qquad \text{find } \sqrt{4} \text{ and then cube}$$
$4^{-3/2}$ is the reciprocal of $4^{3/2}$
So $4^{-3/2} = 1/8$

Test 5

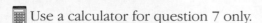 Use a calculator for question 7 only.

1. Work out the value of:
(a) 2^3 (b) 5^4 (c) 3^4
(d) 6^3 (e) 7^4 (f) 2^7

2. Work out the value of:
(a) $2^4 \times 3^2$ (b) $5^3 \times 4^2$
(c) $5^2 \times 2^3$ (d) $7^2 \times 10^3$

3. Work out the value of:
(a) $\sqrt{49}$ (b) $\sqrt[3]{216}$ (c) $\sqrt{225}$
(d) $\sqrt[5]{32}$ (e) $\sqrt[3]{125}$ (f) $\sqrt[5]{243}$

4. Percy Proof says:
'All square numbers are the sum of 2 different prime numbers.'
(a) Check this statement for all square numbers up to 100.
(b) Re-write Percy's statement to make it true for numbers up to 100.

5. Write down the reciprocals of each of these numbers:
(a) 4   (b) 5   (c) $\frac{1}{3}$
(d) $\frac{1}{8}$ (e) $\frac{4}{5}$ (f) $1\frac{1}{4}$
(g) 1.4   (h) 0.7   (i) 2.5

6. Find the value of x in each of the following:
(a) $2^x = 2^2 \times 2^3$ (b) $5^x = 5^4 \times 5^{-6}$
(c) $7^x = 7^4 \div 7^2$ (d) $4^x = 4^7 \div 4^{-4}$
(e) $7^x = (7^4)^2$ (f) $2^x = (2^{-4})^{-2}$

7. Use your calculator to work out:
(a) $2^6 + 2^{-3}$ (b) $10^0 + 10^{-1}$
(c) $(5^2)^{-1} + 10^0$ (d) $\sqrt{16} + \sqrt[3]{125}$
(e) $25^{0.5} + 25^{-0.5}$ (f) $(\sqrt[5]{32})^{-2}$
(g) $4^{1.5}$ (h) $(5^{-1})^2$
(i) 8 to the power $^{-2}/_3$
(j) the reciprocal of $8^{2/3}$

8. (a) $111.11 = 100 + 10 + 1 + \frac{1}{10} + \frac{1}{100}$
Write 111.11 as the sum of powers of 10.
(b) Write 7.5 as the sum of powers of 2.

9. Work out the value of:
(a) 2^{-3} (b) 5^{-2} (c) 10^{-3}
(d) $8^{1/3}$ (e) $32^{1/5}$ (f) $64^{1/2}$
(g) $8^{-1/3}$ (h) $32^{-1/5}$ (i) $64^{-1/2}$
(j) $16^{3/4}$ (k) $25^{3/2}$ (l) $125^{2/3}$
(m) $27^{-2/3}$ (n) $32^{-3/5}$ (o) $64^{-5/6}$

6. STANDARD FORM

Writing a number in standard form

Standard form is a shorthand way of writing very large and very small numbers.
In standard form a number is written as a number between 1 and 10 × a power of 10.
For a large number (greater than 1) the power of 10 is positive.
For a small number (between 0 and 1) the power of 10 is negative.

EXAMPLES

Ordinary number		Standard form
760 000	$7.6 \times 100\ 000$	7.6×10^5
0.00000084	$8.4 \times 0.000\ 000\ 1$	8.4×10^{-7}

Standard form on a calculator

DO THIS
Use your calculator to work out 25 000 × 2 400 000 and 0.000 006 ÷ 2 000 000.
Make sure you understand the entries in this table.

Calculation	Calculator display	Standard form	Ordinary number
25 000 × 2 400 000	6 10	6×10^{10}	60 000 000 000
0.000 006 ÷ 2 000 000	3 ⁻12	3×10^{-12}	0.000 000 000 003

DO THIS
Press this key sequence on your calculator

Your calculator should display 7000.
In standard form this is 7×10^3.

Remember
You can enter numbers in standard form
into your calculator using the
EXP (or EE) button.

Examiner's tip
If your calculator displays an answer in the form | 7.2   08 | *you need to
remember that this is not what you write down. You must either write the answer
in standard form (7.2×10^8) or as an ordinary number (720 000 000).*

Calculating in standard form

When adding and subtracting numbers in standard form change to ordinary numbers first.
When multiplying in standard form: × the numbers and + the powers.
When dividing numbers in standard form: ÷ the numbers and − the powers.

e.g.1 $(3 \times 10^5) + (4 \times 10^{-2})$ $= 300\ 000 + 0.04$
    $= 300\ 000.04$

Calculator

e.g.2

$$(3 \times 10^5) \div (4 \times 10^{-2}) = (3 \div 4) \times (10^5 \div 10^{-2})$$
$$= 0.75 \times 10^{(5 - {}^-2)}$$
$$= 0.75 \times 10^7$$
$$= 7.5 \times 10^6$$

Calculator

e.g.3

$$(5 \times 10^{-2})^2 = (5^2) \times (10^{-2})^2$$
$$= 25 \times 10^{-2 \times 2}$$
$$= 25 \times 10^{-4}$$
$$= 2.5 \times 10^{-3}$$

Calculator

Test 6

Use a calculator for questions 6, 7 and 8 only.

1. Write each of the following numbers in standard form.
   (a) 2400   (b) 1 367 000
   (c) 823 000   (d) 1 213 000 000
   (e) 0.34   (f) 0.0002
   (g) 0.000 005 46   (h) 0.000 000 76

2. Write each of the following as an ordinary number.
   (a) 6×10^5 (b) 3.6×10^7
   (c) 4.23×10^4 (d) 1.234×10^9
   (e) 7×10^{-5} (f) 8.61×10^{-3}
   (g) 1.76×10^{-4} (h) 9.034×10^{-9}

3. Calculate the following giving your answers in standard form.
   (a) $(2 \times 10^{-2}) \times (7 \times 10^4)$
   (b) $(4 \times 10^6) \div (8 \times 10^{-4})$
   (c) $(5 \times 10^3)^2$

4. $p = 2 \times 10^4, q = 4 \times 10^{-2}, r = 5 \times 10^{-3}$.
   Calculate the following giving your answers in standard form.
   (a) $p \times q$ (b) $q \times r$ (c) $p \times q \times r$
   (d) $q \div r$ (e) $q \div p$ (f) r^2

5. 6×10^3 7×10^2 7×10^{-3} 6×10^{-2}
Write down the largest and smallest of these numbers as ordinary numbers.

6. Star A is 40 350 000 000 000 000 km from the Sun.
Star B is 15 300 000 000 000 000 000 km from the Sun.
How much further is it from the Sun to star B than from the Sun to star A?
Give your answers in standard form.

7. Calculate:
(a)   800 000 × 12 000 000
(b)   0.000 000 56 ÷ 20 000 000
(c)   0.000 05³
Give your answers both in standard form and as an ordinary number.

8. Calculate the following:
(a) $(2.6 \times 10^3) \times (7.2 \times 10^4)$
(b) $(5 \times 10^{-3}) \div (7 \times 10^6)$
(c) $(5.6 \times 10^3)^5$
(d) $(1.8 \times 10^3) \times (8.1 \times 10^3)$
(e) $(2.45 \times 10^2) \div (7.1 \times 10^{-1})^3$
(f) $(9.8 \times 10^{-2})^{-4}$
Give your answers in standard form to an accuracy of 3 significant figures.

7. FRACTIONS

4   *Words and meaning*

A whole is divided into 5 equal parts:

1 of the parts is called ¹/₅
¹/₅ can also be thought of as 1 ÷ 5

2 of the parts is called ²/₅
²/₅ can also be thought of as 2 ÷ 5

3 of the parts is called ³/₅
³/₅ can also be thought of as 3 ÷ 5

Remember
The bottom number, called the denominator, is the name of the fraction.
The top number, called the numerator, is the number of parts.
A fraction of a whole, like ²/₅, is called a proper fraction.
A fraction like ⁷/₅ is called an improper fraction.
A fraction like 1²/₅ is called a mixed number.

4

Equivalent fractions and simplest form

To change a fraction to an equivalent fraction multiply or divide both the numerator and denominator by the **same** number.

A fraction in its lowest terms (or simplest form) has a numerator and a denominator that are integers with no common factor apart from 1.

To simplify a fraction in **one step** divide both the numerator and denominator by their highest common factor (HCF); alternatively you can simplify in more than one step.

e.g.1 $\quad ^2/_3 = ^4/_6 \qquad \dfrac{2 \times 2}{3 \times 2}$

e.g.2 $\quad$ The set of equivalent fractions for $^3/_5$ are:
$^3/_5 \qquad ^6/_{10} \quad ^9/_{15} \quad ^{12}/_{20} \quad ^{15}/_{25} \quad \ldots$
The numerators are multiples of **3.**
The denominators are multiples of **5.**

e.g.3 $\quad ^6/_{15}$ is not in simplest form because 6 and 15 have a common factor of 3.
$^6/_{15} = ^2/_5 \qquad \dfrac{6 \div 3}{15 \div 3}$
3 is the HCF of 6 and 15 so the fraction has been simplified in one step.

e.g.4 $\quad ^{70}/_{98} = ^5/_7$
$70 \div 2 = 35 \qquad 35 \div 7 = \mathbf{5}$
$98 \div 2 = 49 \qquad 49 \div 7 = \mathbf{7}$
Divide both the numerator and denominator by 14 (the HCF) to do this in one step.

4

Finding a fraction of a number

e.g.1 $\quad ^3/_5$ of 25

METHOD $\quad 25 \div 5 = 5 \qquad$ finding $^1/_5$ by dividing by 5
$\qquad\qquad 5 \times 3 = 15 \qquad$ multiplying by 3 to find $^3/_5$

ANSWER $\quad$ So $^3/_5$ of 25 $= 15$

> **Examiner's tip**
> *In an exam, you could be asked to write an answer as a mixed number in its lowest terms.*

e.g.2 $\quad ^3/_7$ of 25

METHOD $\quad 25 \div 7 = ^{25}/_7 \qquad$ finding $^1/_7$ by dividing by 7
$\qquad\qquad\qquad\qquad\qquad$ 25 ÷ 7 is not a whole number so leave $^{25}/_7$ as an **improper** fraction
$\qquad ^{25}/_7 \times 3 = ^{75}/_7 \qquad$ multiplying by 3 to find $^3/_7$
$\qquad$ So $^3/_7$ of 25 $= ^{75}/_7$

$\qquad ^{75}/_7$ is an **improper fraction** so change it to a **mixed number.**
$\qquad ^{70}/_7 = 10 \qquad\qquad 70 \div 7$
$\qquad ^{75}/_7 = ^{70}/_7 + ^5/_7$
$\qquad\qquad = 10^5/_7$

ANSWER $\quad$ So as a mixed number the answer is $10^5/_7$

4

Writing one number as a fraction of another

e.g.1 Write 55p as a fraction of 90p.

ANSWER $^{55}/_{90} = {}^{11}/_{18}$ dividing numerator and denominator by 5

e.g.2 Write 800 mm as a fraction of 180 cm.
800 mm = 80 cm first make the units the **same**

ANSWER $^{80}/_{180} = {}^{4}/_{9}$ dividing numerator and denominator by 20

e.g.3 Sam earns £32.
He spends $^{3}/_{8}$ on a DVD and $^{3}/_{10}$ of the rest on a book.
What fraction of Sam's earnings is left?

METHOD $^{3}/_{8}$ of £32 = £12 $(32 \div 8) \times 3$
Sam has £20 left £32 − £12

$^{3}/_{10}$ of £20 = £6 $(20 \div 10) \times 3$
Sam has £14 left £20 − £6

£14 as a fraction of £32 = $^{14}/_{32}$
$^{14}/_{32} = {}^{7}/_{16}$ simplifying

ANSWER So Sam has $^{7}/_{16}$ of his earnings left.

4

Putting fractions in order

To put fractions in order change them to equivalent fractions with a common denominator.

e.g.1 Put the fractions $^{7}/_{12}$, $^{17}/_{30}$ and $^{11}/_{20}$ in order, starting with the smallest.

METHOD 12, 24, 36, 48, **60**, 72, …
30, **60**, 90, …
20, 40, **60**, 80, …
The lowest common denominator is **60.**
Change each fraction to an equivalent fraction with denominator 60.
$^{7}/_{12} = {}^{35}/_{60}$ $^{7 \times 5}/_{12 \times 5}$
$^{17}/_{30} = {}^{34}/_{60}$ $^{17 \times 2}/_{30 \times 2}$
$^{11}/_{20} = {}^{33}/_{60}$ $^{11 \times 3}/_{20 \times 3}$

ANSWER The order of the fractions is $^{11}/_{20}$, $^{17}/_{30}$, $^{7}/_{12}$

4

Multiplying by a proper fraction

e.g.1

$\frac{2}{3} \times \frac{1}{8} = \frac{2 \times 1}{3 \times 8}$ multiplying the numerators
multiplying the denominators

$= \frac{2}{24}$

ANSWER $= \frac{1}{12}$ simplifying

e.g.2

$12 \times \frac{3}{5} = \frac{36}{5}$

ANSWER $= 7\frac{1}{5}$ changing to a mixed number
This is the same as finding $\frac{3}{5}$ of 12.

e.g.3

Amy drinks $\frac{2}{3}$ of a pint of milk a day.
How much milk does she drink in one week?
$\frac{2}{3} \times 7 = \frac{14}{3}$

ANSWER $= 4\frac{2}{3}$ changing to a mixed number
This is the same as finding $\frac{2}{3}$ of 7.

2

Dividing by a proper fraction

To divide by a fraction multiply by its reciprocal.

EXAMPLE
The reciprocal of $\frac{3}{8} = \frac{8}{3}$ so:

e.g.1 $\frac{2}{3} \div \frac{3}{8} = \frac{2}{3} \times \frac{8}{3}$

METHOD $= \frac{2 \times 8}{3 \times 3}$ multiplying the numerators
multiplying the denominators

$= \frac{16}{9}$

ANSWER $= 1\frac{7}{9}$ changing to a mixed number

4

Adding or subtracting proper fractions

To add or subtract fractions change them to equivalent fractions with a common denominator.

e.g.1   Work out the sum and difference of $\frac{2}{3}$ and $\frac{1}{5}$.

METHOD   The lowest common multiple of 5 and 3 is **15**.
$\frac{2}{3} = \frac{10}{15}$ $\frac{1}{5} = \frac{3}{15}$ changing to equivalent fractions with denominator **15**

$\frac{2}{3} + \frac{1}{5} = \frac{10}{15} + \frac{3}{15}$

ANSWER $= \frac{13}{15}$ **adding** the new numerators; do **not** change the denominator

METHOD $\frac{2}{3} - \frac{1}{5} = \frac{10}{15} - \frac{3}{15}$

ANSWER $= \frac{7}{15}$ **subtracting** the new numerators; do **not** change the denominator

FRACTIONS

Calculating with mixed numbers

To calculate with mixed numbers change to improper fractions first.

e.g.1 $3\frac{1}{3} + 1\frac{1}{4}$

METHOD $3\frac{1}{3} = \frac{10}{3}$ $1\frac{1}{4} = \frac{5}{4}$ first change to improper fractions.
The least common multiple of 3 and 4 is **12.**
$\frac{10}{3} = \frac{40}{12}$ $\frac{5}{4} = \frac{15}{12}$ changing to equivalent fractions with denominator **12.**

$\frac{10}{3} + \frac{5}{4} = \frac{40}{12} + \frac{15}{12}$ **adding** the new numerators;
$= \frac{55}{12}$ do **not** change the denominator

ANSWER $= 4\frac{7}{12}$ changing to a mixed number

e.g.2 $5\frac{2}{3} \div 2\frac{1}{2}$

METHOD $5\frac{2}{3} = \frac{17}{3}$ $2\frac{1}{2} = \frac{5}{2}$ first change to improper fractions.
$\frac{17}{3} \div \frac{5}{2} = \frac{17}{3} \times \frac{2}{5}$ the reciprocal of $\frac{5}{2}$ is $\frac{2}{5}$
$= \frac{17 \times 2}{3 \times 5}$ multiplying the numerators
multiplying the denominators
$= \frac{34}{15}$

ANSWER $= 2\frac{4}{15}$ changing to a mixed number

Changing a fraction to a decimal

To change a fraction to a decimal, divide the numerator by the denominator.
For fractions that have denominators with prime factors of 2 and/or 5, first change the fraction to an equivalent fraction with denominator 10, 100, 1000, …
This makes the division possible without a calculator.

e.g.1 $\frac{3}{5} = \frac{6}{10}$ multiplying the numerator and denominator by 2
$= 0.6$ $6 \div 10$

e.g.2 $\frac{17}{40} = \frac{42.5}{100}$ multiplying the numerator and denominator by $\frac{5}{2}$
$= 0.425$ $42.5 \div 100$

e.g.3 $\frac{13}{125} = \frac{104}{1000}$ multiplying the numerator and denominator by 8
$= 0.104$ $104 \div 1000$

Remember
Recurring decimals are written with a dot above the first and last of the recurring digits.

| **e.g.4** | $^2/_3$ | $= 2 \div 3$ |
| | | $= 0.666\ 666\ 6\ldots$ |

This recurring decimal is normally written $0.\dot{6}$.

| **e.g.5** | $^5/_7$ | $= 5 \div 7$ |
| | | $= 0.714285714\ldots$ |

This recurring decimal is normally written $0.\dot{7}1428\dot{5}$.

4 Changing a terminating decimal to a fraction

| **e.g.1** | 0.8 | $= ^8/_{10}$ |
| | $^8/_{10}$ | $= ^4/_5$ simplifying |

ANSWER 0.8 as a fraction is $^4/_5$

| **e.g.2** | $0.24 = ^{24}/_{100}$ |
| | $^{24}/_{100} = ^6/_{25}$ simplifying |

ANSWER 0.24 as a fraction is $^6/_{25}$.

2 The fraction button on your calculator 🖩

The $\boxed{a^b/_c}$ button on your calculator allows you to input fractions.

$\boxed{4 \lrcorner 2 \lrcorner 7}$ on the calculator display means $4^2/_7$

| **e.g.1** | To calculate that $5^1/_3 \div ^2/_5 = 13^1/_3$ |

press $\boxed{5}$ $\boxed{a^b/_c}$ $\boxed{1}$ $\boxed{a^b/_c}$ $\boxed{3}$ $\boxed{\div}$ $\boxed{2}$ $\boxed{a^b/_c}$ $\boxed{5}$ $\boxed{=}$ $\boxed{13 \lrcorner 1 \lrcorner 3}$

1 Changing a recurring decimal to a fraction

Any recurring decimal can be changed to a fraction in its simplest form.

e.g.1	$0.\dot{5}$
	$10 \times 0.\dot{5} = 5.555\ 555\ 5\ldots$
	$ 0.\dot{5} = 0.555\ 555\ 5\ldots$
	$9 \times 0.\dot{5} = 5$ $10 \times 0.\dot{5} - 0.\dot{5}$
	$ 0.\dot{5} = ^5/_9$ dividing by 9

e.g.2	$0.\dot{3}2\dot{7}$
	$1000 \times 0.\dot{3}2\dot{7} = 327.327\ 327\ 3\ldots$
	$ 0.\dot{3}2\dot{7} = 0.327\ 327\ 3\ldots$
	$999 \times 0.\dot{3}2\dot{7} = 327$ $1000 \times 0.\dot{3}2\dot{7} - 0.\dot{3}2\dot{7}$
	$ 0.\dot{3}2\dot{7} = ^{327}/_{999}$ dividing by 999
	$ = ^{109}/_{333}$ dividing numerator and denominator by 3

DO THIS

Check that $0.\dot{5} = ^5/_9$ by calculating $5 \div 9$

Check that $0.\dot{3}2\dot{7} = ^{109}/_{333}$ by calculating $109 \div 333$

Use a calculator for question 10 only.

1. Write these fractions in their lowest terms.
   (a) $^{10}/_{15}$ **(b)** $^{12}/_{30}$ **(c)** $^{21}/_{28}$

2. Calculate each of the following.
   Give your answers as mixed numbers in their lowest terms.
   (a) $^2/_3$ of 15   **(b)** $^4/_9$ of 36 **(c)** $^4/_5$ of 60
   (d) $^2/_3$ of 20   **(e)** $^3/_4$ of 19 **(f)** $^5/_8$ of 12

3. Write the first quantity as a fraction of the second.
   Give your answers in its lowest terms.
   (a) 44 pence, £2   **(b)** 8 mm, 2 cm
   (c) 400 g, 3 kg   **(d)** 75 cm, 4 m

4. Put these fractions in order starting with the smallest.
   $^2/_3$ $^{23}/_{36}$ $^{15}/_{24}$ $^{11}/_{18}$

5. Calculate each of the following.
   Give your answers as mixed numbers in their lowest terms.
   (a) $^2/_3 + ^1/_5$ **(b)** $^2/_3 - ^1/_5$ **(c)** $^2/_3 \times ^1/_5$ **(d)** $^3/_5 + ^5/_8$ **(e)** $^5/_8 - ^7/_{12}$
   (f) $^3/_5 \times ^5/_6$ **(g)** $^7/_{10} - ^2/_3$ **(h)** $^4/_5 + ^5/_6$ **(i)** $^3/_4 \times ^7/_{12}$

6. Calculate each of the following.
   Give your answers as mixed numbers in their lowest terms.
   (a) $^3/_4 \div ^2/_5$ **(b)** $^2/_3 \div ^4/_5$
   (c) $^1/_6 \div ^3/_4$ **(d)** $^7/_{10} \div ^5/_8$
   (e) $2^5/_8 - 1^7/_{12}$ **(f)** $3^3/_5 + 1^3/_4$
   (g) $1^3/_8 \times 1^3/_5$ **(h)** $2^1/_2 \div 3^3/_4$

7. Change these fractions to decimals.
   (a) $^4/_5$ **(b)** $^7/_{20}$ **(c)** $^9/_{25}$
   (d) $^{12}/_{200}$ **(e)** $^{180}/_{300}$ **(f)** $^7/_{40}$

8. Change these decimals to fractions in their lowest terms.
   (a) 0.7   **(b)** 0.12   **(c)** 0.324
   (d) 0.075   **(e)** 0.0005   **(f)** 0.065

9. Change these recurring decimals to fractions in their lowest terms.
   (a) $0.\dot{4}$ **(b)** $0.1\dot{5}$ **(c)** $0.\dot{2}2\dot{5}$
   (d) $0.1\dot{5}$ **(e)** $0.07\dot{5}$ **(f)** $0.3\dot{2}1\dot{5}$

10. Use your calculator to check your answers to questions 5 to 9.

8. PERCENTAGES

The meaning of percentage

A percentage is a fraction with denominator 100.
Fractions, decimals and percentages are different ways of saying the same thing.

EXAMPLES

Percentage	Fraction	Decimal
1%	$^1/_{100}$	0.01
7%	$^7/_{100}$	0.07
23%	$^{23}/_{100}$	0.23

Changing a fraction or a decimal to a percentage

To change a fraction or a decimal to a percentage: **multiply by 100**

e.g.1 $^3/_{20}$ $= 15\%$ $^3/_{20} \times 100 = 15$

e.g.2 $^{17}/_{40}$ $= 42.5\%$ $^{17}/_{40} \times 100 = 42.5$

e.g.3 $0.375 = 37.5\%$ $0.375 \times 100 = 37.5$

e.g.4 $0.15 = 15\%$ $0.15 \times 100 = 15$

Examiner's tip
Learn the percentage equivalents in this table.

$^1/_8$	$^1/_4$	$^1/_3$	$^3/_8$	$^1/_2$	$^5/_8$	$^2/_3$	$^3/_4$	$^7/_8$
12.5%	25%	$33^1/_3\%$	37.5%	50%	62.5%	$66^2/_3\%$	75%	87.5%

Changing a percentage to a fraction or a decimal

To change a percentage to a fraction or a decimal: **divide by 100**

e.g.1 $30\% = {}^{30}/_{100}$
                   $= {}^3/_{10}$ dividing numerator **and** denominator by 10

e.g.2 $24\% = {}^{24}/_{100}$
                   $= {}^6/_{25}$ dividing numerator **and** denominator by 4

e.g.3 $45\% = 0.45$ $45 \div 100$

e.g.4 $7.5\% = 0.075$ $7.5 \div 100$

PERCENTAGES

Writing one number as a percentage of another

To write one number as a percentage of another:

- Change the numbers to the **same units**.
- Write the numbers as a fraction.
- Simplify the fraction.
- Multiply the fraction by 100.

e.g.1   48p as a percentage of £1.60

METHOD   £1.60 = 160p   Change to the **same** units
           48 as a fraction of 160 = $^{48}/_{160}$ Write the numbers as a fraction
           $^{48}/_{160} = {}^{3}/_{10}$ Simplify
           $^{3}/_{10} \times 100 = 30$ Multiply by 100

ANSWER   48p is 30% of £1.60

Finding a percentage increase or decrease

To find a % increase (or decrease):

- Find the actual increase (or decrease).
- Write this as a fraction of the **original** value.
- Simplify the fraction.
- Multiply the fraction by 100.

e.g.1   A computer is bought for £800 and sold for £680.

METHOD   £800 − £680 = £120   Find the actual decrease
           £120 as a fraction of £800 is $^{120}/_{800}$ Write the numbers as a fraction
           $^{120}/_{800} = {}^{3}/_{20}$ Simplify
           $^{3}/_{20} \times 100 = 15$ Multiply by 100 $100 \div 20 \times 3$

ANSWER   % decrease = 15%

Finding a percentage of a quantity

To find x% of a quantity, n:

- Find 1% of n by dividing n by 100.
- Multiply the result by x.

To do this in **one step**, multiply n by $^{x}/_{100}$.

e.g.1   Find 12% of £200.

METHOD   1% of £200 = £2   £200 ÷ 100
           12% of £200 = £24   £2 × 12

One step $200 \times {}^{12}/_{100} = £24$ 200×0.12

e.g.2	Find 35% of 200		
METHOD	$200 \times {}^{35}/_{100} = 70$	200×0.35	
e.g.3	Find 7% of 35		
METHOD	$35 \times {}^{7}/_{100} = 2.45$	35×0.07	

4 Increasing and decreasing quantities by a percentage

To increase (or decrease) a quantity, n, by x%:

- Multiply n by ${}^{x}/_{100}$ to find x% of n.
- Add (or subtract) the result to n.

To do this in **one step**, multiply n by $1 \pm {}^{x}/_{100}$.

> **Examiner's tip**
> *Try to master the one step method.*

e.g.1	Increase 20 by 10%.		
METHOD	10% of 20 $= 2$	20×0.1	
	20 increased by 10% $= 22$	$20 + 2$	
One step	20 increased by 10% $= 22$	20×1.1	$(1 + {}^{10}/_{100} = 1.1)$
e.g.2	20 decreased by 10% $= 18$	20×0.9	$(1 - {}^{10}/_{100} = 0.9)$
e.g.3	4 increased by 7% $= 4.28$	4×1.07	$(1 + {}^{7}/_{100} = 1.07)$
e.g.4	4 decreased by 7% $= 3.72$	4×0.93	$(1 - {}^{7}/_{100} = 0.93)$

2 Reverse percentage problems

When a quantity, n, is changed by x% a new quantity, $n \times (1 \pm {}^{x}/_{100})$, is obtained.
To find the **original** quantity, n, from the new quantity:

- Find 1% of the original quantity by **dividing** the new quantity by $100 \pm x$.
- Multiply by 100.

To do this in **one step**, **divide** by $1 \pm {}^{x}/_{100}$.

e.g.1	A car is sold for £990 at a **loss** of 10%. What was the original price?		
METHOD	1% of original price $= £11$		$£990 \div (100 - 10)$
ANSWER	Original price $= £1100$		11×100
One step	Original price $= £990 \div 0.9$		$1 - {}^{10}/_{100} = 0.9$
	$= £9900 \div 9$		
ANSWER	$= £1100$		

e.g.2   Sam has a 5% wage **increase**. He now earns £252 per week.
What did he earn before?

One step   Sam's previous wage = £252 ÷ 1.05 $1 + {}^5/_{100} = 1.05$

ANSWER   = £240

> **Examiner's tip**
> *Reverse percentage problems are
> easier using the one step method.*

1 Repeated percentage change

A quantity, n, changed by x% for t years becomes $n \times (1 \pm {}^x/_{100})^t$.

e.g.1   A car costs £15 000. It **loses** value at the rate of 3% per year for 10 years.
What is its value after 10 years?

METHOD   To find the value after 1 year multiply by 0.97 $1 - {}^3/_{100}$

ANSWER   So after 10 years the value is £11 061.36 $15\,000 \times 0.97^{10}$

e.g.2   A quantity is **increased** by 5% per week for three weeks.
What is the overall percentage change?

METHOD   To increase by 5% multiply by 1.05 $1 + {}^5/_{100}$
The overall change is 1.05^3 $1.05^3 = 1.157625$

ANSWER   This gives a 15.7625% **increase.** $1.157625 = 1 + \mathbf{0.157625}$
$0.157625 = {}^{15.7625}/_{100}$

e.g.3   A quantity is **increased** by 10% and then **decreased** by 10%.
What is the overall % change?

METHOD   To increase by 10% multiply by 1.1 $1 + {}^{10}/_{100}$
To decrease by 10% multiply by 0.9 $1 - {}^{10}/_{100}$
The overall change is 1.1×0.9 $1.1 \times 0.9 = 0.99$

ANSWER   This gives a 1% **decrease.** $0.99 = 1 - \mathbf{0.01}$
$0.01 = {}^1/_{100}$

Use a calculator for questions 8 and 11 to 15.

1. Change these to percentages:
   (a) $^7/_{10}$ (b) $^9/_{20}$ (c) $^{13}/_{40}$
   (d) $^{87}/_{200}$ (e) $^9/_{25}$ (f) $^{133}/_{500}$
   (g) 0.21   (h) 0.07   (i) 0.125

2. Change these percentages to fractions in simplest form.
   (a) 15%   (b) 36%   (c) 60%
   (d) 12.5%   (e) 62.5%   (f) 7.5%

3. Change each of the percentages in question 2 to a decimal.

4. Work out $^{21}/_{40} - 0.51$.
   Give your answer as a percentage.

5. (a) What is 17 as a percentage of 20?
   (b) Write 24p as a percentage of £3.
   (c) Write 15 cm as a percentage of 4 m.

6. Work out:
   (a) 10% of 200   (b) 20% of 300
   (c) 7% of £220   (d) 17.5% of £50
   (e) 12% of 350   (f) 6% of £4.50

7. (a) Increase £15 by 20%.
   (b) Decrease £300 by 15%.
   (c) Increase £240 by 5%.
   (d) Decrease £175 by 12%.

8. In March 2010 Jean weighed 65 kg.
   In March 2011 she weighed 14% more than this.
   How much did she weigh in March 2011?

9. Bananas cost 40p each.
   Apples cost 15% less than this.
   Find the cost of an apple.

10. (a) James earns £125 per week.
   He gets a wage rise of 18%.
   What is his new weekly wage?
   (b) John's wage rises from £150 per week to £168 per week.
   What is John's percentage wage rise?
   (c) Jenny gets a 7.5% wage rise.
   Her new wage is £150.50 per week.
   What was Jenny's wage before her wage rise?

11.(a) James gets a 15% discount on a theatre ticket.
The normal ticket cost is £13.
How much does James pay for his ticket?

(b) John pays £12.80 for a ticket to a musical.
The normal price is £16.
What percentage discount does John get on his ticket?

(c) Jenny gets a 12.5% discount on a ticket for an exhibition.
She pays £12.25.
What is the normal price of Jenny's ticket?

12.(a) Tom has 8% more marbles than Sam.
Tom has 216 marbles.
How many marbles does Sam have?

(b) Tom is 135 cm tall.
Tom is 10% shorter than Sam.
How tall is Sam?

13.(a) Calculate 5% of 1.8×10^6.
Give your answer in standard form.

(b) Two mice can produce a maximum of 6.25 million mice in 12 months.
Two mice actually produce 2.3×10^4 mice in 12 months.
What percentage of the maximum is this?
Give your answer in standard form.

14. A plant is 12 cm high.
It grows at the rate of 4% a day.
(a) How high is the plant after 8 days?
(b) How many days will the plant have to grow to double its size?

15. The population of a country is 45 million.
The population is increasing at the rate of 2.3% per year.
Assuming the population continues to increase at the same rate, work out:
(a) The population in 20 years time.
(b) How long it takes the population to double.

MONEY

Income tax

A tax allowance is income on which tax is **not** paid.
Income earned **above** the tax allowance is called taxable income.

e.g.1

Billy earns £10 500 per year.
His tax allowance is £4850 per year.
So Billy's taxable income is £5650.   £10 500 − £4850
Billy pays tax at the rates shown in the table.

Taxable income	Tax rate
up to £1000	10%
above £1000	22%

Show that Billy pays £1123 tax per year.

METHOD   Billy's tax = 10% of £1000 + 22% of £4650

10% of £1000 = £100 0.1×1000
22% of £4650 = £1023 0.22×4650

ANSWER   So Billy pays £1123 tax per year.   £100 + £1023

Value Added Tax (VAT)

VAT is a tax paid on goods and services.
The most common rate of VAT is 17.5%.

e.g.1

A computer costs £650 plus VAT at 17.5%.
VAT = £113.75 $0.175 \times £650$ $(^{17.5}/_{100} = 0.175)$

ANSWER   Total cost = £763.75   £650 + £113.75

One step   Total cost = $1.175 \times £650 = £763.75$ $1 + {}^{17.5}/_{100} = 0.175$

Best buy problems

To find a best buy, compare prices for the **same** amounts.

e.g.1

A small pot of yoghurt contains 100 ml and costs 37 pence.
A large pot of yoghurt contains 250 ml and costs 90 pence.

METHOD   Small pot   1 ml costs 0.37 p $37 \div 100$
                Large pot   1 ml costs 0.36 p $90 \div 250$

ANSWER   So the large pot is the better buy.

MONEY

Simple interest

If you invest money you earn interest.
With simple interest you earn the same amount of interest each year.

e.g.1   Suki invests £500 at 3.5% per year simple interest.
She earns interest of 3.5% of £500 each year.

ANSWER   She earns £17.50 interest per year. $0.035 \times £500$

2

Compound interest

With compound interest, the interest you earn is added to your investment.
You then earn interest on the interest.

e.g.1   Suki invests £500 at 3.5% per year compound interest.

Year 1	Suki earns interest of 3.5% of £500.	
	Interest earned = £17.50	$0.035 \times £500$
	The value of Suki's investment = £517.50	£500 + £17.50
One step	Suki's investment	$£500 \times 1.035$
	Interest earned	$£500 \times 1.035 - £500$
Year 2	Suki earns interest of 3.5 % of £517.50.	
	Interest earned = £18.11	$0.035 \times £517.50$
	Total interest earned = £35.61	£17.50 + £18.11
	The value of Suki's investment = £535.61	£517.50 + £18.11
One step	Suki's investment	$£500 \times 1.035^2$
	Interest earned	$£500 \times 1.035^2 - £500$
Year 3	Suki earns interest of 3.5 % of £535.61.	
	Interest earned = £18.75	$0.035 \times £535.61$
	Total interest earned = £54.36	£35.61 + £18.75
	The value of Suki's investment = £554.36	£535.61 + £18.75
One step	Suki's investment	$£500 \times 1.035^3$
	Interest earned	$£500 \times 1.035^3 - £500$
Year t:		
One step	Suki's investment	$£500 \times 1.035^t$
	Interest earned	$£500 \times 1.035^t - £500$

Examiner's tip
Compound interest questions can be tricky. When doing money calculations always remember to give your answer to the nearest penny.

Test 9

Use a calculator for questions 1, 3, 5 and 6.

1. Billy earns £12 600 per year.
His tax allowance is £4500 per year.
How much tax does he pay?
(Use the tax rates in the table on p 49.)

2. A new fitted kitchen is advertised at £1240 plus VAT at 17.5%.
What is the total cost of the kitchen?

3. Chocolate is sold in bars of two sizes.
A large bar weighs 500 g and costs £1.80.
A small bar weighs 350 g and costs £1.25.
Which size bar is the better value?
You **must** show your working.

4. Karen invests £750 at 4% per year simple interest.
How much interest does she earn in 5 years?

5. Helen invests £800 at 3% per year compound interest.
What is the value of her investment after 3 years?

6. Work out the interest earned on these investments.
(a) £5000 at 4.5% compound interest for 2 years.
(b) £350 at 5% compound interest for 10 years.

---

10. RATIO AND PROPORTION

4

Understanding ratio

A ratio compares quantities.
It does not tell you the actual value of the quantities being compared.

e.g.1 The ratio of red beads to blue beads on a necklace is 2 : 3.
This means that 'for every 2 red beads there are 3 blue beads'.

> **Examiner's tip**
> Think of the ratio a : b as 'for every **a** of one quantity there are **b** of the other'.

RATIO AND PROPORTION

Different forms of the same ratio

When you multiply or divide the numbers in a ratio by the **same** number a different form of the ratio, called an equivalent ratio, is obtained.

When the numbers in a ratio are in the same units and are integers with no common factor apart from 1, the ratio is in simplest form.

EXAMPLES

Different forms of the ratio 2 : 3 are shown in this table.

$1 : 1\frac{1}{2}$	$(2 \div 2)$	:	$(3 \div 2)$
$\frac{2}{3} : 1$	$(2 \div 3)$	:	$(3 \div 3)$
$4 : 6$	(2×2)	:	(3×2)
$6 : 9$	(2×3)	:	(3×3)
$8 : 12$	(2×4)	:	(3×4)
$10 : 15$	(2×5)	:	(3×5)

e.g.1

12 : 28 is not in simplest form because 12 and 28 have a common factor of 4.
In simplest form, $12 : 28 = 12 \div 4 : 28 \div 4 = 3 : 7$

e.g.2

24 cm : 1 m is not in simplest form because the quantities in the ratio are in different units.
In simplest form, $24 \text{ cm} : 1 \text{ m} = 24 : 100 = 24 \div 4 : 100 \div 4 = 6 : 25$

Simple proportion problems

When two quantities are always in the same ratio they are said to be in direct proportion.

e.g.1

30 students in Terry's class pay £165 for a trip to the zoo.
Jill's class pay £132.
How many students are in Jill's class?

The total cost of the trip is directly proportional to the number of students.
So the ratio of the number of students to the total cost of the trip is always the same.

METHOD

$30 : £165 = 1 : £5.50$ $30 \div 30 : \mathbf{165 \div 30}$
For every **1** student, the cost is **£5.50**.
$\mathbf{£132 \div £5.50 = 24}$
$1 : £5.50 = 24 : £132$ $1 \times 24 : £5.50 \times 24$

ANSWER

There are 24 students in Jill's class.

Equivalent ratio problems

e.g.1

The ratio of apples to oranges in a box is 3 : 4
For every **3** apples, there are **4** oranges.
There are 15 apples in the box.
How many oranges are in the box?

METHOD $15 = \mathbf{5} \times 3$ (or $15 \div 3 = \mathbf{5}$)

ANSWER   So there must be $\mathbf{5} \times 4 = 20$ oranges in the box.
               15 : 20 and 3 : 4 are equivalent ratios.

e.g.2   A painter makes orange paint by mixing red and
               yellow paint in the ratio 5 : 3
               For every **5** litres of red paint, the painter uses **3**
               litres of yellow paint
               The painter uses 3.5 litres of red paint.
               How much yellow paint does he use?

METHOD $3.5 = \mathbf{0.7} \times 5$ (or $3.5 \div 5 = \mathbf{0.7}$)

ANSWER   So the decorator must use $\mathbf{0.7} \times 3 = 2.1$ litres of yellow paint.
               3.5 : 2.1 and 5 : 3 are equivalent ratios.

3 *Proportional division*

Proportional division means sharing a quantity so that the amounts in each share are in a
given ratio.

e.g.1   Amy and Ben share £93.50 in the ratio 6 : 5
               For every **£6** Amy gets, Ben gets **£5**.
               How much do Amy and Ben get?

METHOD $6 + 5 = 11$
               For every £11 that is shared, Ben gets £5.
               $93.5 \div 11 = 8.5$
               £11 can be shared 8.5 times.
               $6 \times 8.5 = 51$
               $5 \times 8.5 = 42.5$

ANSWER   So Amy gets £51 and Ben gets £42.50
               6 : 5 and £51 : £42.50 are equivalent ratios.

e.g.2   1050 kg of concrete is made by mixing gravel, sand and cement in the
               ratio 4 : 2 : 1.
               For every **4** kg of gravel used, **2** kg of sand and **1** kg of cement are used.
               How much gravel is used?

METHOD $4 + 2 + 1 = 7$
               For every 7 kg of concrete 4 kg of gravel is used.
               $1050 \div 7 = 150$
               7 kg of concrete can be made 150 times.
               $4 \times 150 = 600$

ANSWER   600 kg of gravel is used.

RATIO AND PROPORTION

1

Direct and inverse proportion

When y is **directly** proportional to x^n
the ratio $x^n : y$ is always the same.
When x^n increases, y **increases** at the **same rate**.
Written in symbols: $y \propto x^n$
Written as an equation: $y = kx^n$

When y is **inversely** proportional to x^n
the ratio $1/x^n : y$ is always the same.
When x^n increases, y **decreases** at the **same rate**.
Written in symbols: $y \propto 1/x^n$
Written as an equation: $y = k/x^n$

> **Examiner's tips**
> - *Use corresponding values of the proportional quantities to calculate k.*
> - *This will involve rearranging equations using the balance method (see p. 65)*

The value of k is a constant called the constant of proportionality.

e.g.1

y is directly proportional to x^2
When $x = 5$, $y = 10$
Find y when $x = 3$

METHOD

Write the proportionality as an equation.
$y = kx^2$
Use the corresponding values of x and y to find k.
$10 = k \times 5^2$
$k = 10 \div 25$
$k = 0.4$
So $y = 0.4x^2$
Use the equation to find y when $x = 3$.
$y = 0.4 \times 3^2$

ANSWER

So when $x = 3$, $y = 3.6$

e.g.2

y is inversely proportional to $\sqrt{x}$.
When $x = 16$, $y = 10$
Find x when $y = 100$

METHOD

Write the proportionality as an equation.
$y = k/\sqrt{x}$
Use the corresponding values of x and y to find k.
$10 = k/\sqrt{16}$
$k = 10 \times 4 = 40$
So $y = 40/\sqrt{x}$
Use the equation to find x when $y = 100$.
$100 = 40/\sqrt{x}$
$\sqrt{x} = 40/100 = 0.4$

ANSWER

So when $y = 100$, $x = 0.4^2 = 0.16$

Test 10

Do not use your calculator.

1. 35 : 56   70 : 84   108 : 162
   Write the above ratios:
   (a) In simplest form
   (b) In the form 1 : n
   (c) In the form n : 1.

2. Sue pays £12.50 for 5 boxes of chocolates.
   She then decides to buy 3 more boxes.
   How much does she pay altogether?

3. **(a)** The ratio of a : b is 1 : 3.
        Find b when $a = 28$.
   (b) The ratio c : d is 7 : 4.
        Find d when $c = 56$.

4. The ratio of the amount of drink in a small carton to a large carton is 3 : 5.
   There is 240 ml in the small carton.
   How much is in the large carton?

5. In a recipe the ratio of the weight of butter to the weight of flour is 3 : 8.
   200 g of flour are used in the recipe.
   What weight of butter is used?

6. **(a)** Share 35 in the ratio 2 : 3.
   (b) James and Sue share £55 in the ratio 7 : 4.
   How much does each of them get?

7. **(a)** There are 128 beads on a necklace.
        The ratio of black beads to red beads is 3 : 5.
        How many of each coloured bead is on the necklace?
   (b) 20 red beads are added to the necklace.
        What is the new ratio of black to red beads?
        Give your answer in simplest form.

8. The ratio of the angles in a triangle is 7 : 10 : 13.
   Work out the largest angle.

9. £1000 is shared between 4 people in the ratio 4 : 6 : 7 : 8.
   How much is in each share?

10. y is directly proportional to x^3.
   When $x = 2$, $y = 16$.
   (a) Find y when $x = 1$.
   (b) Find x when $y = 128$.

11. y is inversely proportional to x^2.
   When $x = 5$, $y = 4$.
   (a) Find y when $x = 2$.
   (b) Find x when $y = 900$.

11. TIME, SPEED AND OTHER COMPOUND MEASURES

4

Time and timetables

Time can be given using either the 12-hour clock or 24-hour clock.
Timetables normally use the 24-hour clock.

EXAMPLES

1140 on the 24-hour clock is the same as 11.40 am on the 12-hour clock.
1525 on the 24-hour clock is the same as 3.25 pm on the 12-hour clock.

The timetable below shows the times of trains from Norwich to London.

NORWICH	Dep	0500	0520	0530	0600	0630	0655	0710	0755	0805	0835	0905
Diss	Dep	0518	......	0547	0618	0647	0713	0728	......	0823	0852	0922
Stowmarket	Dep	0531	......	0558	0630	0658	0725	0740	......	0835	0903	0933
IPSWICH	Arr	0542	0553	0610	0641	0709	0736	0751	0828	0846	0913	0944
	Dep	0543	0555	0612	0642	0710	0737	0752	0830	0847	0915	0945
Manningtree	Dep	0553	......	0620	0652	0721	......	0802	......	......	0925	......
COLCHESTER	Dep	0604	0610	0632	0704	0732	......	0812	......	0906	0935	1003
Chelmsford	Arr	......	......	......	......	......	......	......	......	......	......	1020
LONDON		0653	0700	0721	0756	0824	0848	0903	0933	0955	1025	1054

e.g.1   You need to travel from Ipswich and get to London by 8.30 am. What train should you catch?

ANSWER   You should catch the 0709.

e.g.2   You arrive at Stowmarket at 0720 to catch a train to Colchester. How long do you have to wait?

ANSWER   20 minutes   You need to catch the 0740.

e.g.3   How long does the quickest train from Norwich to London take?

ANSWER   1 hour 38 minutes   The 0755 is the quickest train; it arrives at 0933.

3

Speed and average speed

Speed measures how fast something is moving.
Speed involves two other measures: distance and time.
In most situations speed is not constant and average speed is used.

Remember

These formulae link average speed (S), total distance travelled (D) and total time taken (T).

$$S = D \div T \qquad D = S \times T \qquad T = D \div S$$

e.g.1

A cheetah takes 10 seconds to run 180 metres.
$180 \div 10 = 18$
The cheetah runs at a speed of 18 metres per second.

e.g.2

Ben cycles for 20 minutes at an average speed of 15 km/h.
20 minutes = $\frac{1}{3}$ of an hour
$15 \times \frac{1}{3} = 5$
Ben cycles 5 km.

e.g.3

Kalam drives 20 miles at an average speed of 50 mph.
$20 \div 50 = 0.4$
$0.4 \times 60 = 24$
Kalam drives for 24 minutes.

Examiner's tip
*To change hours to
minutes multiply by 60.
Remember that 6
minutes = 0.1 hours.
For example, 1 hour 24
minutes = 1.4 hours
(**not** 1.24 hours).*

3 ## Compound measures

Measures like speed, that involve two other measures, are called compound measures.
Another compound measure you could be asked questions about is density.
Density (*D*) links the two measures, mass (*M*) and volume (*V*).

$$D = M \div V \quad M = D \times V \quad V = M \div D$$

e.g.1

The volume of a block of gold is 540 cm³.
Its mass is 6155 g.
The density of the block = $6155 \div 540 = 11.4$ g/cm³.
This means that every cubic centimetre of the gold block has a
mass of 11.4 g.

Do not use a calculator on questions 1 and 2.

1. Change these times to hours and minutes.
   (a) 0.2 hours   **(b)** 5.3 hours
   (c) 3.75 hours **(d)** 2.35 hours

2. Change these times to a time in hours.
   (a) 24 minutes
   (b) 5 hours 48 minutes
   (c) 3 hours 15 minutes
   (d) 6 hours 57 minutes

3. A train travels at 60 km/h for 2.5 hours.
   It then travels at 50 km/h for a further 3 hours 18 minutes.
   (a) How far does the train travel altogether?
   (b) How long does the total journey take?
   (c) What is the average speed of the train?

4. Jenny sets out on a journey at 1020.
   She completes it at 1305.
   She travels for a total distance of 165 km.
   Work out her average speed in km/h.

5. Ruth sets out on a journey at 1145.
   She completes her journey at 1330.
   She travels at an average speed of 80 km/h.
   Work out the distance she travels.

6. Bill starts a journey at 0810.
   He drives 38 km at an average speed of 63 km/h.
   Find the time his journey ends.
   Give your answer to the nearest minute.

7. Use the timetable of trains from Norwich to London on page 56 to answer these questions.
   The distance the train travels between Norwich and London is 200 km.
   (a) What is the average speed between Norwich and London of the 0630 from Norwich?
   (b) The 0955 from Norwich travels at an average speed of 120 km/h.
       What time does the train arrive in London?
   (c) The 0500 from Norwich travels at an average speed of 110 km/h between Norwich and Ipswich.
       What distance does the train travel between Norwich and Ipswich?

8. The density of aluminium is 2590 kg/m³.
   (a) A piece of aluminium has a mass of 1500 kg.
       Work out its volume.
   (b) The volume of a piece of aluminium is 4.5 m³.
       Work out its mass.

12. SURDS

1 Rational, irrational numbers and surds

A rational number is a number that can be written in the form $^a/_b$ where a and b are integers. For example, $^4/_2$, $^2/_3$ and $^{11}/_4$ are all rational numbers. All rational numbers can be written either as terminating or recurring decimals (see pages 40–41).
Numbers that are not rational are called irrational numbers.
Irrational numbers include $\sqrt{2}$, $\sqrt{3}$, $\sqrt[3]{50}$, π, ...
Irrational numbers with square roots are called surds.

2 Exact answers

Irrational numbers cannot be written in the form $^a/_b$ and cannot be written as either recurring or terminating decimals.
Their exact values cannot be written in decimal form.

> ### Examiner's tips
> - Watch out for questions that say 'Give your answer in terms of π' and questions on Pythagoras that have an answer that is a surd.
> - When asked for an exact answer, leave your answer in irrational form, e.g. $\sqrt{20}$ or 4π.

1 Simplifying surds

A surd is in its simplest form when:
The number under the square root sign does **not** have a **square** factor.
The smallest possible number is underneath the square root sign.
There is no surd in the denominator of a fraction.

e.g.1
$$\begin{aligned}\sqrt{32} &= \sqrt{(16 \times 2)} \\ &= \sqrt{16} \times \sqrt{2} \\ &= 4\sqrt{2}\end{aligned}$$
16 is a **square** factor of 32

$\sqrt{16} = 4$

e.g.2
$$\begin{aligned}\sqrt{8} \times \sqrt{24} &= \sqrt{(8 \times 24)} \\ &= \sqrt{(8 \times 8 \times 3)} \\ &= \sqrt{8^2} \times \sqrt{3} \\ &= 8\sqrt{3}\end{aligned}$$
$24 = 8 \times 3$

$\sqrt{8^2} = 8$

e.g.3
$$\begin{aligned}\sqrt{8} + \sqrt{18} &= \sqrt{(4 \times 2)} + \sqrt{(9 \times 2)} \\ &= \sqrt{4} \times \sqrt{2} + \sqrt{9} \times \sqrt{2} \\ &= 2\sqrt{2} + 3\sqrt{2} \\ &= 5\sqrt{2}\end{aligned}$$
4 and 9 are **square** factors of 8 and 18

e.g.4
$$\begin{aligned}\frac{4}{\sqrt{2}} &= \frac{4 \times \sqrt{2}}{(\sqrt{2})^2} \\ &= \frac{4 \times \sqrt{2}}{2} \\ &= 2\sqrt{2}\end{aligned}$$
multiplying numerator and denominator by $\sqrt{2}$

> ### Examiner's tip
> In example 4, simplifying involves 'rationalising the denominator'.
> To rationalise the denominator get rid of the surd in the denominator of the fraction.

SURDS

Do not use a calculator.

1. Simplify:
 (a) $\sqrt{12}$ (b) $\sqrt{20}$ (c) $\sqrt{45}$
 (d) $\sqrt{80}$ (e) $\sqrt{27}$ (f) $\sqrt{50}$

2. Simplify:
 (a) $\sqrt{3} \times \sqrt{12}$ (b) $\sqrt{3} \times \sqrt{27}$
 (c) $\sqrt{8} \times \sqrt{5}$ (d) $\sqrt{24} \times \sqrt{32}$
 (e) $\sqrt{18} \times \sqrt{4}$ (f) $\sqrt{10} \times \sqrt{18}$

3. Simplify:
 (a) $2\sqrt{3} + \sqrt{12}$ (b) $\sqrt{27} \times 4\sqrt{3}$
 (c) $\sqrt{50} - \sqrt{8}$ (d) $\sqrt{24} + \sqrt{54}$
 (e) $\sqrt{10} \times 2\sqrt{5}$ (f) $\sqrt{90} - \sqrt{40}$

4. Simplify:
 (a) $(3 - \sqrt{2})^2$ (b) $(1 + \sqrt{5})^2$
 (c) $(\sqrt{3} - \sqrt{2})^2$ (d) $(\sqrt{3} + \sqrt{27})^2$
 (e) $(3 + \sqrt{2})(3 - \sqrt{2})$
 (f) $(2 + \sqrt{3})(3 + \sqrt{27})$

5. Simplify by rationalising the denominator:
 (a) $\dfrac{1}{\sqrt{3}}$ (b) $\dfrac{5}{\sqrt{10}}$ (c) $\dfrac{10}{\sqrt{5}}$

 (d) $\dfrac{8}{\sqrt{2}}$ (e) $\dfrac{9}{\sqrt{3}}$ (f) $\dfrac{8}{\sqrt{8}}$

Section 2: Algebra
INTRODUCING ALGEBRA

1.

Algebra

Simple algebraic expressions

Algebraic expressions are made up of terms.
Algebraic expressions that contain like terms can be simplified.
When algebraic expressions are simplified the rules of arithmetic are used.

> ### Remember
>
> $5 \times n$ and $n \times 5$ are both written $5n$
>
> $a \times b$ and $b \times a$ are both written ab
>
> $^4/_p$ means $4 \div p$ $^t/_2$ means $t \div 2$
>
> $5a, 7a, a, 12a, \ldots$ are examples of **like** terms
>
> $5a, 7b, x, 12y, \ldots$ are examples of **unlike** terms

e.g.1 $3x + 5x = 8x$ $3 \times$ a number $(x) + 5 \times$ a number $(x) = 8 \times$ a number (x)

e.g.2 $3a + 5b$ cannot be simplified a and b are different numbers

e.g.3 $x + 4y + 3x - 5y = 4x - y$

e.g.4 $2a \times 3 = 2 \times 3 \times a = 6a$

> ### Examiner's tip
> Writing $x \times 3$ as $x3$ is incorrect
> because $x3$ can be confused with x^3.

Writing algebraic expressions

e.g.1   There are n people on a bus.
If 3 people get off the bus there are
$n - 3$ people on the bus.
If 5 people get on the bus there are
$n + 5$ people on the bus.

e.g.2   A packet of sweets contains x sweets.
Ben has 5 packets, so he has $5x$ sweets.
After Ben eats 4 sweets he has $5x - 4$ sweets left.

e.g.3   The sum of the angles in this triangle is
$x + 3x - 20 + 2x + 50$.

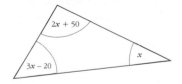

This expression can be simplified to $6x + 30$.

2

Algebraic expressions involving powers

$x \times x$ is written x^2 and read 'x squared'.

$y \times y \times y$ is written y^3 and read 'y cubed'.

$w \times w \times w \times w \times w$ is written w^5 and read 'w to the power 5'.

In the expression x^y, y is the power and x is the base.

x^y is read 'x to the power of y'.

y is the number of times that x is multiplied together.

The rules of powers

To multiply powers of numbers with the same base add the powers. $\qquad a^m \times a^n = a^{m+n}$

To divide powers of numbers with the same base subtract the powers. $\qquad a^m \div a^n = a^{m-n}$

To raise a power to a power multiply the powers. $\qquad (a^m)^n = a^{mn}$

Any number raised to the power zero = 1. $\qquad a^0 = 1$

Any number raised to the power 1 is the number itself. $\qquad a^1 = a$

e.g.1 $\qquad x^2 \times x^3 = x^5 \qquad\qquad x^{2+3}$

e.g.2 $\qquad y \times y^3 = y^4 \qquad\qquad y^{1+3}$

e.g.3 $\qquad x^3y^5 \times xy^3 = x^4y^8 \qquad x^3 \times x \times y^5 \times y^3 = x^{3+1} \times y^{5+3}$

e.g.4 $\qquad x^7 \div x^3 = x^4 \qquad\qquad x^{7-3}$

e.g.5 $\qquad 2x^7 \times 4x^3 = 8x^{10} \qquad 2 \times 4 \times x^{7+3}$

e.g.6 $\qquad 8x^7 \div 2x^2 = 4x^5 \qquad (8 \div 2) \times (x^7 \div x^2)$

e.g.7 $\qquad (2x^3)^2 = 4x^6 \qquad\qquad 2^2 \times (x^3)^2$

e.g.8 $\qquad \dfrac{3x^2y^3 \times 4x^3y^2}{2xy^4} = 6x^4y \qquad (3 \times 4 \div 2) \times (x^2 \times x^3 \div x) \times (y^3 \times y^2 \div y^4)$

3

Expanding brackets

The process of removing brackets from an algebraic expression is called expanding.

METHOD 1 Multiply each term in the bracket by the term outside the bracket

$a(b + c) = ab + ac \quad a \times b + a \times c$

METHOD 2 **The box method**

×	b	c
a	ab	ac

$a(b + c) = ab + ac$

e.g.1 $\qquad 2(x + 5) = 2x + 10 \quad 2 \times x + 2 \times 5$ or

×	x	5
2	2x	10

e.g.2

$y(y-1) = y^2 - y$ $y \times y - y \times 1$ or

$\times$	y	$^{-}1$
y	y^2	^{-}y

e.g.3

$3a(2a + 5) = 6a^2 + 15a$ $3a \times 2a + 3a \times 5$

or

$\times$	$2a$	5
$3a$	$6a^2$	$15a$

2 *Factorising*

Factorising is the inverse (opposite) of expanding brackets.

EXAMPLES

$6x - 15$	$= 3(2x - 5)$	$6x$ and 15 have a **common factor** of 3
$p^2 + 2p$	$= p(p + 2)$	p^2 and $2p$ have a **common factor** of p
$3a^2 + 6a$	$= 3a(a + 2)$	$3a^2$ and $6a$ have a **common factor** of $3a$

Examiner's tip

If you expand your factorised expression you should get the expression you started with. Use this idea to check your answers.

Test 13

Do not use a calculator.

1. Simplify:
  (a) $t + 3t + 5t$ **(b)** $3x - 4 + 2x$
  (c) $3p + 2q - 4q$ **(d)** $3x - 2y - 4y$
  (e) $5a + ab - a - 3b - 3ab + 2a$

2. Sam is x years older than Emma.
  Write an expression for:
  (a) Sam's age when Emma is 5 years old.
  (b) Sam's age when Emma is y years old.
  (c) The age of Jenny who is twice Sam's age.

3. Boxes of marbles each contain 10 marbles.
  Bill buys b boxes of marbles.
  He gives Jenny a marbles.
  Write down an expression for the number of marbles Bill has.

4. A packet of sweets cost x pence.
  Tom buys 5 packets of sweets.
  He pays with a £10 note.
  Write down an expression for the change Tom receives in pence.

SOLVING
LINEAR EQUATIONS

5. Which of these algebraic expressions are equivalent?

$y \times y$ $y + y + y$ $y^2 + y$

$2y + y$ $2y \times y$ y^2

$y^5 \div y^3$ $y \times y + y$ $y(y + 1)$

6. Simplify:

  (a) $t \times t^5$ **(b)** $x^3 \times x^2$

  (c) $4x^3 \times 3x^2$ **(d)** $y^4 \div y$

  (e) $y^7 \div y^2$ **(f)** $10y^5 \div 2y^3$

  (g) $xy^3 \times x^2y^4$ **(h)** $a^4b^5 \div a^2b^3$

  (i) $(2x^2)^3$ **(j)** $2p^3 \times 8p^5 \div 4p$

7. Expand:

  (a) $3(a + 5)$ **(b)** $5(x - 4)$

  (c) $p(p - 4)$ **(d)** $3x(2x + 4)$

  (e) $5ab(a - 3b + 2)$

8. Expand and simplify:

  (a) $3(t + 1) + 2(t - 4)$

  (b) $2(3q - 4) + 3(q - 2)$

  (c) $5(2a + b) - 3(a - 3b)$

9. Factorise:

  (a) $6a + 3$ **(b)** $10x - 15$

  (c) $3r^2 - 4r$ **(d)** $x^2 - x$

  (e) $5a^2 + 10a$ **(f)** $2a^3b + 10ab$

2.

Solving by inspection

If an algebraic expression is made equal to a number (or another algebraic expression) an equation is formed.

The solution of the equation is the value of the letter symbol that fits the equation.

Finding the value of the letter symbol in an equation is called solving.

Some simple equations can be solved by inspection.

This means looking at the equation and spotting the solution.

e.g.1

$$x + 3 = 8$$
$$5 + 3 = 8$$
$$x = 5$$

e.g.2

$$y - 4 = 7$$
$$11 - 4 = 7$$
$$y = 11$$

e.g.3

$$3p = 12$$
$$3 \times 4 = 12$$
$$p = 4$$

e.g.4

$$^1/_3 = 4$$
$$12 \div 3 = 4$$
$$t = 12$$

4 Working backwards

Equations can be written in the form of word problems.
One way of solving these is to work backwards.

e.g.1

Sara thinks of a number.
She multiplies it by 4 and then adds 5.
She gets the answer 33.
What number did Sara think of?

$$? \rightarrow \boxed{\times 4} \rightarrow \boxed{+ 5} \rightarrow 33$$
$$7 \leftarrow \boxed{\div 4} \leftarrow \boxed{- 5} \leftarrow 33$$

ANSWER   Sara thought of the number 7

4 Using the balance method

The balance method can be used to change an equation to a simpler equation that is still true.

The balance method means doing the same thing to both sides of an equation.

e.g.1 $4x + 3 = 9$

METHOD

$$4x = 6 \qquad \text{subtracting 3 from both sides}$$
$$x = {}^6/_4 \qquad \text{dividing both sides by 4}$$

ANSWER $x = 1.5$

e.g.2 $2 - {}^1/_2\,a = 10$

METHOD

$${}^-1/_2\,a = 8 \qquad \text{subtracting 2 from both sides}$$
$$a = 8 \times {}^-2 \qquad \text{multiplying both sides by } {}^-2$$

ANSWER $a = {}^-16$

> ### Examiner's tips
> - *Show the steps you use in solving an equation.*
> - *Check your answer by seeing if your solution fits the equation.*

SOLVING LINEAR EQUATIONS

Algebra

4 Solving equations with brackets

e.g.1 $2(5x - 3) = 9$

METHOD $10x - 6 = 9$ expanding brackets
$10x = 15$ adding 6 to both sides
$x = 15 \div 10$ dividing both sides by 10

ANSWER $x = 1.5$

Remember
Expand the brackets first and then use the balance method.

3 Solving equations with the unknown on 'both sides'

e.g.1 $5x + 2 = 3x - 2$

METHOD $2x + 2 = {}^-2$ subtracting $3x$ from both sides
$2x = {}^-4$ subtracting 2 from both sides
$x = {}^-4 \div 2$ dividing both sides by 2

ANSWER $x = {}^-2$

e.g.2 $3(4x - 1) = 2(4x + 5)$

METHOD $12x - 3 = 8x + 10$ expanding brackets
$4x - 3 = 10$ subtracting $8x$ from both sides
$4x = 13$ adding 3 to both sides
$x = {}^{13}/_4$ dividing both sides by 4

ANSWER $x = 3.25$

2 Equations with fractions

e.g.1 $\frac{1}{2}x + 2 = 5 - \frac{1}{3}x$ the lowest common multiple of 2 and 3 is **6**

METHOD $3x + 12 = 30 - 2x$ multiplying both sides by **6**
$5x + 12 = 30$ adding $2x$ to both sides
$5x = 18$ subtracting 12 from both sides
$x = 18 \div 5$ dividing both sides by 5

ANSWER $x = 2\frac{1}{4}$

Remember
To solve equations with fractions:
Multiply both sides of the equation by the lowest common multiple of the denominators.
Then use the balance method.

e.g.2

$$\frac{x+2}{6} = \frac{4x-3}{4} + 1$$

The lowest common multiple of 6 and 4 is **12**

METHOD

$2(x+2) = 3(4x-3) + 12$ multiplying both sides by **12**

$2x+4 = 12x - 9 + 12$ expanding brackets

$2x+4 = 12x + 3$ simplifying

$4 = 10x + 3$ subtracting $2x$ from both sides

$1 = 10x$ subtracting 3 from both sides

ANSWER $x = 0.1$ dividing both sides by 10

> ### Examiner's tip
> *Normally, letter terms are collected on the left-hand side of the equation.*
> *However, it is sometimes more convenient to collect them on the right-hand side.*

3   *Writing equations*

e.g.1

In bag A there are n marbles.
In bag B there are 3 more marbles than in bag A.
The total number of marbles is 43.

METHOD

Bag $A = n$ marbles

Bag $B = n + 3$ marbles

Total $= n + n + 3 = 2n + 3$ marbles

So $2n + 3 = 43$

ANSWER $n = 20$ by inspection

e.g.2

Rectangles A and B have the same perimeter.

$x + 5$

$2x + 3$ A

$x + 3$

$8x + 2$ B

METHOD

Perimeter of $A = 2(x + 5) + 2(2x + 3)$

$= 6x + 16$ $2x + 10 + 4x + 6$

Perimeter of $B = 2(x + 3) + 2(8x + 2)$

$= 18x + 10$ $2x + 6 + 16x + 4$

So $18x + 10 = 6x + 16$

$18x = 6x + 6$ subtracting 10 from both sides

$12x = 6$ subtracting 6 from both sides

ANSWER $x = 0.5$ dividing both sides by 12

Do not use a calculator.

1. Write down the solutions to these equations.
 (a) $x + 12 = 20$ **(b)** $x - 7 = 1$
 (c) $x + 15 = 20$ **(d)** $x - 12 = {}^-2$
 (e) $5x = 20$ **(f)** $7x = 28$
 (g) $x/2 = 4$ **(h)** $x/5 = 20$

2. Tom thinks of a number.
 He multiplies it by 5 and then adds 3.
 He gets the answer 38.
 What number did Tom think of?

3. For an emergency call a plumber charges £18 per hour plus a fixed charge of £50.
 The plumber charges Mrs Jones £131.
 How many hours did the plumber work on Mrs Jones' emergency?

4. Solve these equations.
 (a) $2x + 1 = 9$ **(b)** $3x - 5 = 16$
 (c) $5x + 15 = 30$ **(d)** $4x - 1 = 35$
 (e) $1 - 2x = 21$ **(f)** $3 - 5x = 37$
 (g) $1 + x/3 = 3$ **(h)** $4 + x/2 = 5$
 (i) $2 - x/4 = 5$ **(j)** $3 - x/4 = {}^-2$

5. Solve these equations.
 (a) $2(x + 1) = 9$ **(b)** $5(x - 3) = 16$
 (c) $2(3x + 1) = 44$ **(d)** $4(x - 1) = 10$
 (e) $5(1 - x) = 21$ **(f)** $2(1 - 5x) = 3$
 (g) $6(1 + x/3) = 5$ **(h)** $4(1 + x/2) = 1$

6. Solve these equations.
 (a) $2x + 5 = 5x - 4$ **(b)** $5x - 3 = x$
 (c) $3x + 1 = x - 4$ **(d)** $4(x - 1) = 2x$
 (e) $3(5 - 2x) = 2(2x + 7)$
 (f) $3(1 + 5x) = 3(2x + 7) + 2(2x + 3)$
 (g) $2(2x + 7) - 4(2x + 7) = 2(7 - 3x)$

7. Solve these equations.
 (a) $\frac{1}{2}x + 1 = \frac{3}{4}x - 3$
 (b) $\frac{1}{5}x - 1 = \frac{1}{3}x$
 (c) $\frac{1}{3}x - 4 = \frac{1}{4}x - 7$
 (d) $\frac{1}{4}(x - 1) = \frac{1}{5}x$
 (e) $\dfrac{1 + 3x}{2} = \dfrac{2x + 7}{3} + 3$
 (f) $\dfrac{(x + 7)}{2} - \dfrac{3(2x + 7)}{4} = \dfrac{2(7 - 3x)}{5}$

8. (a) Use the fact that these two rectangles have the same area to form an equation in terms of x.

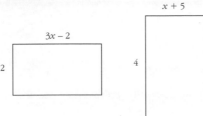

$x + 5$

$3x - 2$

2

4

(b) Solve the equation and find the area of the rectangle.

9. A quadrilateral has angles $x°$, $(2x - 55)°$, $(2x + 40)°$ and $(x + 45)°$.
(a) Form and solve an equation in x.
(b) Find the largest angle in the quadrilateral.

3. FORMULAE

Writing expressions and formulae

An algebraic expression contains letter symbols and numbers.
A formula is a rule that uses letter symbols and numbers, and always has an equals sign.

e.g.1   A TV engineer charges a basic fee of £40 plus £18 per hour for repairs.
The charge, £C, for n hours work is given by the formula $C = 40 + 18n$.

e.g.2   Tickets for a school concert are £5 for adults and £3 for children.
The total value, £T, of ticket sales for x adults and y children is $T = 5x + 3y$.

Substitution into formulae

Substitution means replacing the letter symbols in a formula by numbers.

e.g.1 $A = 2x + 5y$
Work out the value of A when
$x = 4$ and $y = 3$.

METHOD $A = 2 \times 4 + 5 \times 3 = 8 + 15$

ANSWER $A = 23$

e.g.2

$B = 3a + 4b - 5c$
Work out B when $a = 2$, $b = {}^-1$ and $c = 2.4$.

METHOD

$B = 3 \times 2 + 4 \times {}^-1 - 5 \times 2.4$
$\quad = 6 + {}^-4 - 12$

ANSWER

$B = {}^-10$

2 More substitution

e.g.1

$V = \dfrac{a^2 + b^2}{a - b}$

METHOD

Work out V when $a = 2.45$ and $b = {}^-1.3$.
$V = (2.45^2 + {}^-1.3^2) \div (2.45 - {}^-1.3)$
$\quad = 7.6925 \div 3.75$

ANSWER

$V = 2.0513 \ldots$

e.g.2

$W = \sqrt{a^3 + b^2}$
Find the value of W when $a = 2$ and $b = 3.5$.

METHOD

$W = \sqrt{2^3 + 3.5^2}$
$\quad = \sqrt{8 + 12.25}$
$\quad = \sqrt{20.25}$

ANSWER

$W = 4.5$

2 Rearranging formulae

a is the subject of the formula $a = bc + d$.
The formula can be rearranged to make b, c or d the subject.
Rearranging a formula is similar to solving an equation using the balance method.

e.g.1

Rearrange the formula $a = bc + d$ to make b the subject.

METHOD

$a = bc + d$
$a - d = bc$ subtracting d from both sides
$\dfrac{a - d}{c} = b$ dividing both sides by c

ANSWER

$b = \dfrac{a - d}{c}$

e.g.2

Rearrange the formula $V = \sqrt{pq}$ to make q the subject.

METHOD

$V = \sqrt{pq}$
$V^2 = pq$ squaring both sides
$\dfrac{V^2}{p} = q$ dividing both sides by p

ANSWER

$q = \dfrac{V^2}{p}$

2 Finding values from a formula

e.g.1

The volume, V, of a square-based cuboid of base length x and height h is x^2h.
A square-based cuboid has base length 5 cm and volume 320 cm³.

METHOD

$V = x^2h$
When $V = 320$ and $x = 5$
$\quad 320 = 5^2 \times h$
$\quad 320 = 25 \times h$
$\quad\quad h = 320 \div 25$ dividing both sides by 25

ANSWER

$\quad\quad h = 12.8$

e.g.2

s is given by the formula $s = ut + \frac{1}{2}at^2$
Work out a when $s = 2.4$, $u = 5.6$ and $t = 4$

METHOD

$2.4 = 5.6 \times 4 + \frac{1}{2} \times a \times 4^2$
$2.4 = 22.4 + 8 \times a$
$2.4 - 22.4 = 8 \times a$ subtracting 22.4 from both sides
$\quad {}^-20 = 8 \times a$
$\quad\quad a = {}^-20 \div 8$ dividing both sides by 8

ANSWER

$\quad\quad a = {}^-2.5$

1 More rearranging formulae

In some formulae the subject occurs in **more than one term**.
Rearranging these formulae could involve both factorising and expanding brackets.

e.g.1

Make y the subject of the formula $a = \dfrac{y + 1}{y}$

METHOD

Remove the fractions
$\quad\quad ay = y + 1$ multiplying both sides by y
Collect terms involving the subject
$\quad\quad ay - y = 1$ subtracting y from both sides
$\quad y(a - 1) = 1$ factorising

ANSWER

$\quad\quad y = \dfrac{1}{a - 1}$ dividing both sides by $a - 1$

e.g.2

Make x the subject of the formula $q = \dfrac{x^2 + p}{x^2 - p}$

METHOD

Remove the fractions
$\quad q(x^2 - p) = x^2 + p$ multiplying both sides by $x^2 - p$
$\quad qx^2 - qp = x^2 + p$ expanding brackets
Collect terms involving the subject
$\quad qx^2 - x^2 = qp + p$ adding qp to both sides and subtracting x^2
                        from both sides
$\quad x^2(q - 1) = p(q + 1)$ factorising
$\quad\quad x^2 = \dfrac{p(q + 1)}{q - 1}$ dividing both sides by $q^2 - 1$
$\quad\quad x = \sqrt{\dfrac{p(q + 1)}{q - 1}}$ taking the square root of both sides

Test 15

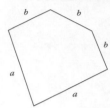 Use a calculator for questions 7 and 10.

1. Write a formula for P, the perimeter of this polygon.

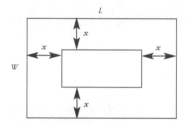

2. A train has x first class carriages and y standard-class carriages.
There are a seats in a first class carriage and b seats in a standard-class carriage.
Write a formula for N, the number of seats on the train.

3. A garden in the shape of a rectangle has length L and width W.
The garden is made up of a rectangular lawn surrounded by a flowerbed of width x.

(a) Write a formula for P, the perimeter of the lawn.
(b) Write a formula for A, the area of the lawn.

4. The formula $F = 1.8C + 32$ is used to change temperatures from degrees Celsius, C, to degrees Fahrenheit, F.
Find F when:
(a) $C = 10$ **(b)** $C = 20$ **(c)** $C = {}^-10$

5. You are told that $A = 2a + 3b$.
Work out A when:
(a) $a = 10$ and $b = 5$
(b) $a = 20$ and $b = {}^-4$

6. You are told that $X = a^2 + 2b^2$.
Work out X when:
(a) $a = 10$ and $b = {}^-3$
(b) $a = {}^-2$ and $b = 4$

7. Use the formula $P = \sqrt{\dfrac{a^3}{2b}}$ to calculate P when $a = 1.2$ and $b = {}^2/_5$
Give your answer to an accuracy of 3 significant figures.

8. Make x the subject of each of the following formulae.
(a) $y = 5x$ **(b)** $y = 3x + 2$
(c) $y = 5x - 3$ **(d)** $y = ax + c$
(e) $y = 3x + a$ **(f)** $y = {}^x/_a + b$

9. Make x the subject of each of the following formulae.
   (a) $p = \sqrt{x/y}$ **(b)** $p = \sqrt{y/x}$

   (c) $p = \sqrt{5/x}$ **(d)** $p = \sqrt{x + y}$

10.(a) You are told that $u = \sqrt{gR}$.
        Work out R when $u = 6$ and $g = 10$.

   (b) You are told that $p = \sqrt{\dfrac{x + y}{x - y}}$.

        Work out x when $p = 2.5$ and $y = 6$
        Give your answer to an accuracy of 3 significant figures.

11. Make z the subject of the following formulae.
   (a) $az - 3 = z + b$
   (b) $az - b = cz + d$
   (c) $a(z - 3) = b(z - 1)$
   (d) $x(z - y) = z + y$
   (e) $y = \dfrac{az - b}{bz - a}$
   (f) $y = \sqrt{\dfrac{z + a}{z - a}}$

4. SEQUENCES

Continuing sequences using term-to-term rules

A sequence is a set of numbers that follow a rule.
The numbers in a sequence are called terms.
A term-to-term rule connects one term in a sequence to the next term in the sequence.
Term-to-term rules can be used to continue sequences.

e.g.1

The sequence   1, 3, 7, 15, ... has the term-to-term rule:
$\times$ the last term by 2 and then $+1$
The next term in the sequence is $15 \times 2 + 1 = 31$.

e.g.2

The 4th, 5th and 6th terms of a sequence are 1, 4 and 7.
The term-to-term rule is add 3.
7th term $= 7 + 3 = 10$
3rd term $= 1 - 3 = {}^-2$
Using the term-to-term rule 4 times gives:
10th term $= 7 + 4 \times 3 = 19$
Using the term-to-term rule -3 times gives:
1st term $= 1 - 3 \times 3 = {}^-8$

TERM ᴛᴏTERM
RULES

SEQUENCES

2

The nth term of a linear sequence

The term-to-term rule of a linear sequence involves either adding or subtracting the same number.

The nth term is a rule from which any term in the sequence can be found.

e.g.1

The nth term of a sequence is $4n + 1$.
The **1**st term is $4 \times \mathbf{1} + 1 = 5$.
The **2**nd term is $4 \times \mathbf{2} + 1 = 9$.
The **3**rd term is $4 \times \mathbf{3} + 1 = 13$.
The sequence is a linear sequence with term-to-term rule add 4.

e.g.2

The sequence   2,   7,   12,   17, …   is a linear sequence
with term-to-term rule add **5.**
The nth term rule is connected to the multiples of **5.**

n	1	2	3	4 …
Term	2	7	12	17 …
5n	5	10	15	20 …
5n – 3	2	7	12	17 …

So the nth term is $5n - 3$.

e.g.3

Percy Proof says that 2003 is a term in the sequence with n^{th} term $4n + 1$.
Explain why he is wrong.

$4n$ is the nth term for the multiples of 4.
So $4n + 1$ is 1 more than a multiple of 4.

$2003 = 4 \times 500 + 3$
So 2003 is 3 more than a multiple of 4, so it can't be in the sequence.

2

Quadratic sequences

A sequence that is connected to n^2 is called a quadratic sequence.

e.g.1

n^{th} term $= n^2 + 3$
The **1**st term is $\mathbf{1}^2 + 3 = 4$
The **2**nd term is $\mathbf{2}^2 + 3 = 7$ $7 - 4 = \mathbf{3}$
The **3**rd term is $\mathbf{3}^2 + 3 = 12$ $12 - 7 = \mathbf{5}$
The **4**th term is $\mathbf{4}^2 + 3 = 19$ $19 - 12 = \mathbf{7}$
The **5**th term is $\mathbf{5}^2 + 3 = 28$ $28 - 19 = \mathbf{9}$
The differences between the terms of this quadratic sequence are 3, 5, 7, 9, …

> **Examiner's tip**
> If you have to find the nth term of a quadratic sequence the connection to n^2 will be simple.

e.g.2

The sequence 2,   6,   12,   20,   30, …   has differences 4, 6, 8, 10, …
This is a quadratic sequence and has an nth term rule connected to n^2.

n	1	2	3	4	5 …
Term	2	6	12	20	30 …
n^2	1	4	9	16	25 …
$n^2 + n$	2	6	12	20	30 …

So the nth term is $n^2 + n$.

2 *Sequences from patterns of shapes*

Patterns of shapes can be used to represent sequences.

e.g.1

This sequence of patterns is made from matchsticks.

Pattern **1**   Pattern **2**   Pattern **3**

Pattern **1** 2 vertical matchsticks and 3×1 horizontal matchsticks
Pattern **2** 2 vertical matchsticks and 3×2 horizontal matchsticks
Pattern **3** 2 vertical matchsticks and 3×3 horizontal matchsticks
Pattern **n** 2 vertical matchsticks and $3 \times n$ horizontal matchsticks
So the number of matchsticks in Pattern $n = 3n + 2$
The number of matchsticks in Pattern n is the nth term rule for the sequence 5, 8, 11,…

> **Examiner's tip**
> *You might be asked to use a sequence of patterns*
> *to explain why the nth term rule works.*

Test 16

Do not use a calculator.

1. Write down the missing numbers in the following sequences.
   (a)   1,   5,   11,   19,   ?,   ?   …
   (b) 27,   24,   19,   12,   ?,   ?   …
   (c)   7,   10,   16,   ?,   37,   ?   …
   (d) ⁻1,   ?,   11,   23,   ?,   59, …

2. The first four terms of a sequence are
   3,   5,   7,   9, …
   One number in the sequence is x.
   In terms of x:
   (a) What is the number before x in the sequence?
   (b) What is the third number after x in the sequence?

3. Write the first five terms in each of these sequences.
  (a) 1st term = 5.
    Term-to-term rule: add 3
  (b) 3rd term = ⁻1.
    Term-to-term rule: add 4
  (c) 1st term = 1.
    Term-to-term rule: multiply by ⁻2
  (d) 4th term = 16.
    Term-to-term rule: multiply by 4

4. A sequence has n^{th} term $3n + 1$.
  (a) Find the first three terms of this sequence.
  (b) Repeat **(a)** for each of these sequences.
    (i) $5n - 3$ **(ii)** $7n - 4$
    (iii) $n^2 + 2n$ **(iv)** $n(n + 1)$
  (c) Is 930 a term in any of the sequences in **(a)** and **(b)**?
    Explain your answers.

5. Find the nth term of each of the following sequences.
  (a) 3,   5,   7,   9, ...
  (b) 4,   7,   10,   13, ...
  (c) 1,   5,   9,   13, ...
  (d) 3,   9,   15,   21, ...
  (e) $\frac{1}{3}$, $\frac{3}{7}$, $\frac{5}{11}$, $\frac{7}{15}$, ...

6. Find the nth term of each of the following sequences.
  (a) 1,   4,   9,   16, ...
  (b) 3,   6,   11,   18, ...
  (c) 0,   3,   8,   15, ...
  (d) 2,   8,   18,   32, ...

7. The diagram shows a sequence of patterns.

Pattern 1

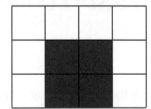

Pattern 2

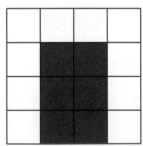

Pattern 3

  (a) How many white squares are in Pattern n?
  (b) Use the pattern of squares to explain your answer to **(a)**.
  (c) In which pattern number are there 2000 white squares?
  (d) Percy Proof says there is a pattern with 381 white squares.
    Explain why he is wrong.

5.   LINEAR GRAPHS

Coordinates

Coordinates are pairs of numbers used to describe the
position of a point on a grid.

The 1ˢᵗ number is the distance moved along the x-axis.
The 2ⁿᵈ number is the distance moved along the y-axis.
The x-axis and y-axis cross at the origin, O.
The coordinates (x, y) describe the position of a point
x units across, left or right, and y units up or down **from**
the origin.

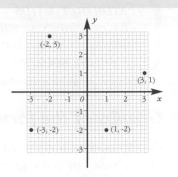

Straight line graphs

A set of points whose coordinates follow a rule can be plotted and joined to make a graph.
The rule is usually written as an equation.

e.g.1   Equation $y = 2$
The graph joins **all** points where the
y-coordinate equals 2.

e.g.2   Equation $x = {}^-3$
The graph joins **all** points where the
x-coordinate equals ⁻3.

e.g.3   Equation $y = x$
The graph joins **all** points where the
y-coordinate equals the x-coordinate.

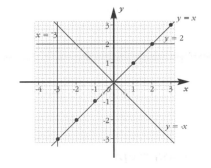

e.g.4   Equation $y = {}^-x$
The graph joins **all** points where the
y-coordinate equals the negative value of
the x-coordinate.

Drawing a graph from its equation

To plot a graph from its equation:
    Work out pairs of values of x and y that fit the equation.
    Write the values of x and y as coordinates.
    Plot and join the points.

e.g.1   Equation $y = 3x + 2$
To find each y-coordinate multiply the
x-coordinate by 3 and then add 2
The values of x and y can be put in a table.

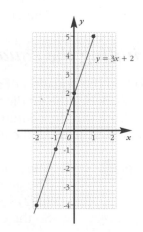

x	⁻2	⁻1	0	1
y	⁻4	⁻1	2	5

Coordinates $({}^-2, {}^-4), ({}^-1, {}^-1), (0, 2), (1, 5)$

77

2

Graphs of the form $y = mx + c$

Graphs of the form $y = mx + c$ are linear (straight line) graphs.
The value of m is the gradient of the graph.
The value of c is the y-intercept.

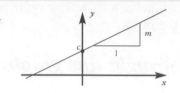

Gradient
The gradient of a line (m) is defined as:

$$\frac{\text{distance up}}{\text{distance along}}$$

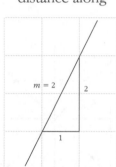

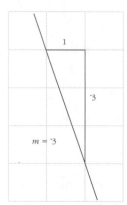

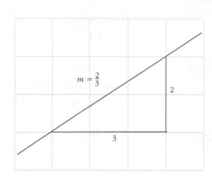

y-intercept
The y-intercept (c) is the value of y where the graph
crosses the y-axis.

e.g.1   Equation $y = 2x - 1$

The graph crosses the y-axis at the point
$(0, {}^-1)$ so $c = {}^-1$
The gradient $= {}^2/_1$ so $m = 2$

2

Finding the equations of linear graphs

To find the equation of a straight line graph:
    Work out the gradient (m)
    Work out the y-intercept (c)
    Substitute m and c in $y = mx + c$

e.g.1   The gradient of the line is ${}^3/_2$ so $m = 1.5$
               The graph crosses the y-axis at the point
               $(0, 2)$ so $c = {}^-2$
               So the equation of the line is $y = 1.5x - 2$

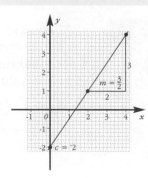

2 Practical applications of linear graphs

e.g.1

The graph shows how TV repair charges
(£C) depend on the time taken for the
repairs (t minutes).
£20 ÷ 40 minutes
The gradient of the line = £0.50 per minute
The 'y-intercept' = £20
Equation of the line $C = 0.5t + 20$
Cost for a 2-hour repair = £80 $0.5 \times 120 + 20$

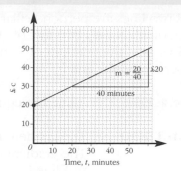

Time, t, minutes

2 Drawing graphs of the form px + qy = r

Equations of linear graphs can also be written with the equation in the form **px + qy = r**
The coordinates of points where the line crosses the axes can be found by substituting
$x = 0$ and $y = 0$ into the equation.

e.g.1   Equation $2x - 3y = 6$

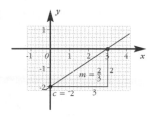

METHOD

When $x = 0$ $^-3y = 6$
So $y = ^-2$ $6 ÷ ^-3$
Graph crosses y-axis at $(0, ^-2)$.
When $y = 0$ $2x = 6$
So $x = 3$ $6 ÷ 2$
Graph crosses x-axis at $(3, 0)$.

So the graph of $2x - 3y = 6$ passes through $(0, ^-2)$ and $(3, 0)$.

The graph has gradient (m), $^2/_3$, and y-intercept (c), $^-2$.
So the equation $2x - 3y = 6$ can also be written in the form $y = ^2/_3 x - 2$.

2 Rearranging px + qy = r to y = mx + c

Equations of the form **px + qy = r** can be rearranged to the form $y = mx + c$

e.g.1   Rewrite the equation $3y - 2x = 6$ in the form $y = mx + c$

METHOD $3y - 2x = 6$
Add $2x$ to both sides.
$3y = 2x + 6$
Divide both sides by 3.
$y = ^2/_3 x + 2$

The line has gradient (m) $^2/_3$ and y-intercept (c) 2.

1

The gradients and equations of perpendicular lines

If two lines are perpendicular to each other then their
gradients have a product of ⁻**1**.
So if **m** is the gradient of a line then the gradient of a
perpendicular line is ⁻¹/**m**.

$m = \frac{1}{2}$

$m = ⁻2$

e.g.1   A line has equation $y = ⁻4x + 5$.

METHOD   The gradient **(m)** of this line is ⁻4.
The gradient of the line perpendicular to
this line is ¼ .   ⁻¹/₋₄

ANSWER   The equation of the line perpendicular to this line and passing through
(0, 5) is $y = \frac{1}{4}x + 5$.

Test 17

Do not use a calculator.

1. (a) Copy and complete the table of values for $y = 3x - 4$.

x	⁻1	0	1	2	3
y		⁻4			

(b) Draw the line $y = 3x - 4$ for values of x from ⁻1 to 3.
(c) Write down the coordinates of the point where the line $y = 3x - 4$ crosses the
y-axis.

2. On the same axes draw the lines $x = ⁻3$, $y = 2$, $x + y = 0$ and $y - x = 0$.
One of these lines has a negative gradient.
Work out the value of this gradient.

3. On the same set of axes draw these lines for values of x from ⁻3 to 3.
(a) $y = 3x + 1$ **(b)** $y = 3x + 4$
(c) $y = 3x$ **(d)** $y = 3x - 2$
What do you notice?

4. On the same set of axes draw these lines for values of x from ⁻3 to 3.
(a) $y = x + 1$ **(b)** $y = 2x + 1$
(c) $y = 3x + 1$ **(d)** $y = ⁻3x + 1$
What do you notice?

5. Draw lines passing through these pairs of points.
(i) (0, 2) and (1, 4)
(ii) (0, ⁻1) and (2, 5)
(iii) (1, 3) and (2, 2)
(iv) (⁻1, 6) and (1, 2)

(v) (⁻1, 8) and (1, 5)
(a) Write down the gradient and *y*-intercept of each line.
(b) Write down the equation of each line.

2 **6.** Each of the following graphs pass through the points (0, *a*) and (*b*, 0)
(a) $x + 2y = 4$ **(b)** $2x - y = 8$
(c) $2x + 3y = 12$ **(d)** $4x + 5y = 10$
(e) $3x - 2y = 12$ **(f)** $5x - 3y = ⁻30$
In each case, find the values of *a* and *b*.

2 **7.** Rearrange each of the equations in question 6 to give *y* in terms of *x*.

2 **8.** Draw intersecting lines with gradients of:
(a) ⁻3 and ¹/₃ **(b)** ⁻1.5 and ²/₃
(c) 2.5 and ⁻0.4 **(d)** ⁻5 and 0.2
In each case what do you notice?
Explain your answer.

2 **9.** Percy Proof says that the lines
$2y = 3 - x$ and $y - 2x = 7$ are perpendicular.
Show that he is right.

2 **10.** A line perpendicular to the line with equation $5x - 2y = 4$ passes through the
point (0, 3).
Find the equation of this line.

---

6. # SOME APPLICATIONS OF GRAPHS

2 ## 'Real-life' graphs

e.g.1   Water is poured into the container at a constant rate.
The graph shows the depth of the water plotted against time.

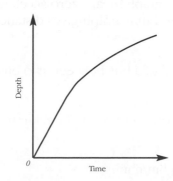

SOME APPLICATIONS OF GRAPHS

e.g.2

The graph shows the volume of water in a bath plotted against time.

O to A hot tap on

$200 \div 2 = 100$

Water fills at the rate of 100 litres/min

A to B cold tap on

$100 \div 2 = 50$

Water fills at the rate of 50 litres/min

C to D plug out

$300 \div 2 = 150$

Water empties at the rate of 150 litres/min

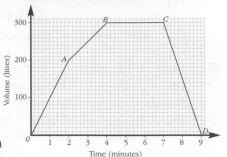

The gradient shows the rate of filling and emptying the bath.

The straight lines show a constant rate.

The horizontal line shows the volume of water stays the same.

4   *Distance-time graphs*

Speed is the rate of change of distance with respect to time. So:

The gradient of a distance-time graph gives the speed.

A linear distance-time graph means constant speed.

A horizontal distance-time graph means zero speed.

> **Remember**
>
> 6 minutes = 0.1 hours

e.g.1

Tom goes on a bike ride.

The graph shows his journey.

The total distance Tom cycles is 8 km.

He does this in two stages.

$5 \div 0.5 = 10$

Stage 1:   speed = 10 km/hour

He stops for 30 minutes.

$3 \div 0.25 = 12$

Stage 2:   speed = 12 km/hour

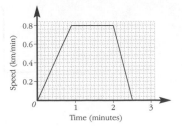

1   *Speed-time graphs*

Acceleration is the rate of change of speed with respect to time. So:

The gradient of a speed-time graph gives acceleration.

A linear speed-time graph means constant acceleration.

A horizontal speed-time graph means zero acceleration.

The area beneath a speed-time graph gives distance travelled.

> **Examiner's tip**
>
> *You will not be asked to find the area beneath a curved graph.*

e.g.1

The graph shows the speed of a bus between two bus stops.

$0.8 \div 1 = 0.8$

The bus accelerates at 0.8 km/min².

The bus then travels at a constant speed of 0.8 km/minute for 1 minute.

$^-0.8 \div 0.5 = ^-1.6$

The bus decelerates at 1.6 km/min².

$0.5 \times (1 + 2.5) \times 0.8$

Distance travelled by the bus = 1.4 km

Test 18

Do not use a calculator.

2 1. The following diagrams show the cross-sections of a number of containers.

(a)   **(b)**   **(c)**   **(d)**   **(e)**   **(f)**

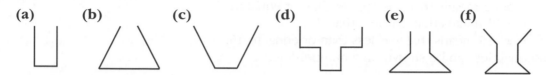

Water flows into each container at a constant rate.
Sketch a graph of the depth of water against time for each container.

2 2. Water flows into a container at a constant rate.
The graph shows the depth of the water against time.

Sketch the cross-section of the container.

4 3. Sam walks from Corfe to Wareham and then
returns to Corfe.
The graph shows her journey.
  (a) At what time did Sam leave Corfe?
  (b) How far from Wareham did Sam make
       her first stop?
  (c) Sam had lunch at Wareham.
       How many minutes did she stop for lunch?
  (d) At what average speed did Sam walk
       back from Wareham to Corfe?

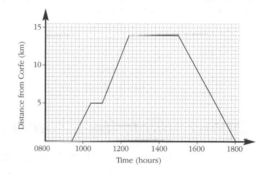

4 4. Hannah goes to a shop to buy a loaf of bread.
The shop is 800 m from her home.
She leaves home at 1512 and walks to the shop at a steady speed.
She takes 12 minutes to reach the shop and 3 minutes to buy a loaf of bread.
She then walks home at a steady speed arriving at 1542.
  (a) Draw a distance-time graph to represent her journey.
  (b) Find the average speed in km/hour at which she walks home.

1 5. The diagrams show speed-time graphs for two trains.
  (a) Which train goes the fastest?
       By how much?
  (b) Which train accelerates the fastest?
       By how much?
  (c) Which train travels the furthest?
       By how much?

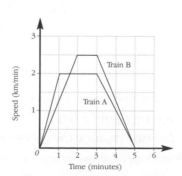

83

7. INEQUALITIES

Showing inequalities on a number line

An inequality involves one of these symbols $>$ $\geq$ $<$ $\leq$

$x > 1$ means that x is greater than 1.

$x \geq {}^{-}2$ means that x is greater than or equal to $^{-}2$.

$x < 1$ means that x is less than 1.

$x \leq 15$ means that x is less than or equal to 15.

Inequalities can be shown on a number line.

e.g.1 $x > 3$

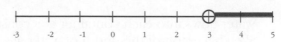

The hollow circle at 3 shows that 3 is **not included**.

e.g.2 $x < 2$

The hollow circle at 2 shows that 2 **is not included**.

e.g.3 $x \geq 1$

The solid circle at 1 shows that 1 **is included**.

e.g.4   Double inequalities can also be shown.

${}^{-}3 < x \leq 2$

The solid circle at 2 shows that 2 **is included**.

The hollow circle at $^{-}3$ shows that $^{-}3$ **is not included**.

Solving simple linear inequalities

Values of x can be found that fit inequalities like $5x - 3 < 7$.

The method is similar to the balance method used to solve equations.

e.g.1
$$5x - 3 < 7$$
$$5x < 10 \qquad \text{adding 3 to both sides}$$
$$x < 2 \qquad \text{dividing both sides by 5}$$

e.g.2
$$5x + 4 \geq 2x - 5$$
$$3x + 4 \geq {}^{-}5 \qquad \text{subtracting } 2x \text{ from both sides}$$
$$3x \geq {}^{-}9 \qquad \text{subtracting 4 from both sides}$$
$$x \geq {}^{-}3 \qquad \text{dividing both sides by 3}$$

DO THIS

Show the solutions to $5x - 3 < 7$ and $5x + 4 < 2x - 5$ on a number line.

> **Examiner's tip**
> Do **not** replace the inequality symbol with an equals sign!

2 Solving harder linear inequalities

There is one important exception when using the balance method to solve inequalities.
If you multiply or divide the inequality by a **negative** number **reverse** the inequality.

e.g.1

$$^-5x - 3 < 7$$
$$^-5x < 10 \qquad \text{adding 3 to both sides}$$
$$x > ^-10 \qquad \text{dividing both sides by } ^-5$$

e.g.2

$$4 - x \geq 2x - 5$$
$$4 - 3x \geq ^-5 \qquad \text{subtracting } 2x \text{ from both sides}$$
$$^-3x \geq ^-9 \qquad \text{subtracting 4 from both sides}$$
$$x \leq 3 \qquad \text{dividing both sides by } ^-3$$

DO THIS

Show the solutions of $^-5x - 3 < 7$ and $4 - x \geq 2x - 5$ on a number line.

2 Double inequalities

Inequalities like $^-10 \leq 6x + 2 < 26$ are called double inequalities.
To solve these use the balance method on **each part** of the inequality.

Answers: Can be written as a double inequality
Can be shown on a number line
Can be written as the set of integers satisfying the inequality

e.g.1

$$^-10 \leq 6x + 2 < 26$$
$$^-12 \leq 6x < 24 \qquad \text{subtracting 2 from each part}$$
$$^-2 \leq x < 4 \qquad \text{dividing each part by 6}$$

ANSWER   As a double inequality $^-2 \leq x < 4$

On a number line

-3   -2   -1   0   1   2   3   4   5

As a set of integers $^-2, ^-1, 0, 1, 2, 3$

2 Showing inequalities on a graph

Inequalities involving two variables can be shown as a region on a graph.

e.g.1   Show the region that satisfies the inequality $x + y < 4$.
Label the region **R**.

METHOD   Step 1 Draw the line with equation $x + y = 4$.
Draw a **dotted line** to show that points on the line **are
not included**.
Step 2 Test a point on either side of the line to see if its coordinates
fit the inequality.

For example: Test (0, 0)
$x = 0, y = 0$ which gives $x + y = 0$.
So (0, 0) satisfies the inequality because $0 < 4$.
So (0, 0) lies in the region $x + y < 4$.

Step 3 Shade **out** the region **not** required.

Step 4 Label the required region **R**.

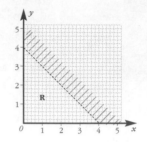

> ### Examiner's tip
> *Remember to label the*
> *required region clearly.*

e.g.2

Show the region that satisfies the inequalities $y \leq 5$, $^-2 \leq x < 4$ and $x + 2y \geq 4$

Label the region **R**.

METHOD

Step 1 Draw the line with equation $y = 5$
Draw a **full line** to show that points on the line **are included**.

Step 2 Test a point on either side of the line to see if its coordinates fit the inequality.

Step 3 Shade **out** the region **not** required.

Step 4 Repeat for the other inequalities.

Step 5 Label the required region **R**.

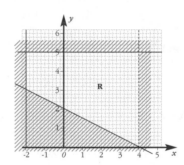

Test 19

Do not use a calculator.

1. Show each of the following inequalities on a number line.
   (a) $x > ^-2$ (b) $x < 3$
   (c) $x \leq 2$ (d) $x \geq ^-2$
   (e) $^-2 < x < 1$ (f) $^-1 \leq x < 3$
   (g) $^-4 \leq x \leq 3$ (h) $0 < x \leq 4$

2. List all the integers that satisfy the following inequalities.
   (a) $^-1 \leq x \leq 1$ (b) $^-1 \leq x < 3$
   (c) $^-4 < x < 3$ (d) $^-8 < x \leq ^-3$

2 3. Write down the inequality describing the numbers shown on each of these number lines.

(a)

(b)

(c)

(d)

2 4. Solve each of the following inequalities.
(a) $4x + 2 \le 18$ (b) $5x - 3 \ge 22$
(c) $6x + 1 < 25$ (d) $5x - 3 \ge {}^{-}13$
(e) $2(2x - 3) < {}^{-}8$ (f) $3 - 3x \ge {}^{-}12$
(g) $5 - 6x \le {}^{-}7$ (h) $4(2 - x) \ge {}^{-}12$

2 5. Solve each of the following inequalities.
(a) $5 \le 3x + 2 < 11$
(b) $3 \le 4x - 5 < 19$
(c) $11 < 4x + 3 \le 27$
(d) $7 \le 6x - 5 \le 13$
(e) ${}^{-}12 \le 3x - 9 \le {}^{-}6$
(f) ${}^{-}3 \le 4x + 5 < 17$

2 6. Find the integer values that satisfy each of the inequalities in question 5.

2 7. Show clearly each of the following regions.
Represent each solution on a number line.
(a) $y \le 3$ (b) $y > x + 2$
(c) $y \le x + 2$ (d) $x + y \le 2$
(e) $x + y \ge 3$ (f) $3x + y > 6$

2 8. For each set of inequalities, show clearly the region that they all satisfy.
Label the region **R**.
(a) $x \le 2, y \ge x + 2, y < 3x$
(b) $x \ge 0, x \le 4, y \le x$
(c) $y \le 2, y \le 2x, y \ge x - 1$

2 9. Each diagram shows a region, **R**, which satisfies three inequalities.
In each case find the three inequalities.

(a)

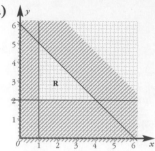

(b)

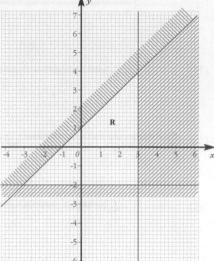

(c)

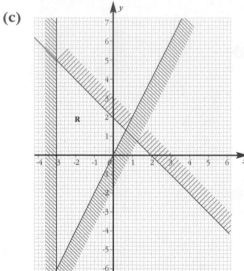

---

8. NON-LINEAR EQUATIONS AND THEIR GRAPHS

1 Recognising graphs

Linear (straight line) graphs
General equation $y = mx + c$

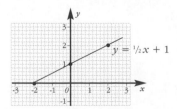

$y = \frac{1}{2}x + 1$

m is the gradient.
c is the y-intercept.

Quadratic graphs

General equation $y = ax^2 + bx + c$

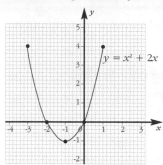

a cannot be zero.
The graph is **symmetrical**.
It has a **maximum** or **minimum** value.
Points are joined with a **smooth curve**.

Cubic graphs

General equation $y = ax^3 + bx^2 + cx + d$

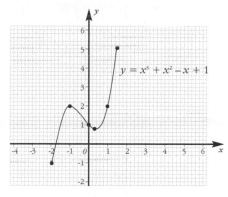

a cannot be zero.
The graph has **rotational symmetry.**
Points are joined with a **smooth curve**.
The graph crosses the *x*-axis at one or three points.

Reciprocal graphs

General equation $y = {}^a/_x + b$

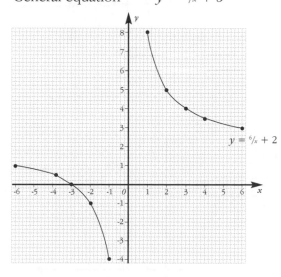

> ### Examiner's tip
> *Questions could ask you to match graphs with their equations.*

x cannot be zero.
The graph has **rotational symmetry.**

Points are joined with a **smooth curve**.
The graph does **not** cross the *y*-axis.

2

Drawing non-linear graphs

Drawing a non-linear graph is similar to drawing a linear graph:

Use the equation of the graph to work out pairs of values of x and y that fit the equation.

Write the values of x and y as coordinates.

Plot and join the points with a **smooth curve.**

In most cases you will be given a table to complete to help find the coordinates.

EXAMPLES

Quadratic graphs

e.g.1 Equation $y = x^2 - 2x - 1$

x	-2	-1	0	1	2	3	4
y	7	2	-1	-2	-1	2	7
	(-2, 7)	(-1, 2)	(0, -1)	(1, -2)	(2, -1)	(3, 2),	(4, 7)

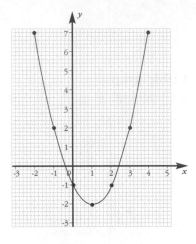

e.g.2 Equation $y = 2x - x^2$

x	-2	-1	0	1	2	3	4
y	-8	-3	0	1	0	-3	-8
	(-2, -8)	(-1, -3)	(0, 0)	(1, 1)	(2, 0)	(3, -3)	(4, -8)

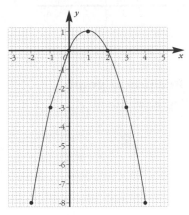

Cubic graphs

e.g.1 Equation $y = x^3 - 7x^2 + 14x - 8$

x	0.5	1	1.5	2	2.5	3	3.5	4	4.5
y	-2.625	0	0.625	0	-1.125	-2	-1.875	0	4.375

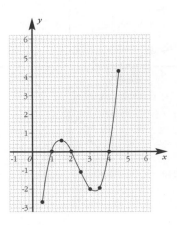

Reciprocal graphs

e.g.1   Equation $y = {}^{12}/_x + 1$

x	⁻6	⁻4	⁻2	⁻1	0	1	2	3	6
y	⁻1	⁻2	⁻5	⁻11		13	7	5	3

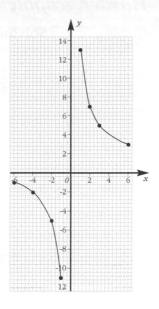

> ### Examiner's tips
> - If your curve does not look right, re-calculate the values in your table.
> - Normally you will be given **axes** and a **table** with some of the values filled in. Use the completed values to check your method.

2   *Using graphs to solve quadratic equations*

e.g.1   To solve the quadratic equation $x^2 - 2x - 1 = 0$
Draw the graph of $y = x^2 - 2x - 1$.
Find the points where this graph intersects the line $y = 0$.
Write down the **x-coordinates** of these points.

So the **approximate** solutions of
$x^2 - 2x - 1 = 0$ are:
$x = 2.4$ and $x = ⁻0.4$.

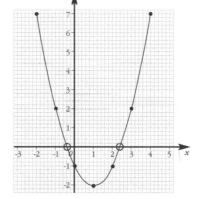

e.g.2   **Solving** the quadratic equation $2x - x^2 = ⁻4$
Draw the graph of $y = 2x - x^2$.
Find the points where this graph intersects the line $y = ⁻4$.
Write down the **x-coordinates** of these points.

So the **approximate** solutions of
$2x - x^2 = ⁻4$ are:
$x = 3.2$ and $x = ⁻1.2$.

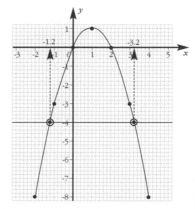

> ### Examiner's tip
> If there are **two** points of intersection, there are **two** solutions; make sure you give **both**.

1 *Harder graphical solutions*

e.g.1

Solving the quadratic equation $2x^2 - x - 2 = 2x + 1$
Draw the graph of $y = 2x^2 - x - 2$.
Find the points where this graph intersects the line $y = 2x + 1$.
Write down the **x-coordinates** of these points.

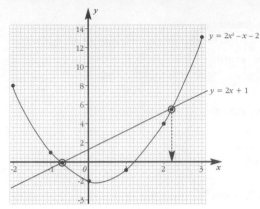

So the **approximate** solutions of $2x^2 - x - 2 = 2x + 1$ are:
$x = 2.2$ and $x = {}^-0.7$.

e.g.2

You are given the graphs of $y = 3x - 1$ and $y = {}^8/x$.
Show that the points of intersection of these graphs are the solutions of
$3x^2 - x - 8 = 0$.
At the points of intersection:

$\qquad 3x - 1 = {}^8/x$
$\qquad 3x^2 - x = 8 \qquad\qquad$ multiplying both sides by x
$3x^2 - x - 8 = 0 \qquad\qquad$ subtracting 8 from both sides

e.g.3

You are given the graph of $y = x^2 - 4x - 1$.
You want to use this graph and a straight line to solve the equation
$y = x^2 - x - 7$.
Let the line have equation $y = ax + b$.
At the points of intersection
$x^2 - 4x - 1 = ax + b$
$x^2 - 4x - ax - 1 - b = 0 \qquad\qquad$ subtracting ax **and** b from both sides

Comparing $x^2 - 4x - ax - 1 - b = 0$ with $x^2 - x - 7 = 0$
$\qquad {}^-4 - a = {}^-1 \qquad\qquad$ comparing the number of x's
$\qquad$ So $a = {}^-3$

$\qquad {}^-1 - b = {}^-7 \qquad\qquad$ comparing the number terms
$\qquad$ So $b = 6$

So the equation of the straight line you need to draw is $y = 6 - 3x$.

1 *Exponential graphs*

General equation $y = a^x$

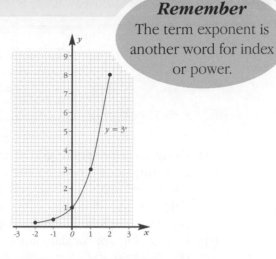

a cannot be zero.
Points are joined with a **smooth curve**.
The graph does not cross the x-axis.
The graph crosses the y-axis at the point $(0, 1)$.

The graph of $y = 3^x$ is shown.
This table shows values of y to 2 decimal places.

x	$^-2$	$^-1$	0	1	2
y	0.11	0.33	1	3	9

1 *The equation of a circle*

General equation $x^2 + y^2 = r^2$

This circle has centre $(0, 0)$ and radius r.

The graph of $x^2 + y^2 = 9$ is shown.
The graph is a circle of radius 3 with centre $(0, 0)$.

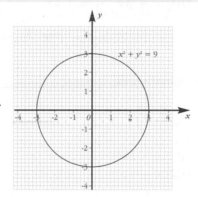

Test 20

Use a calculator for questions 3 and 7 only.

1. For each graph state whether it is linear, quadratic, cubic or reciprocal.

(a)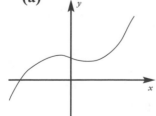

(b)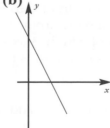

(c)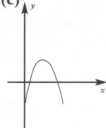

(d)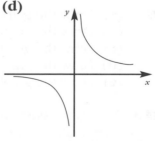

2. State whether these equations will produce a linear, quadratic, cubic or reciprocal graph.

$y = {}^4/_x$ $y = x^2 - 3$ $y = 3 - 2x$ $y = x + x^2 - x^3$ $y = (x + 1)(x - 2)$

NON-LINEAR EQUATIONS
AND THEIR GRAPHS

Algebra

3. **(a)** Copy and complete these tables for the equations given.

$y = 5 - x^2$

x	-3	-2	-1	0	1	2	3
y							

$y = x^2 - x + 3$

x	-2	-1	0	1	2	3
y						

$y = x^2 + 3x - 1$

x	-4	-3	-2	-1	0	1
y						

(b) Using an appropriate grid, draw a graph for each equation.
(c) Use your graphs to solve these equations.
   (i) $5 - x^2 = 0$ **(ii)** $x^2 - x + 3 = 0$
   (iii) $x^2 + 3x - 1 = 0$ **(iv)** $5 - x^2 = 3$
   (v) $x^2 - x + 3 = 7$ **(vi)** $x^2 + 3x - 1 = 2$
(d) By drawing appropriate lines on your graphs solve these equations.
   (i) $5 - x^2 = x$
   (ii) $x^2 - x + 3 = 2x + 1$
   (iii) $x^2 + 3x - 1 = 1 - x$

4. **(a)** Copy and complete the table for the equation:

$y = x^2 - 4x + 3$

x	-1	0	1	2	3	4	5
y			0			3	

(b) Draw the graph of $y = x^2 - 4x + 3$ for values of x from -1 to 4.
(c) Use your graph to solve these equations.
   (i) $x^2 - 4x + 3 = 0$
   (ii) $x^2 - 4x + 3 = 2$
   (iii) $x^2 - 4x + 3 = x + 2$

5. **(a)** Show that the points of intersection of the graphs of $y = x^2$ and $y = 1 - 3x$ give the solution of the equation $x^2 + 3x - 1 = 0$
(b) Show that the equation:
$x^2 - 3x - 1 = 0$ can also be solved using the graphs of $y = x$ and
$y = 3x + 1/x$.

6. You are given the graph of $y = x^2 + 3x - 1$
Give the equation of the line you need to draw to solve the equation
$y = x^2 + x - 5$

7. **(a)** Draw the graph of $xy = 6$ for values of x from -6 to 6.
(b) Draw the graph of $y = x^3 - x$ for values of x from -2 to 2.
(c) Draw the graph of $y = 2^x$ for values of x from -3 to 3.
(d) Draw the graph of $y = 0.5^x$ for values of x from -3 to 3.
(e) Draw the graph of $x^2 + y^2 = 4$.

8. What is the equation of the circle with centre $(0, 0)$ and radius 5?

9. QUADRATIC EXPRESSIONS AND EQUATIONS

2

More expanding brackets

The process of removing brackets from an algebraic expression is called expanding.

To expand brackets:

Term × bracket
Multiply **each** term in the bracket
by the term outside the bracket.

Bracket × bracket
Multiply **each** term in the first bracket
by **each** term in the second bracket.

You can use the box method in both cases (see page 62).

e.g.1 $3(x + 2) = 3x + 6$

METHOD $3 \times x + 3 \times 2$ or

×	x	2
3	$3x$	6

e.g.2 $x(x - 2) = x^2 - 2x$

METHOD $x \times x - x \times 2$ or

×	x	‾2
x	x^2	‾$2x$

e.g.3 $(x + 3)(x + 4) = x^2 + 7x + 12$

METHOD $x(x + 4) + 3(x + 4)$
Expand each bracket
$x^2 + 4x + 3x + 12$ or

×	x	3
x	x^2	$3x$
4	$4x$	12

Then collect like terms and **simplify.**

e.g.4 $(2x + 3)(x - 4) = 2x^2 - 5x - 12$

METHOD $2x(x - 4) + 3(x - 4)$
Expand each bracket
$2x^2 - 8x + 3x - 12$ or

×	$2x$	3
x	$2x^2$	$3x$
‾4	‾$8x$	‾12

Then collect like terms and **simplify.**

> ## Examiner's tip
> *- Questions will ask you either to 'expand' or to 'expand and simplify'.*
> *Make sure you remember what each of these instructions means.*

QUADRATIC EXPRESSIONS AND EQUATIONS

2

Factorising

Factorising is the inverse (opposite) of expanding.

e.g.1 $x^2 + 2x = x(x + 2)$ x^2 and $2x$ have a common factor of x

e.g.2 $4x^2 - 6x = 2x(2x - 3)$ $4x^2$ and $6x$ have a common factor of $2x$

2

Factorising quadratics of the form $x^2 + bx + c$

e.g.1   **Factorise** $x^2 + 5x + 6$.

METHOD   Start from what you know $(x + ?)(x + ?)$
The unknown numbers have a **product** of 6 and a **sum** of 5

1×6 $1 + 6 = 7$ ✗
2×3   **$2 + 3 = 5$** ✓

ANSWER $x^2 + 5x + 6 = (x + 2)(x + 3)$

e.g.2   **Factorise** $x^2 + 4x - 12$.

METHOD   Start from what you know $(x + ?)(x + ?)$
The unknown numbers have a **product** of ⁻12 and a **sum** of 4

$1 \times {}^-12$ $1 + {}^-12 = {}^-11$ ✗
${}^-1 \times 12$ ${}^-1 + 12 = 11$ ✗
$2 \times {}^-6$ $2 + {}^-6 = {}^-4$ ✗
${}^-2 \times 6$ **${}^-2 + 6 = 4$** ✓

ANSWER $x^2 + 4x - 12 = (x - 2)(x + 6)$

e.g.3   **Factorise** $x^2 - 3x + 2$.

METHOD $(x + ?)(x + ?)$
The unknown numbers have a **product** of 2 and a **sum** of ⁻3

1×2 $1 + 2 = 3$ ✗
${}^-1 \times {}^-2$ **${}^-1 + {}^-2 = {}^-3$** ✓

ANSWER $x^2 - 3x + 2 = (x - 1)(x - 2)$

2

Solving quadratic equations

e.g.1   **Solving** $x^2 + 5x = 0$

METHOD   Step 1 Factorise $x^2 + 5x$.
                 $x^2 + 5x = x(x + 5)$
Step 2 Rewrite equation:
                 $x(x + 5) = 0$
                 So either $x = 0$ or $x + 5 = 0$.

ANSWER $x = 0$ and $x = {}^-5$

e.g.2

Solving $x^2 - 5x + 6 = 0$
Step 1 Factorise $x^2 - 5x + 6$.
$$(x + ?)(x + ?)$$
The unknown numbers have a **product** of 6 and a **sum** of ⁻5

$$1 \times 6 \qquad 1 + 6 = 7 \ ✗$$
$$2 \times 3 \qquad 2 + 3 = 5 \ ✗$$
$$\text{⁻}1 \times \text{⁻}6 \qquad \text{⁻}1 + \text{⁻}6 = \text{⁻}7 \ ✗$$
$$\mathbf{\text{⁻}2 \times \text{⁻}3} \qquad \mathbf{\text{⁻}2 + \text{⁻}3 = \text{⁻}5} \ ✓$$

So $x^2 - 5x + 6 = (x - 2)(x - 3)$
Step 2 Rewrite equation:
$$(x - 2)(x - 3) = 0$$
So either $x - 2 = 0$ or $x - 3 = 0$.

ANSWER $x = 2$ and $x = 3$

---

1 *Quadratics of the form $ax^2 + bx + c$*

e.g.1 **Factorise** $2x^2 + 5x - 3$.

METHOD Start from what you know $\qquad (2x + ?)(x + ?)$
The unknown numbers have a **product** of ⁻3
Possible combinations are:
$(2x + 1)(x - 3)$	This gives $2x^2 - 5x - 3$ ✗
$(2x + 3)(x - 1)$	This gives $2x^2 + x - 3$ ✗
$(2x - 1)(x + 3)$	This gives $2x^2 + 5x - 3$ ✓

ANSWER So $2x^2 + 5x - 3 = (2x - 1)(x + 3)$

e.g.2 **Solving** the equation $2x^2 + 5x - 3 = 0$.

METHOD After factorising rewrite the equation as:
$$(2x - 1)(x + 3) = 0$$
So either $2x - 1 = 0$ or $x + 3 = 0$.

ANSWER $x = 0.5$ and $x = \text{⁻}3$

e.g.3 **Factorise** $6x^2 + 13x + 5$.

METHOD $(6x + ?)(x + ?)$ or $(2x + ?)(3x + ?)$

The unknown numbers have a **product** of 5
Possible combinations are:
$(6x + 1)(x + 5)$	This gives $6x^2 + 31x + 5$ ✗
$(6x + 5)(x + 1)$	This gives $6x^2 + 11x + 5$ ✗
$(3x + 1)(2x + 5)$	This gives $6x^2 + 17x + 5$ ✗
$(3x + 5)(2x + 1)$	This gives $6x^2 + 13x + 5$ ✓

ANSWER So $6x^2 + 13x + 5 = (3x + 5)(2x + 1)$

e.g.4   **Solving** $6x^2 + 13x + 5 = 0$

METHOD   After factorising rewrite the equation as:
$(3x + 5)(2x + 1) = 0$
So either $3x + 5 = 0$ or $2x + 1 = 0$.

ANSWER $x = {}^-5/_3 = {}^-1^2/_3$ and $x = {}^-0.5$

1   *Special cases*

Difference of two squares
$(x - \boldsymbol{a})(x + \boldsymbol{a}) = x^2 - \boldsymbol{a}^2$

×	x	^-a
x	x^2	^-ax
a	ax	$^-a^2$

e.g.1 $x^2 - 9 = (x - 3)(x + 3)$ $x^2 - 3^2$

e.g.2 $(2x - 5)(2x + 5) = 4x^2 - 25$ $(2x)^2 - 5^2$

Perfect squares
$(x + \boldsymbol{a})^2$ is a perfect square
$(x + \boldsymbol{a})^2 = x^2 + 2\boldsymbol{a}x + \boldsymbol{a}^2$

×	x	a
x	x^2	ax
a	ax	a^2

$(\boldsymbol{a}x + \boldsymbol{b})^2$ is a perfect square
$(\boldsymbol{a}x + \boldsymbol{b})^2 = \boldsymbol{a}^2x^2 + 2\boldsymbol{a}\boldsymbol{b}x + \boldsymbol{b}^2$

×	ax	b
ax	a^2x^2	abx
b	abx	b^2

e.g.1 $(x - 3)^2 = x^2 - \boldsymbol{6}x + \boldsymbol{9}$
$2 \times {}^-3 = {}^-\boldsymbol{6}$ and $^-3^2 = \boldsymbol{9}$

e.g.2 $(3x - 2)^2 = \boldsymbol{9}x^2 - \boldsymbol{12}x + \boldsymbol{4}$
$3^2 = \boldsymbol{9}$, $2 \times 3 \times {}^-2 = {}^-\boldsymbol{12}$, $(^-2)^2 = \boldsymbol{4}$

e.g.3 $x^2 + 6x + \boldsymbol{9} = (x + 3)^2$
$1/_2$ of $\boldsymbol{6}$ is 3 and $3^2 = \boldsymbol{9}$

Completing the square
Any quadratic can be written in the form $(x + \boldsymbol{a})^2 + \boldsymbol{c}$ or $(\boldsymbol{a}x + \boldsymbol{b})^2 + \boldsymbol{c}$.
Use the patterns in the perfect square forms to find $\boldsymbol{a}$, $\boldsymbol{b}$ and $\boldsymbol{c}$.

e.g.1 $x^2 + 6x + 4 = (x + 3)^2 - 5$
STEP 1 ↑   ↑ STEP 2
$\boxed{1/_2 \text{ of } 6}$ $\boxed{4 - 3^2}$

e.g.2 $9x^2 - 12x - 7 = (3x - 2)^2 - 11$
STEP 1 ↑   ↑ STEP 3
$\boxed{\sqrt{9}}$ $\boxed{^-7 - (^-2)^2}$
STEP 2 $\boxed{1/_2 \text{ of } ^-12 \div \sqrt{9}}$

Solving quadratic equations by completing the square

Completing the square can be used to solve quadratics that do **not** factorise.

e.g.1　　**Solving** $x^2 + 6x + 4 = 0$

METHOD　Step 1　Change $x^2 + 6x + 4$ to completed square form.
　　　　　　　$x^2 + 6x + 4 = (x + 3)^2 - 5$
　　　　　Step 2　Rewrite the equation using the completed square form.
　　　　　　　$(x + 3)^2 - 5 = 0$
　　　　　Step 3　Use the balance method to solve the equation
　　　　　　　$(x + 3)^2 - 5 = 0$
　　　　　　　　$(x + 3)^2 = 5$　　　　adding 5 to both sides
　　　　　　　　$x + 3 = \pm\sqrt{5}$　　　taking the square root of both sides
　　　　　　　　$x = {}^-3 \pm\sqrt{5}$　　subtracting 3 from both sides

ANSWER　So $x = {}^-0.76$ and ${}^-5.24$ to an accuracy of 2 decimal places

> ### Examiner's tips
> - Answers are normally required to an accuracy of 2 decimal places.
> - If you are asked for an accurate answer leave it in surd form, $({}^-3 \pm\sqrt{5})$.

Using the quadratic formula

A quadratic equation written in the form $ax^2 + bx + c = 0$ can be solved using this formula:

$$x = \frac{{}^-b \pm\sqrt{b^2 - 4ac}}{2a}$$

e.g.1　　**Solving** $2x^2 - 3x - 7 = 0$
　　　　　Step 1　Write down the values of a, b and c
　　　　　　　$a = 2, b = {}^-3, c = {}^-7$
　　　　　Step 2　Substitute in the formula and simplify

$$x = \frac{3 \pm\sqrt{({}^-3)^2 - 4 \times 2 \times {}^-7}}{2 \times 2}$$

$$x = \frac{3 \pm\sqrt{65}}{4}$$

　　　　　Step 3　Calculate solutions
　　　　　　　$x = 2.77$ and ${}^-1.27$ to an accuracy of 2 decimal places

> ### Examiner's tip
> Master the formula method. You can use it
> to solve **all** quadratic equations unless you
> are asked for a particular method.

1 *Solving problems using quadratic equations*

e.g.1   These two rectangles have the same area.
What is the area?

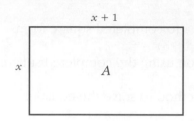

METHOD   Step 1 Form a quadratic equation
Area of rectangle $A = x \times (x + 1)$
$= x^2 + x$
Area of rectangle $B = (x - 1)(3x - 5)$
$= 3x^2 - 8x + 5$

The areas are equal so:
$$3x^2 - 8x + 5 = x^2 + x$$

Step 2 Rearrange quadratic equation to the form $ax^2 + bx + c = 0$
$3x^2 - 8x + 5 = x^2 + x$
$2x^2 - 8x + 5 = x$ subtracting x^2 from both sides
$2x^2 - 9x + 5 = 0$ subtracting x from both sides

Step 3 Solve the quadratic equation
Using the formula $a = 2, b = {}^-9, c = 5$

$$x = \frac{9 \pm \sqrt{({}^-9)^2 - 4 \times 2 \times 5}}{2 \times 2}$$

$$x = \frac{9 \pm \sqrt{41}}{4}$$

$x = 3.85$ and 0.65 to 2 decimal places

Step 4 Use the solution to solve the original problem.

If $x = 0.65$ then rectangle B would have two negative lengths!
This is impossible so x must be 3.85.

So the area of rectangle $A = 18.67...$ 3.85×4.85
Checking rectangle B 18.67

ANSWER   So the area of each rectangle is 18.7 cm² to 3 significant figures

Use a calculator for questions 11 to 16.

1. Expand:
    (a) $2(a + 3)$ **(b)** $4(x - 1)$
    (c) $x(x - 1)$ **(d)** $2x(x + 1)$
    (e) $2x(4x + 1)$ **(f)** $3y(5y + 3)$

2. Expand and simplify:
    (a) $(a + 3)(a + 2)$ **(b)** $(x + 2)(x + 5)$
    (c) $(x - 2)(2x + 3)$ **(d)** $(y - 2)(y - 5)$
    (e) $(2x + 1)(x + 5)$ **(f)** $(5p + 3)(p - 1)$

3. Factorise:
    (a) $x^2 + 2x$ **(b)** $a^2 + a$
    (c) $x^2 - 6x$ **(d)** $2y^2 - 4y$
    (e) $10x^2 - 15x$ **(f)** $2a^2x^2 + 4ax$

4. Factorise:
    (a) $x^2 + 3x + 2$ **(b)** $x^2 + 7x + 6$
    (c) $x^2 + 8x + 12$ **(d)** $x^2 - 5x + 6$
    (e) $x^2 - 5x - 14$ **(f)** $x^2 - 9x + 20$
    (g) $x^2 + 15x - 54$ **(h)** $x^2 - 20x - 44$

5. Factorise:
    (a) $2x^2 + 7x + 3$ **(b)** $3x^2 + 5x + 2$
    (c) $2x^2 + 5x - 3$ **(d)** $4x^2 + 11x - 3$
    (e) $12x^2 - 11x + 2$ **(f)** $6x^2 + x - 2$

6. Solve these quadratic equations by factorising.
    (a) $x^2 + 2x = 0$
    (b) $6x^2 - 9x = 0$
    (c) $x^2 + 3x - 28 = 0$
    (d) $x^2 + 5x - 24 = 0$
    (e) $x^2 - 6x + 8 = 0$
    (f) $x^2 - 4x - 60 = 0$

7. Solve these quadratic equations by factorising.
    (a) $2x^2 + 5x - 12 = 0$
    (b) $2x^2 + 5x - 3 = 0$
    (c) $3x^2 - 7x + 4 = 0$
    (d) $4x^2 + x - 3 = 0$

8. Factorise:
    (a) $x^2 - 16$ **(b)** $a^2 - 100$
    (c) $4x^2 - 9$ **(d)** $x^2 - y^2$
    (e) $5x^2 - 20$ **(f)** $18x^2 - 8y^2$

1 9. Factorise:
   (a) $x^2 + 16x + 64$ **(b)** $x^2 - 16x + 64$
   (c) $x^2 + 10x + 25$ **(d)** $x^2 - 10x + 25$
   (e) $4x^2 + 12x + 9$ **(f)** $9x^2 - 24x + 16$

1 10. Write each of the following in the form $(ax + b)^2 + c$.
   (a) $x^2 + 16x + 70$ **(b)** $x^2 - 16x + 70$
   (c) $x^2 + 10x + 20$ **(d)** $x^2 - 10x - 5$
   (e) $4x^2 + 12x + 7$ **(f)** $9x^2 - 24x - 5$

1 11. Solve each of the following by completing the square.
   (a) $x^2 + 8x + 8 = 0$ **(b)** $x^2 - 6x - 4 = 0$
   (c) $x^2 + 10x - 2 = 0$ **(d)** $x^2 - 2x - 5 = 0$
   (e) $4x^2 + 4x - 2 = 0$ **(f)** $9x^2 - 6x - 2 = 0$
   Give both exact solutions and answers to 2 decimal places.

1 12. Check the solutions to the equations in questions 6, 7 and 11 using the formula.
   What do you notice?

1 13.(a) Factorise $4x^2 - 5x - 6$.
   (b) Hence, or otherwise, solve the equation $4x^2 - 5x - 6 = 0$.

1 14. Three integers are in the sequence x, $x + 1$ and $x + 2$
   The sum of the squares of the two smaller numbers equals the square of the
   larger number.
   (a) Use this information to write a quadratic equation.
       Simplify your equation.
   (b) Solve the equation to find the three integers.

1 15. The length of a rectangle is 10 cm more than its width.
   If the area of the rectangle is 80 cm², calculate its perimeter.
   Give your answer to 2 decimal places.

1 16. Rectangles A and B have equal areas.

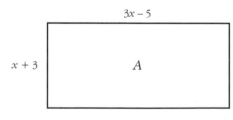
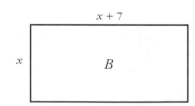

   (a) Form an equation in x.
   (b) Solve the equation.
   (c) Find the difference between the perimeters of the rectangles.

SIMULTANEOUS EQUATIONS

2

Understanding simultaneous equations

There are many pairs of values of x and y that fit the equation $x + y = 6$.
There are also many pairs of values that fit the equation $y = 2x$.
However, there is only **one pair** of values of x and y that fits **both** of these equations.
$x + y = 9$ and $y = 2x$ are called simultaneous equations; the solution is the pair of values that fits them **both**.

2

Solving simultaneous equations graphically

You need to be able to draw straight line graphs (see page 77).

To solve a pair of simultaneous equations graphically:
    Draw the graphs of both lines on the same diagram.
    Find the x-coordinate and y-coordinate at the point where the two lines intersect.

e.g.1   The diagram shows the graphs of
$y = 2x + 1$ and $x + y = 7$

METHOD   The values of the x-coordinate and the
y-coordinate at the point where the lines
intersect gives the solution to the
simultaneous equations $y = 2x + 1$ and
$x + y = 7$
The lines cross at the point $(2, 5)$.

ANSWER   This gives the solution $x = 2, y = 5$

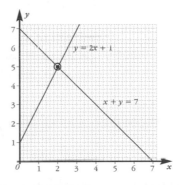

Remember
Some pairs of simultaneous
equations have no solution.
If their graphs are drawn the
lines are parallel.
If the equations are rearranged to
the form $y = mx + c$ then the
values of m are equal.

2

The substitution method

One way to solve a pair of simultaneous
equations is by substituting an unknown from
one equation into the other.

e.g.1 $y = 3x$ A
            $x + 2y = 21$ B

METHOD   Substitute y from A into B
            $x + 6x = 21$
            $7x = 21$
            $x = 3$
            Substituting $x = 3$ in A
            $y = 9$

ANSWER $x = 3$
                $y = 9$

2 *The elimination method*

A useful method for solving simultaneous equations is the elimination method.
This uses the balance method to form a new equation that is still true and in which one
of the letter symbols has been eliminated.

e.g.1

$$3x + y = 14$$
$$2x + y = 10$$

METHOD Label each equation
$3x + y = 14$ **A**
$2x + y = 10$ **B**

The number of y's are the **same**
To eliminate the y's **subtract** the equations
$\quad x = 4 \quad$ **A – B**

Substitute $x = 4$ in **B** to find y
$2 \times 4 + y = 10$
$\quad\quad y = 2 \;$ by inspection

ANSWER So $x = 4$ and $y = 2$

e.g.2

$$3x + y = 17$$
$$2x - y = 8$$

METHOD Label each equation
$3x + y = 14$ **A**
$2x - y = 11$ **B**

The number of y's are the **same** but the **signs** are **different**
To eliminate the y's **add** the equations
$5x = 25 \quad\quad$ **C = A + B**
$\;x = 5 \quad\quad$ dividing both sides by 5

Substitute $x = 5$ in **A** to find y
$3 \times 5 + y = 14$
$\quad\quad y = {}^{-}1 \quad\quad$ by inspection

ANSWER So $x = 5$ and $y = {}^{-}1$

e.g.3

$$3x + 2y = 10 \quad \textbf{A}$$
$$\;x + 4y = 5 \quad \textbf{B}$$

METHOD The number of x's and the number of y's are **different**
Make the number of y's the same by multiplying **A** by 2
$6x + 4y = 20 \;$ **2A**

To eliminate the y's **subtract B** from **2A**
$5x = 15 \quad\quad$ **2A – B**
$\;x = 3 \quad\quad$ dividing both sides by 5

Substitute $x = 3$ in A to find y

$3 \times 3 + 2y = 10$

$\quad 2y = 1 \qquad$ subtracting 9 from both sides

$\quad y = 0.5 \quad$ dividing both sides by 2

ANSWER So $x = 3$ and $y = 0.5$

Alternatively, eliminate the x's.

Do this with $3B - A$

e.g.4

$3x + 2y = 19 \quad A$

$2x - 3y = 4 \quad\;\; B$

METHOD The number of x's and the number of y's are **different**.

Make the number of y's the same by multiplying A by 3 and B by 2.

$9x + 6y = 57 \quad 3A$

$4x - 6y = 8 \qquad 2B$

To eliminate the y's **add** $3A$ to $2B$

$13x = 65 \qquad\quad 3A + 2B$

$\quad x = 5 \qquad\quad\;$ dividing both sides by 13

Substitute $x = 5$ in A to find y.

$3 \times 5 + 2y = 19$

$\qquad 2y = 4 \quad$ subtracting 15 from both sides

$\qquad y = 2 \quad$ dividing both sides by 2

ANSWER So $x = 5$ and $y = 2$

Alternatively, eliminate the x's.

Do this with $2A - 3B$

> **Examiner's tip**
> *When there is a choice of which unknown letter to eliminate, there is usually less chance of error if you **add** equations rather than subtract. So eliminate the letter symbol which has different signs.*

2 | Using simultaneous equations to solve problems

e.g.1 There are x seats in a first-class carriage and y seats in a standard-class carriage. Train A has three first-class carriages and four standard-class carriages and a total of 515 seats.

Train B has two first-class carriages and six standard-class carriages and a total of 610 seats.

METHOD Step 1 Form the equations

$\qquad 3x + 4y = 515$

$\qquad 2x + 6y = 610$

Step 2 Solve the equations

$\qquad 3x + 4y = 515 \qquad A$

$\qquad 2x + 6y = 610 \qquad B$

$\qquad 6x + 8y = 1030 \qquad 2A$

$\qquad 6x + 18y = 1830 \qquad 3B$

$\qquad\quad 10y = 800 \qquad 3B - 2A$

$\qquad\quad\; y = 80$

Substituting $y = 80$ in **A**

$$3x + 4 \times 80 = 515$$
$$3x = 195 \qquad \text{subtracting 320 from both sides}$$
$$x = 65 \qquad \text{dividing both sides by 3}$$

ANSWER   A first-class carriage has 65 seats and a standard-class carriage has 80 seats.

Solving simultaneous equations when one is linear and one is quadratic

Graphical method

e.g.1   The diagram shows the graphs of $y = 2x + 1$ and $y = x^2 - 2$.

METHOD   The values of the x-coordinate and the y-coordinate at the points where the lines intersect give the solutions to the simultaneous equations $y = 2x + 1$ and $y = x^2 - 2$.

ANSWER   The lines cross at the points $(3, 7)$ and $(^-1, ^-1)$. This gives the solutions $x = 3, y = 7$ and $x = ^-1, y = ^-1$.

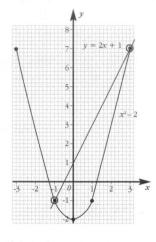

> ### Remember
> There are two solutions to simultaneous equations when one is linear and one is quadratic

Method of substitution

e.g.1
$$x^2 + y^2 = 9 \qquad \textbf{A}$$
$$y - 3x = 1 \qquad \textbf{B}$$

Rearrange equation **B** to make y the subject.
$$y = 3x + 1 \qquad \text{adding } 3x \text{ to both sides}$$

Substitute $y = 3x + 1$ into equation **A.**
$$x^2 + (3x + 1)^2 = 9$$

Simplify and rearrange into form $ax^2 + bx + c = 0$.
$$x^2 + 9x^2 + 6x + 1 = 9 \qquad \text{expanding brackets}$$
$$10x^2 + 6x - 8 = 0 \qquad \text{simplifying and rearranging}$$

Use the formula
$a = 10, b = 6, c = ^-8$

> ### Remember
> Use the substitution method if you are asked to work out the points of intersection of a circle and a line.

$$x = \frac{^-6 \pm \sqrt{6^2 - 4 \times 10 \times ^-8}}{2 \times 10}$$

$$x = \frac{^-6 \pm \sqrt{356}}{20}$$

$x = 0.64$ and $^-1.24$ to an accuracy of 2 decimal places

Substitute these values into $y = 3x + 1$ to give …
When $x = 0.64$, $y = 2.92$ and when $x = {}^-1.24$, $y = {}^-2.72$.

$x^2 + y^2 = 9$ is the equation of a circle centre $(0, 0$, and radius 3).
The points of intersection of $y = 3x + 1$ and this circle are $(0.64, 2.92)$
and $(^-1.24, ^-2.72)$.

Test 22

Use a calculator for questions 5 to 7.

1. Use graphs to solve these pairs of simultaneous equations.
   (a) $y = 3x - 2$ and $x + 2y = 10$
   (b) $2y = 3x + 6$ and $y = 8 - x$
   (c) $y = 4x + 1$ and $y - 2x = 3$

2. Solve each of these pairs of simultaneous equations.
   (a) $5x - 4y = 20$ **(b)** $2x + 3y - 14$
   $2x + 4y = 1$ $4x - y = 21$
   (c) $2x - 3y = 14$ **(d)** $2y - 3x = 6$
   $x + 6y = {}^-8$ $4y + x = 19$
   (e) $3x + 4y = 2$ **(f)** $3x + 2y = 9$
   $^-x + 2y = 6$ $2x - 4y = {}^-26$
You **must** show your method.
Do not use trial and improvement.

3. Use the method of substitution to solve these pairs of simultaneous equations.
   (a) $y = 2x$ and $x + 2y = {}^-5$
   (b) $y = 3x + 1$ and $2x + y = 6$
   (c) $y - 3x = 2$ and $3x + 2y = {}^-14$

4. Cinema tickets cost £x for an adult and £y for a child.
   1 adult and 4 children cost a total of £19.
   3 adults and 2 children cost a total of £22.
   (a) Form a pair of simultaneous equations to show this information.
   (b) Solve the simultaneous equations to find the cost for an adult and a child.

5. Use a graphical method to solve the simultaneous equations
   $y = x^2 - x - 1$ and $y - x = 2$
   Confirm your solution using substitution.

6. Solve the following pairs of simultaneous equations.

(a) $y^2 - 3x^2 = 10$ (b) $2x^2 + y^2 = 8$
$\quad y = 2x + 1$ $\qquad y = x + 1$

(c) $x^2 + y^2 = 10$ (d) $x^2 + y^2 = 5$
$\quad y - 2x = 1$ $\qquad x + 2y = 2$

Give your answers to 2 decimal places.

7. Find the points of intersection of the circle $x^2 + y^2 = 16$ and the line $y = x - 1$
Give your answers to 2 decimal places.

---

11.   ALGEBRAIC METHODS

2

Solving cubic equations using trial and improvement

The method of trial and improvement can be used to solve cubic equations.

e.g.1 Use trial and improvement **to solve** $x^3 - 3x = 24$ to an accuracy of 1 decimal place.

METHOD Step 1 Work with whole numbers.

Trial	$x^3 - 3x$	Result
$x = 2$	$2^3 - 3 \times 2$	2 too small
$x = 3$	$3^3 - 3 \times 3$	18 too small
$x = 4$	$4^3 - 3 \times 4$	52 too big

The solution lies between $x = 3$ and $x = 4$.
Step 2 Work with numbers to one decimal place.

Trial	$x^3 - 3x$	Result
$x = 3.5$	$3.5^3 - 3 \times 3.5$	32.375 too big
$x = 3.4$	$3.4^3 - 3 \times 3.4$	29.104 too big
$x = 3.3$	$3.3^3 - 3 \times 3.3$	26.037 too big
$x = 3.2$	$3.2^3 - 3 \times 3.2$	23.168 too small

The solution lies between $x = 3.2$ and $x = 3.3$.
Step 3 Try 3.25

Trial	$x^3 - 3x$	Result
$x = 3.25$	$3.25^3 - 3 \times 3.25$	24.578125 too big

ANSWER The solution lies between $x = 3.2$ and $x = 3.25$.
So to an accuracy of 1 decimal place the solution is 3.2.

1 Simplifying expressions

e.g.1 Simplify $(x + 2)(x + 3) + (x + 3)(x + 4)$

$x^2 + 5x + 6 + x^2 + 7x + 12$ expanding brackets

$2x^2 + 12x + 18$ collecting terms

$2(x^2 + 6x + 9)$ factorising

$2(x + 3)^2$ factorising

e.g.2 Show that $(x - y)^2 = (x + y)^2 - 4xy$

Expand the left-hand side.

$(x - y)^2 = x^2 - 2xy + y^2$

Expand and simplify the right-hand side.

$(x + y)^2 - 4xy = x^2 + 2xy + y^2 - 4xy$

$= x^2 - 2xy + y^2$

So $(x - y)^2 = (x + y)^2 - 4xy$

1 Simplifying algebraic fractions

An algebraic fraction simplifies if the numerator and denominator have a common factor.

e.g.1 Simplify $\dfrac{x^2 - 4}{x^2 - x - 2}$

Factorise numerator **and** denominator.

$\dfrac{(x - 2)(x + 2)}{(x - 2)(x + 1)}$

Divide both the numerator and denominator by $(x - 2)$.

$\dfrac{(x + 2)}{(x + 1)}$

e.g.2 Simplify $\dfrac{x^2 - 3x}{2x^2 - 5x - 3}$

Factorise numerator **and** denominator.

$\dfrac{x(x - 3)}{(x - 3)(2x + 1)}$

Divide numerator and denominator by $(x - 3)$.

$\dfrac{x}{2x + 1}$

1

Adding and subtracting algebraic fractions

e.g.1

$$\frac{4}{x-2} + \frac{2}{x+3}$$

METHOD   Write each fraction with a **common denominator.**

$$\frac{4(x+3)}{(x-2)(x+3)} + \frac{2(x-2)}{(x-2)(x+3)}$$

Write as a **single fraction.**

$$\frac{4(x+3) + 2(x-2)}{(x-2)(x+3)}$$

Expand the numerator and simplify.

$$\frac{4x+12+2x-4}{(x-2)(x+3)}$$

$$\frac{6x+8}{(x-2)(x+3)}$$

ANSWER   Factorise the numerator.

$$\frac{2(3x+4)}{(x-2)(x+3)}$$

e.g.2

$$\frac{x}{x+1} - \frac{2}{x-1}$$

METHOD   Write each fraction with a **common denominator.**

$$\frac{x(x-1)}{(x+1)(x-1)} - \frac{2(x+1)}{(x-1)(x+1)}$$

Write as a **single fraction.**

$$\frac{x(x-1) - 2(x+1)}{(x-1)(x+1)}$$

Expand the numerator and simplify.

$$\frac{x^2 - x - 2x - 2}{(x-1)(x+1)}$$

ANSWER $\dfrac{x^2 - 3x - 2}{x^2 - 1}$

1 | *Equations involving algebraic fractions*

e.g.1

$$\frac{2}{x-1} + \frac{3}{x+2} = 1$$

METHOD

Multiply through by $(x-1)(x+2)$.

$$\frac{2(x-1)(x+2)}{x-1} + \frac{3(x-1)(x+2)}{x+2} = (x-1)(x+2)$$

$$2(x+2) + 3(x-1) = (x-1)(x+2)$$

Expand, simplify and rearrange to form $ax^2 + bx + c = 0$.

$$2x + 4 + 3x - 3 = x^2 + x - 2$$
$$5x + 1 = x^2 + x - 2$$
$$x^2 - 4x - 3 = 0$$

Use the formula.
$a = 1, b = {}^-4, c = {}^-3$

$$x = \frac{4 \pm \sqrt{({}^-4)^2 - 4 \times 1 \times {}^-3}}{2 \times 1}$$

$$x = \frac{4 \pm \sqrt{28}}{2}$$

ANSWER $x = 4.65$ and ${}^-0.65$ to an accuracy of 2 decimal places

Test 23

 Use a calculator for questions 1 and 6.

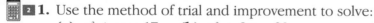 **1.** Use the method of trial and improvement to solve:
  (a) $x^3 + x = 17$ **(b)** $x^3 + 2x = 90$
  (c) $x^3 - x = 31$ **(d)** $x^3 - 4x = 7$
  Give your solutions to 1 decimal place.
  You **must** show all your trials.

2. Simplify:
  (a) $(3x + y)(x - y) + 2y(x - y)$
  (b) $(x - 3)^2 + (x - 5)^2 - 2$
  (c) $(x + 7)(x - 7) - (x + 4)(x - 4)$
  (d) $(2x + y)(3x - 4y) - (6x + 5y)(x - 3y)$

3. In each case show that expression A is equivalent to expression B:

(a) A $(x + y)^2 + (x - y)^2$
    B $2(x^2 + y^2)$

(b) A $(x + y)^2 - (x - y)^2$
    B $4xy$

(c) A $(a + bx)^2 + (ab - x)^2$
    B $(b^2 + 1)(x^2 + a^2)$

(d) A $(a + bx)^2 - (ab + x)^2$
    B $(b^2 - 1)(x^2 - a^2)$

(e) A $4(2x + y)(2x - y)$
    B $8y(2x - y) + 4(2x - y)^2$

4. Simplify:

(a) $\dfrac{x - 3}{2x - 6}$

(b) $\dfrac{x^2 - 1}{x + 1}$

(c) $\dfrac{x + 5}{3x + 15}$

(d) $\dfrac{2x + 3y}{4x^2 - 9y^2}$

(e) $\dfrac{x^2 + 9x + 20}{x + 4}$

(f) $\dfrac{x^2 - 3x - 4}{x^2 - 1}$

(g) $\dfrac{x^2 - 4x - 5}{x^2 - 3x - 10}$

(h) $\dfrac{x^2 - 2x + 1}{x^2 + 3x - 4}$

(i) $\dfrac{2x^2 + 9x + 10}{3x^2 - 12}$

(j) $\dfrac{6x^2 + 13x - 5}{2x^2 + 3x - 5}$

5. Simplify :

(a) $\dfrac{1}{x - 3} + \dfrac{1}{x - 1}$

(b) $\dfrac{x}{x - 1} - \dfrac{1}{x + 1}$

(c) $\dfrac{1}{x + 1} + \dfrac{2}{2x - 1}$

(d) $\dfrac{3}{3x + 2} - \dfrac{x}{x^2 + 1}$

(e) $\dfrac{3x}{x^2 + 2} - \dfrac{2}{x - 1}$

6. Solve the following equations:

(a) $\dfrac{4}{x} + \dfrac{3}{10 - x} = 2$

(b) $\dfrac{3}{x + 1} + \dfrac{7}{x - 6} = 5$

(c) $\dfrac{8x}{x + 3} - \dfrac{x}{x - 2} = 1$

(d) $\dfrac{x}{x + 2} - \dfrac{x - 1}{x} = 4$

(e) $\dfrac{1}{2x + 3} + \dfrac{1}{6 - x} = \dfrac{2}{5}$

Give your answers to an accuracy of 2 decimal places.

2. TRANSFORMING GRAPHS

Function notation

Function notation can be used to show a relationship between two variables.

In this example $f(x) = x^2$

$f(x)$ means a function of x.
$f(x) = x^2$ means that $y = x^2$ where y is a function of x.

e.g.1

$f(x) = 2x + 5$
$f(3) = 2 \times 3 + 5 = 11$

e.g.2

$f(x) = (x + 3)^3$
$f(1) = (1 + 3)^3 = 4^3 = 64$

e.g.3

$f(x) = 2x^2 + 4$
$f(4) = 2 \times 4^2 + 5 = 32 + 5 = 37$

Translating a graph

When the position or shape of a graph is changed by a transformation (see p. 143) then the equation of the transformed graph is related to the equation of the original graph.

When a graph is translated all points on the graph move by the same vector (see p. 144).

Original equation	New equation	Transformation
$y = f(x)$	$y = f(x) + a$	Translation by vector $\begin{pmatrix} 0 \\ a \end{pmatrix}$
$y = f(x)$	$y = f(x + a)$	Translation by vector $\begin{pmatrix} \bar{a} \\ 0 \end{pmatrix}$

e.g.1

The diagram shows the graphs of $y = x^2$ and the graphs of the related functions $y = x^2 + 2$ and $y = (x - 3)^2$

Original equation	New equation	Transformation	
$y = x^2$	$y = x^2 + 2$	Translation by vector $\begin{pmatrix} 0 \\ 2 \end{pmatrix}$ This means that all y-coordinates on the original graph are increased by 2.	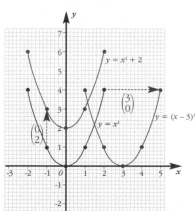
$y = x^2$	$y = (x - 3)^2$	Translation by vector $\begin{pmatrix} 3 \\ 0 \end{pmatrix}$ This means that all x-coordinates on the original graph are increased by 3.	

Remember
The direction in which the graph is translated depends upon the sign of a.

TRANSFORMING GRAPHS

1 Stretching a graph

A graph can be stretched either from the x-axis, parallel to the y-axis or from the y-axis, parallel to the x-axis.

Original equation	New equation	Transformation
$y = f(x)$	$y = af(x)$	Stretch from the x-axis, parallel to the y-axis, scale factor **a**. This means that all y-coordinates on the original graph are multiplied by **a** to give the y-coordinates on the new graph.
$y = f(x)$	$y = f(ax)$	Stretch from the y-axis, parallel to the x-axis, scale factor $^1/_a$. This means that all x-coordinates on the original graph are divided by **a** to give the x-coordinates on the new graph.

e.g.1

The diagram shows the graphs of $y = \sin x$ and the graphs of the related functions $y = 2\sin x$ and $y = \sin 3x$.

Original equation	New equation	Transformation
$y = \sin x$	$y = 2\sin x$	Stretch from x-axis, scale factor 2. All y-coordinates on the original graph are multiplied by 2 to give the y-coordinates on the new graph.
$y = \sin x$	$y = \sin 3x$	Stretch from y-axis, scale factor $^1/_3$. All x-coordinates on the original graph are divided by 3 to give the x-coordinates on the new graph.

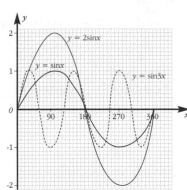

1 Reflecting a graph

A graph can be reflected in either the x-axis or the y-axis.

Original equation	New equation	Transformation
$y = f(x)$	$y = {}^-f(x)$	Reflection in the x-axis. This means that the y-coordinates on the original graph change signs.
$y = f(x)$	$y = f({}^-x)$	Reflection in the y-axis. This means that the x-coordinates on the original graph change signs.

The diagram shows the graphs of $y = (x - 2)^2$ and the graphs of the related functions $y = {}^-(x + 2)^2$ and $y = ({}^-x + 2)^2$

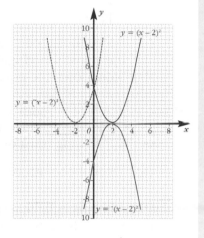

Original equation	New equation	Transformation
$y = (x - 2)^2$	$y = {}^-(x - 2)^2$	Reflection in the x-axis
$y = (x - 2)^2$	$y = ({}^-x - 2)^2$ *	Reflection in the y-axis

* The new equation $y = ({}^-x - 2)^2$ is equivalent to the equation $y = (x + 2)^2$

> **Examiner's tip**
> Transformations of the graphs of
> $y = x^2$, $y = x^3$, $y = \sin x$ and $y = \cos x$
> are common exam questions.

Test 24

Do not use a calculator.

1. You are told that:
  $f(x) = 3x - 2$
  $g(x) = x^2 + 3x - 1$
  $h(x) = x^3 + x^2 + x + 1$
  Work out the values of $f(x)$, $g(x)$ and $h(x)$ when:
  (a) $x = 0$ **(b)** $x = 2$ **(c)** $x = {}^-2$

■2. Each of the following diagrams shows the graph of $y = x^2$ together with the graph of a related function.

(i) 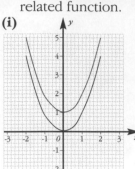 (ii) 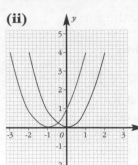 (iii) 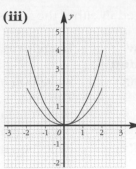 (iv)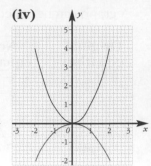

(a) For each diagram describe the transformation that maps the graph of $y = x^2$ on to the transformed graph.

(b) Write down the equation of each related graph.

■3. The graph of $y = \sin x$ for values of x from 0 to 180^0 is shown. Draw diagrams to show the graph of $y = \sin x$ together with each of the following transformations of this graph:

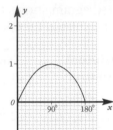

(a) Translation with vector $\begin{pmatrix} 0 \\ 2 \end{pmatrix}$

(b) Translation with vector $\begin{pmatrix} 90^0 \\ 0 \end{pmatrix}$

(c) Stretch from the x-axis with scale factor 3

(d) Stretch from the y-axis with scale factor $^1/_2$

In each case give the equation of the transformed graph.

■4. A sketch of the graph of $y = x^3$ is shown.

(a) Use the graph to sketch the following graphs.

(i) $y = ^1/_2 x^3$ (ii) $y = ^-1/_2 x^3$
(iii) $y = x^3 + 2$ (iv) $y = (x + 2)^3$
(v) $y = ^1/_2 (x^3 + 2)$
(vi) $y = ^-1/_2 (x + 2)^3$

(b) The graph of $y = x^3$ passes through the point (2, 8). Write down the coordinates to which the point (2, 8) moves in each of your sketch graphs.

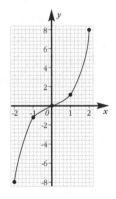

■5. The diagram shows the graph of $y = \cos x$.

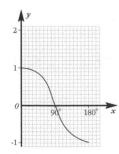

(a)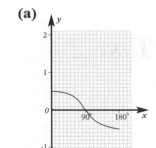

(b)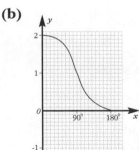

Each of the graphs (a) and (b) is a transformation of the graph of $y = \cos x$.
Give the equation for each one.

Section 3: Shape, Space and Measures
ANGLES, PARALLEL LINES AND POLYGONS

Angles at a point and on a straight line

Angles at a point add up to 360°.
Angles on a straight line add up to 180°.

$a + b + c + d = 360°$
$a + b = 180°$
$c + d = 180°$

e.g.1

$x = 95°$ $x + 85° = 180°$ (angles on a straight line)
$y = 65°$ $y + 115° + 180° = 360°$ (angles at a point)

> **Remember**
> **Acute** angles are angles less than 90°.
> **Obtuse** angles are angles between 90° and 180°.
> **Reflex** angles are angles between 180° and 360°.
> Angles that add up to 90° are called **complementary** angles.
> Angles that add up to 180° are called **supplementary** angles.

Intersecting and parallel lines

When two straight lines cross the **opposite angles** are equal.
When two **parallel lines** are crossed by a **transversal** two sets of equal angles are formed.

The following pairs of **corresponding angles** are equal:
a and e
b and f
c and g
d and h

The following pairs of **alternate angles** are equal:
a and h
b and g
d and e
c and f

The following pairs of **allied angles** add up to 180°, so:
$d + f = 180°$
$c + e = 180°$

> **Remember**
> **Arrow heads** are used to show that lines are parallel.

e.g.1

$a = 20°$ **corresponding** angles are equal
$b = 32°$ **alternate** angles are equal
$c = 128°$ **supplementary angles** add up to 180°

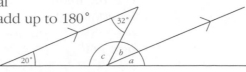

4 · Angles in triangles and quadrilaterals

The angles of a triangle add up to $180°$.
$a + b + c = 180°$
The exterior angle of a triangle equals the sum of the interior opposite angles.
$d = b + c$
The angles of a quadrilateral add up to $360°$.
$p + q + r + s = 360°$

e.g.1

$w = 150°$ $110 + 40$
$x = 30°$ $180 - (110 + 40)$
$y = 70°$ $180 - 110$
$z = 100°$ $360 - (110 + 80 + 70)$

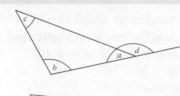

4 · Angles in polygons

The exterior angles of any polygon add up to $360°$.
So: $a + b + c + d + e + f = 360°$
At each vertex, the interior and exterior angles are supplementary.
So: $a + u = b + v = c + w = \dots = 180°$
The interior angles of a polygon with n sides add up to $\mathbf{180° \times (n - 2)}$.
So, for a six-sided polygon:
   The interior angles add up to $720°$ $180° \times (6 - 2)$

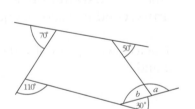

e.g.1 $a = 100°$ sum of exterior angles = $360°$
                   so $a = 360 - (70 + 50 + 30 + 110)$
        $b = 80°$ the interior and exterior
                  angles are supplementary,
                  so $b = 180 - 100$

3 · Regular polygons

A regular polygon has equal angles and equal sides.
For a regular n-sided polygon:
   The exterior angle = $\mathbf{360° \div n}$
   The interior angle = $\mathbf{180° - (360° \div n)}$
   The centre angle = $\mathbf{360° \div n}$
Joining lines from each vertex to the centre forms n isosceles triangles (see page 124).

Regular pentagon
$^{360}/_5 = 72°$
$180 - 72 = 108°$

Regular octagon
$^{360}/_8 = 45°$
$180 - 45 = 135°$

e.g.1 $ABCDE$ is a regular pentagon with centre O.
        CDF and AEF are straight lines.
        G is the mid-point of BC.
        Exterior angle = centre angle = $72°$ $^{360}/_5$
        $a = 36°$ $^1/_2$ of 72
        $b = 144°$ 2×72
        $c = 36°$ In triangle DEF $180 - 2 \times 72$

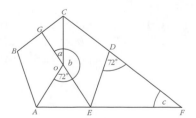

Tessellations

A tessellation is a repeating pattern of shapes.
A shape tessellates if it covers a surface without overlapping and without gaps.

EXAMPLES

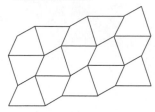
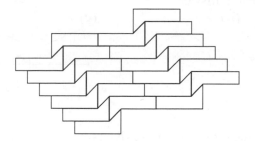

Three-figure bearings

Bearings are used to describe the direction of one place from another.
A bearing is an angle, between 0° and 360°, measured clockwise from the North direction.
It is always written as a three-figure number.

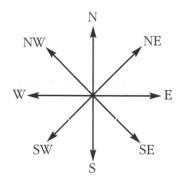

Remember

The bearing of North is 000°.
The bearing of East is 090°.
The bearing of South is 180°.
The bearing of West is 270°.

EXAMPLES

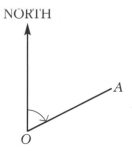 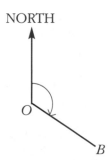 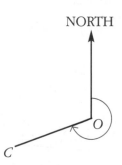 

The bearing of *A* from *O* is 075°.
The bearing of *B* from *O* is 115°.
The bearing of *C* from *O* is 260°.
The bearing of *D* from *O* is 330°.

Examiner's tip
*You will need to
use a protractor to
draw and measure
bearings.*

ANGLES, PARALLEL LINES
AND POLYGONS

Test 25

Diagrams in questions 1 to 5 have not been drawn accurately.

1. Find the size of angles *a* to *c* in these diagrams.
Give a reason for each answer.

(a)

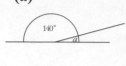

(b)

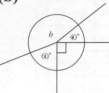

(c)

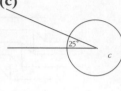

2. Find the size of angles *a* to *c* in these diagrams.
Give a reason for each answer.

(a)

(b)

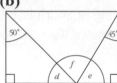

(c)

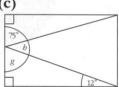

3. Find the size of angles *a* to *h* in these diagrams.
Give a reason for each answer.

(a)

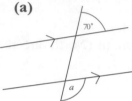

(b)

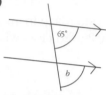

(c)

4. Find the size of angles *a* to *e* in these diagrams.
Give a reason for each answer.

(a)

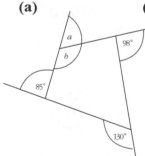

(b)

(c)

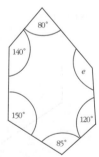

5. Find the size of angles *a* to *n* in these regular polygons.

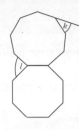
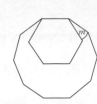
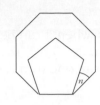

6. Show how each of the following shapes tessellate.

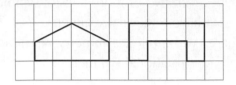

7. (a) Use a protractor to measure the bearings of A, B, C and D from O.

(i)   (ii)   (iii)   (iv)

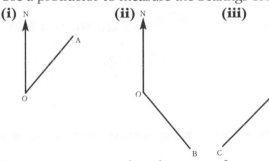

(b) Use a protractor to draw bearings of:
  (i) 080°   **(ii)** 115° **(iii)** 160°
  (iv) 210°   **(v)** 265° **(vi)** 320°

2. SYMMETRY

Line symmetry

A shape with line symmetry can be folded so that one half fits exactly over the other.
The fold line is called a line of symmetry or a mirror line.

EXAMPLES
A rectangle has 2 lines of symmetry   A hexagon has 6 lines of symmetry

> **Examiner's tip**
> *When you are first learning about symmetry, using tracing paper can help.*

Rotational symmetry

A shape has rotational symmetry when it can be rotated about its centre so that it fits exactly on to its original position.

The number of times it does this in one turn is called the order of rotational symmetry.

EXAMPLES

Equilateral triangle
Rotational symmetry order 3
3 lines of symmetry.

Remember

All shapes with two or more lines of symmetry have rotational symmetry.
Shapes with no line symmetry can have rotational symmetry.

Rotational symmetry order 4
0 lines of symmetry

Examiner's tips

Learn how to use tracing paper to check rotational symmetry.

Symmetries in 3-D shapes

A plane of symmetry divides a solid into two equal halves.
An axis of symmetry is a line about which a solid shape has rotational symmetry.

e.g.1

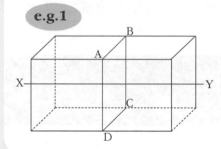

ABCD is a plane of symmetry
A cuboid has 3 planes of symmetry.

XY is an axis of symmetry
The cuboid has rotational symmetry of order 2 about *XY*.

Test 26

1. Which of the following shapes have:
   (a) Line symmetry
   (b) Rotational symmetry
   For a shape with line symmetry, give the number of lines of symmetry.
   For a shape with rotational symmetry, give the order of rotational symmetry.

(a) 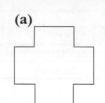　(b) 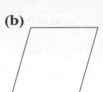　(c) 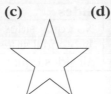　(d) 　(e)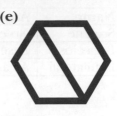

2. (a) Copy and complete each of these shapes so that the blue lines are lines of symmetry.

　　　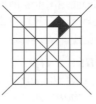

(b) Copy and complete each of the shapes in **(a)** so that they have rotational symmetry of order 2.

(c) Copy and complete each of the shapes in **(a)** so that they have rotational symmetry of order 4.

3. For each of the shapes below draw diagrams to show **all** the planes of symmetry.

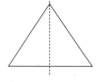　

---

3. # TRIANGLES AND QUADRILATERALS

4

Special triangles and their properties

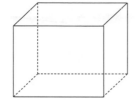　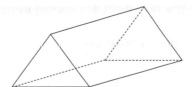

Isosceles　**Equilateral**　**Scalene**

　　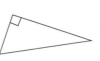

Obtuse angled　Acute angled　Right-angled

123

TRIANGLES AND QUADRILATERALS

Name	Angles	Sides	Symmetry
Scalene	No equal angles	No equal sides	No lines of symmetry
Isosceles	Base angles are equal	Two equal sides	One line of symmetry
Equilateral	All angles equal 60°	All sides equal	Three lines of symmetry

e.g.1

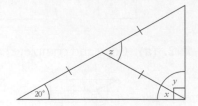

$x = 20°$ base angles of an isosceles triangle
$y = 70°$ angles x and y add up to 90°
$z = 40°$ base angles in the isosceles triangle = 70°
          so $z = 180 - (2 \times 70)$

> ### Examiner's tip
> *Working out the angles on the diagram is fine,*
> *but write them on the answer line as well.*
> *If you are asked for a reason for your answer,*
> *make sure you try to give one.*

> ### Remember
> Equal lengths in diagrams are
> marked with dashes.

4

Constructing triangles

Triangles with given lengths and angles are constructed
using a ruler, protractor and a pair of compasses.
In the diagrams below construction lines are shown in red.

e.g.1

Two angles and a side given
$AB = 3$ cm, $x = 45°$, $z = 55°$

Use a ruler to construct AB.
Use a protractor to construct angle x and y.
Continue the lengths of sides AC and BC
until they cross.

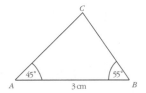

e.g.2

Two sides and an included angle given
$AB = 3$ cm, $AC = 2$ cm, $x = 30°$

Use a ruler to construct AB.
Use a protractor to construct angle x.
Use a ruler to construct AC.
Join B to C.

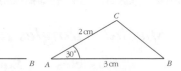

e.g.3

Three sides given
$AB = 3$ cm, $AC = 4.5$ cm, $BC = 3.5$ cm

Use a ruler to construct AB.
Use a compass to construct an arc at A of radius 4.5 cm.
Use a compass to construct an arc at B of radius 3.5 cm.
Draw the arcs so they cross at C.
Join both A and B to C.

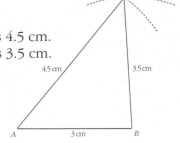

e.g.4

An equilateral triangle of given side length
$AB = 4$ cm, $AC = 4$ cm, $BC = 4$ cm

Use a ruler to construct *AB*.
Use a compass to construct an arc at *A* of radius 4 cm.
Use a compass to construct an arc at *B* of radius 4 cm.
Draw the arcs so they cross at *C*
Join both *A* and *B* to *C*.

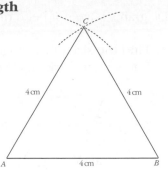

4

Special quadrilaterals and their properties

Square   Rectangle   Parallelogram   Trapezium   Rhombus   Kite

Name	Sides	Angles	Diagonals	Lines of Symmetry	Rotational Symmetry
Square	All sides equal Opposite sides parallel	All 90°	Equal and bisect each other at right angles	4	Order 4
Rectangle	Opposite sides equal and parallel	All 90°	Equal and bisect each other	2	Order 2
Parallelogram	Opposite sides equal and parallel	Opposite angles equal	Bisect each other	0	Order 2
Trapezium	One pair of parallel sides			0	No
Rhombus	All sides equal Opposite sides parallel	Opposite angles equal	Bisect each other at right angles	2	Order 2
Kite	2 pairs of sides equal	1 pair of opposite angles equal	One bisects the other at right angles	1	No

Remember
The sum of the angles in any quadrilateral is 360°.

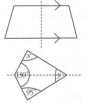

EXAMPLES
This quadrilateral has one line of symmetry and one pair of opposite sides parallel.
> The only quadrilateral that has one pair of opposite sides parallel is a trapezium.
> So the quadrilateral is a symmetrical trapezium.

The diagram shows a kite.
> $x = 95°$ a kite has one line of symmetry (shown)
> $y = 40°$ $360 - (2 \times 95 + 130)$

Diagrams have not been drawn accurately.

1. Find the size of the angles marked a to j in these diagrams.
Show your working clearly.

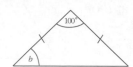

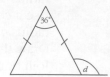

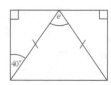
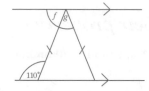
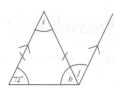

2. Triangle *ABC* is not drawn to scale.

Construct accurately the following triangles where:
(a) $AB = 8$ cm, $x = 30°$ and $y = 110°$.
(b) $AB = 7.5$ cm, $AC = 5.5$ cm and $x = 55°$.
(c) $AB = 6.5$ cm, $AC = 4.5$ cm, $AC = 7$ cm.

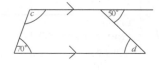

3. Construct an equilateral triangle of side length 6 cm.

4. Find the size of the angles marked a to i in these diagrams.
Show your working clearly.

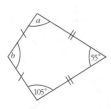
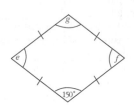
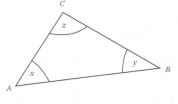
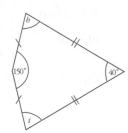

5. Identify each of the following quadrilaterals:
(a) One pair of opposite sides parallel
The other pair of opposite sides **not** parallel
(b) Both opposite pairs of angles equal
Diagonals **not** equal but bisect each other
2 lines of symmetry
(c) Rotational symmetry order 2 and no line symmetry

6. Percy Proof says he has drawn a quadrilateral with exactly three right angles.
Explain why this is impossible.

ANGLES AND CIRCLES

2 | *Parts of a circle*

2 | *Angles and circles*

Angles drawn from a diameter to the circumference

When a triangle is drawn from a diameter
the angle on the circumference is **always**
a right angle.

x is always $90°$

Angles drawn from an arc to the circumference

When an angle is drawn from an arc to any
point on the circumference of a circle, the
angle at the circumference is **always** the same.

$x = y$

Angle drawn from an arc to the centre

When an angle is drawn from an arc to the
centre of a circle, the angle at the centre is
always double any angle at the circumference
drawn from the **same** arc.

$x = 2y$

Angles in a cyclic quadrilateral

The vertices of a cyclic quadrilateral are on the
circumference of a circle.
The opposite angles of a cyclic quadrilateral add up to $180°$.

$a + c = b + d = 180°$

EXAMPLES

$a = 43°$ angles drawn from same arc
$b = 40°$ angle at circumference $= 90°$
           angles in a triangle add up to $180°$
$c = 110°$ $180 - 2 \times 35$ (isosceles triangle)
$d = 55°$ angle at centre $= 2 \times$ angle at circumference
$e = 95°$ opposite angles of cyclic quadrilateral

2

Circles and tangents

A tangent to a circle is a line that touches the circle.

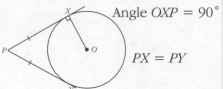

Angle $OXP = 90°$

Tangents drawn to a circle from
the same point are equal.

$PX = PY$

Where a tangent and radius meet on the circumference of a
circle, the angle between them is a right angle.

e.g.1

The diagram shows a circle with centre O.
PA and PB are tangents to the circle at A and B.
C is a point on the circumference of the circle.

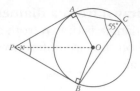

Angle at centre is double angle at circumference
    So angle $AOB = 2 \times 55 = 110°$
PO is a line of symmetry
    So angle $AOP = 55°$
Angle between tangent and radius = 90°
    So angle $APO = 180 - (90 + 55) = 35°$
    So $x = 70°$ 2×35

1

More circles and tangents

The angle between a tangent and a chord is equal to
any angle at the circumference drawn from the chord.

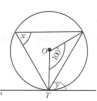

$x = y$

x **must** be in the opposite segment to y.

e.g.1

The diagram shows a circle with centre O.
PT is a tangent to the circle at T.

Angle at centre is double angle at circumference
    So $x = 50°$ ½ of 100
Angle between tangent and chord = angle in opposite segment
    So $y = 50°$

Do not use a calculator.

2 1. Work out each of the lettered angles in the following diagrams.
Give a reason for your answers.

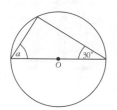 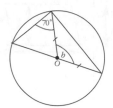 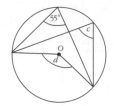 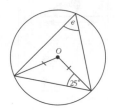

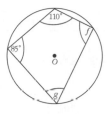 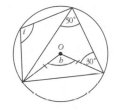 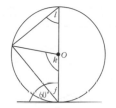 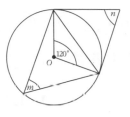

1 2. Work out each of the lettered angles in the following diagrams.
Give a reason for your answers.

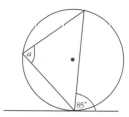 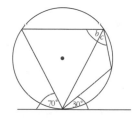

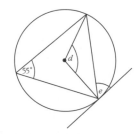 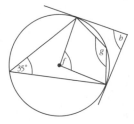

5. AREA AND PERIMETER

Formulae for the area of triangles and quadrilaterals

Shape	Triangle	Square	Rectangle	Parallelogram	Trapezium
	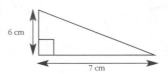				
Area	$^1/_2 \times b \times h$	l^2	$l \times w$	$b \times h$	$^1/_2 \times (a + b) \times h$

e.g.1

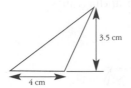

6 cm

7 cm

Area = 21 cm² $^1/_2 \times 7 \times 6$

e.g.2

3.5 cm

4 cm

Area = 7 cm² $^1/_2 \times 4 \times 3.5$

e.g.3

5 m

6 cm

Area = 30 m² 5×6

e.g.4

2 m

5 m

4 m

Area = 15 cm² $^1/_2 \times (2 + 4) \times 5$

Examiner's tip

On some exam papers, the units of the answer (eg. cm²)may already be written in for you. If they are not, always remember to write them in yourself. If the question asks you to find the area of something, your answer will make no sense if it does not have an area unit attached to it, it will just be a meaningless number!

Shape, Space and Measures

Area and perimeter of composite shapes

e.g.1

Area

The L-shape can be divided into a square (*A*) and a rectangle (*B*).
Area of A = 21.16 cm²   4.6 × 4.6
Area of B = 15.64 cm²   4.6 × 3.4
Area of L-shape = 36.8 cm²   21.16 + 15.64

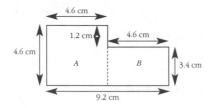

Perimeter   4.6 + 1.2 + 4.6 + 3.4 + 9.2 + 4.6
Perimeter = 27.6 cm

e.g.2

Area

The shape can be divided into a square (*C*) and a trapezium (*D*).
Area of C = 10.24 cm²   3.2 × 3.2
Area of D = 6.88 cm²   ½ × (3.2 + 1.1) × 3.2
Area of L-shape = 17.12 cm²   10.24 + 6.88

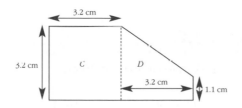

Perimeter   Use Pythagoras' rule to find the length of the sloping side (see page 154).
3.2 + (sloping side) + 1.1 + 6.4 + 3.2

Remember
The perimeter of a shape is the length of all its sides added together.
When finding the area of a compound shape show **all** your working.

3

Area and circumference of a circle

Circumference	**Area**
π × diameter	π × (radius)²
2 × π × radius	

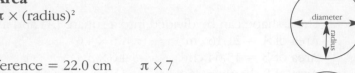

e.g.1

Circumference = 22.0 cm	π × 7
Circumference = 7 × π	**in terms of π**
Radius = 3.5 cm	½ of 7
Area = 38.5 cm²	π × (3.5)²
Area = 12.25 × π	**in terms of π**

e.g.2

Circumference = 20.1 cm	6.4 × π
Circumference = 6.4 × π	**in terms of π**
Area = 32.2 cm²	π × (3.2)²
Area = 10.24 × π	**in terms of π**

3.2 cm

e.g.3

Perimeter = 25.7 cm	10 + ½ of π × 10
Perimeter = 10 + 5 × π	**in terms of π**
Radius = 5 cm	½ of 10
Area = 39.3 cm²	½ of π × (5)²
Area = 12.5 × π	**in terms of π**

10 cm

Examiner's tip
- Use the π button on your scientific calculator or use π = 3.14

2

Harder circle problems

e.g.1

What is the circumference of a circle of area of 25 cm²?

π × (radius)²	= 25	
(radius)²	= 25 ÷ π	dividing both sides by π
radius	= √(25 ÷ π)	taking the square root of both sides
radius	= 2.82 cm	to 3 significant figures
diameter	= 5.64 cm	2 × 2.82
circumference	= 17.7 cm	5.64 × π

1

The area of sectors and the length of arcs

A sector is the area enclosed between an arc and two radii.
a is the angle between the radii.

Arc length

Minor arc length	= $^a/_{360}$ × π × diameter
	= $^a/_{360}$ × 2 × π × radius

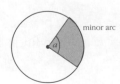

minor arc

Area of sector

Area of minor sector	= $^a/_{360}$ × π × (radius)²

e.g.1

| Length of minor arc | = 3.14 cm | $^{30}/_{360} \times 2 \times \pi \times 6$ |
| | = π | **in terms of π** |

| Area of minor sector | = 9.42 cm² | $^{30}/_{360} \times \pi \times 6^2$ |
| | = 3 × π | **in terms of π** |

Test 29

Do not use a calculator for questions 1, 3 and 6.

1. Work out the area of each of these shapes.

(a)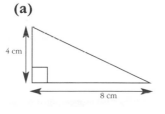

(b)

(c)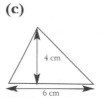

(d)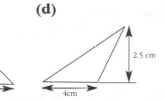

(e)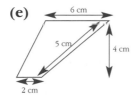

(f)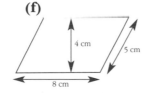

(g)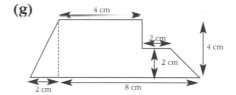

2. Work out the area and perimeter of each of these shapes.
Give the units of your answers.

(a)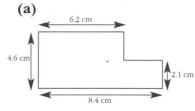

(b)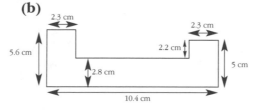

(c)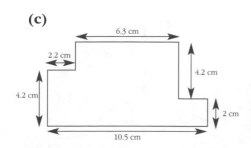

3. Work out the area and perimeter of each of these shapes.
Give your answers in terms of π.

(a)

(b)

(c)

(d)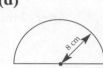

4. The diagram shows the inside of a running track.
(a) Find the length of its perimeter..
(b) What is the area enclosed by the running track?

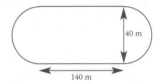

5. (a) Find the area of a circle with circumference 20 cm.
(b) Find the circumference of a circle with area 20 cm².

6. Work out the shaded area in this shape.
Give your answer in terms of π.

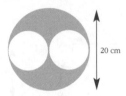

7. Find the area and perimeter of each of these sectors.

(a)

(b)

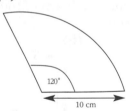

(c)

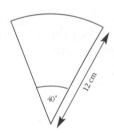

8. Find the area and perimeter of the shaded part of each of these diagrams.
Give your answers in terms of π.

(a)

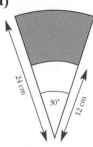

(b)

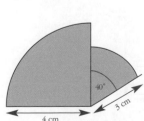

(c)

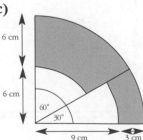

VOLUME AND SURFACE AREA

3-D shapes and their nets

A solid is a three-dimensional shape.
Some common solids are shown in the table.

Name	Cuboid	Triangular prism	Cylinder	Triangular pyramid	Sphere
	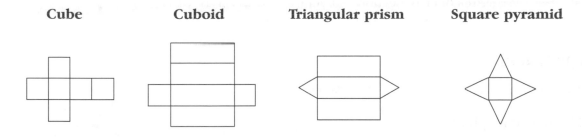				
Faces	6	5	3	4	1
Edges	12	9	2	6	0
Vertices	8	6	0	4	0

The cuboid, triangular prism and cylinder are all examples of prisms.
All prisms have a constant cross-section – shaded in the diagrams.

A net is a flat shape that can be folded to form a solid.
Some common nets are shown below.

Cube	Cuboid	Triangular prism	Square pyramid

Isometric drawings and plans and elevations

Isometric paper is used to make 2D drawings of 3D shapes.
A plan is the view of a 3D shape looking from above.
An elevation is the view of a 3D shape looking from the front or side.

EXAMPLES

Isometric drawing   Plan   Elevation A   Elevation B

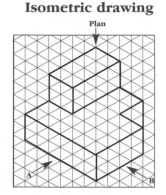

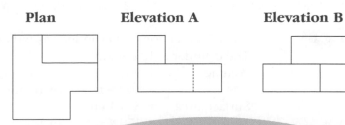

Remember
Full lines on plans and elevations are used to
show edges you can see.
Dotted lines are used to show edges that are
hidden.

VOLUME AND SURFACE AREA

4

The volume and surface area of a cuboid

Volume is the amount of space occupied by a 3D shape.
Surface area is the area of **all** the surfaces of a solid shape.

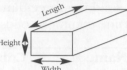

Volume of a cuboid
length × width × height

Surface area of a cuboid
2 × length × width + 2 × length × height + 2 × width × height

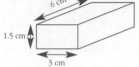

e.g.1

| Volume = 27 cm³ | 6 × 3 × 1.5 |
| Surface area = 63 cm² | 2 × 6 × 3 + 2 × 6 × 1.5 + 2 × 3 × 1.5 |

2

Prisms

Volume of a prism
area of cross-section × length

e.g.1

The diagram shows the cross-section of a prism in
the shape of a trapezium.
The prism is 3 cm long.
Area of cross-section = 1.7cm²   ½ × (2 + 1.4) × 1
Volume of prism = 5.1 cm³   3 × 1.7

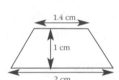

2

Cylinders

A cylinder is a prism with a circular cross-section.

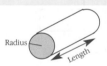

The net of a cylinder

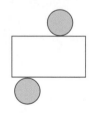

Volume of a cylinder
π × (radius)² × length

Surface area of a cylinder
2 × π × (radius)² + π × diameter × length

e.g.1

The cross-section of a cylinder has radius 5 cm.
The cylinder is 12 cm long.

Volume	= 942.5 cm³	π × 5² × 12
	= 300 × π	**in terms of π**
Surface area	= 534.1 cm²	2 × π × 5² + π × 10 × 12
	= 170 × π	**in terms of π**

1

Volume and surface area of cones, pyramids and spheres

Cone	Pyramid	Sphere

Volume

$\frac{1}{3} \times$ base area $\times$ height

$\frac{1}{3}\pi r^2 h$

Volume

$\frac{1}{3} \times$ base area $\times$ height

Volume

$\frac{4}{3}\pi r^3$

Curved surface area

πrl

Surface area

$4\pi r^2$

e.g.1
A sphere has radius 6 cm.

Volume	$= 904.8$ cm^3	$\frac{4}{3} \times \pi \times 6^3$	
	$- 288 \times \pi$	**in terms of** π	
Surface area	$= 452.4$ cm^3	$4 \times \pi \times 6^2$	
	$= 144 \times \pi$	**in terms of** π	

e.g.2
A cone has base radius 5 cm and height 12 cm.

Volume $\quad = 314.2$ cm$^3 \quad \frac{1}{3} \times \pi \times 5^2 \times 12$

$\quad\quad\quad = 100 \times \pi \quad$ **in terms of** π

The formula for the curved surface area uses the slant height of the cone.
To calculate the slant height use Pythagoras' rule (see page 154).

Slant height $\quad = 13$ cm $\quad \sqrt{5^2 + 12^2}$

Curved surface area $= 204.2$ cm$^3 \quad \pi \times 5 \times 13$

$\quad\quad\quad\quad\quad\quad = 65 \times \pi \quad$ **in terms of** π

Examiner's tip
*Note that the formula given
for the pyramid is for a
square-based pyramid.
Pyramids with different bases
will need different formulae.*

Test 30

Use a calculator for questions 5 onwards.

1.(a) 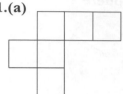 **(b)** 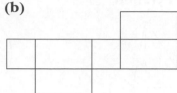 **(c)**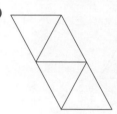

Which of the above is:
(a) the net of a prism?
(b) the net of a pyramid?
(c) **not** the net of a solid?

2.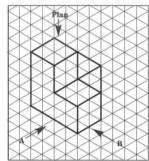

The diagram shows two solids.
(a) Draw plan views of each solid.
(b) Draw elevations from the directions shown.

3.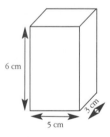

Which of the above cuboids:
(a) has the larger volume?
(b) has the smaller surface area?

4. A cuboid has integer lengths.
The area of its base is 5 cm².
Its volume is 20 cm³.
What is its surface area?

5. The cross-section of a triangular based prism is shown.
The length of the prism is 4.5 cm.
Work out the volume of the prism.
State the units of your answer.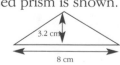

6. The diagram shows a cylinder.
The radius of the cylinder is 8 cm.
The height of the cylinder is 10 cm.

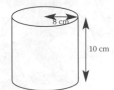

(a) Calculate the volume of the cylinder.
(b) Calculate the surface area of the cylinder.

7. Two cylinders, *A* and *B*, each have volume 300 cm³.
(a) The radius of cylinder *A* is 5 cm.
Find the height of cylinder *A*.
(b) The height of cylinder *B* is 10 cm.
Find the radius of cylinder *B*.

8. The following shapes are made up of cones, cylinders and hemispheres.
Find their volumes.

(a) (b) (c) (d) (e)

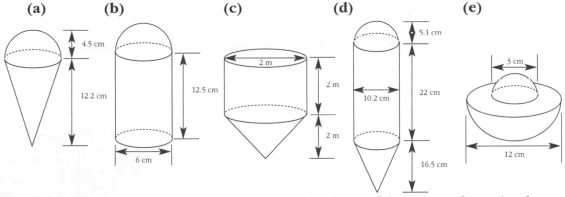

9. The diagram shows a piece of cheese cut in the shape of the sector of a circle of radius 8 cm.
The thickness of the cheese is 6.5 cm.

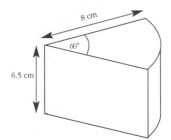

(a) Find the volume of the cheese.
The curved surface of the cheese is covered in a red wax.
(b) Find the area of the wax covering.

LOCI AND CONSTRUCTIONS

4

Scale drawings

Distance on maps and plans are drawn to scale. For example:

Scale   **Means ...**
1 to 500   Real length = 500 × distance on a map or plan
1 cm to 2 km   1 cm on the map or plan = an actual length of 2 km

e.g.1

The scale of a map is 1 cm represents 5 km.
A road on the map is 2.4 cm long.
2.4 × 5
The actual length of the road is 12 km.

e.g.2

A plan is drawn to a scale of 1 to 5000.
A church on the plan is 1.2 cm long.
1.2 × 5000 = 6000 cm
6000 ÷ 100
The actual length of the church is 60 m.

2

The idea of a locus

A locus is the path followed by a point that moves according to a rule.

e.g.1

Rule   P is 1 cm from the point X
Locus   The dotted line

e.g.2

Rule   Q is 1 cm from the line AB
Locus   The dotted line

> **Remember**
> The word 'loci' means more than one locus.

2

Other simple loci

Points equidistant from two fixed points (*A* and *B*)
The locus is the perpendicular bisector of the line *AB*.

Points equidistant from two fixed lines (*AB* and *AC*)
The locus is the line that bisects angle *CAB*.

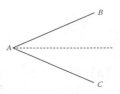

> **Remember**
> The word 'equidistant' might be used in locus questions; it means 'an equal distance from'.
> Bisect means 'cut in half'.

2

Constructions

Accurate constructions are done using **only** a straight edge and a pair of compasses.
In the diagrams below construction lines are shown in red.
The constructions are in blue.

The perpendicular bisector of a line
Draw equal arcs with centres A and B.
The arcs intersect at C and D.
CD is the perpendicular bisector of AB.
Points on CD are equidistant from A and B.

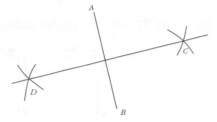

The bisector of an angle
Draw equal arcs with centre A.
The arcs intersect AB and AC at D and E.
Draw equal arcs with centres D and E.
The arcs intersect at F.
AF is the angle bisector of angle BAC.
Points on AF are equidistant from AB and AC.

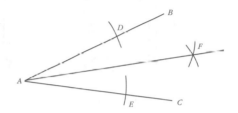

The perpendicular from a point to a line
Draw equal arcs with centre P.
The arcs intersect the line at A and B.
Draw equal arcs with centres A and B.
The arcs intersect at C.
PC is the perpendicular from P to the line.

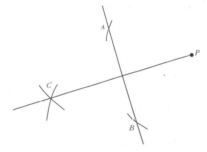

The perpendicular from a point on a line
Draw equal arcs with centre P.
The arcs intersect the line at A and B.
Draw equal arcs with centres A and B.
The arcs intersect at C and D.
CD is the perpendicular to the line passing through P.

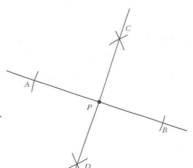

Examiner's tips
- *When drawing accurate loci show your construction arcs. Try to draw them with faint lines but make sure they can be seen.*
- *If you are asked to construct an angle of 60°, use the equilateral angle construction on page 125.*

1. A boat sails due east from a port *P* for a distance of 10 km.
It then changes course and sails for 8 km on a bearing of 150° to lighthouse, *L*.
Using a scale of 1 cm to represent 2 km make a scale drawing of the boat's journey.
Use your drawing to measure the distance and bearing of *L* from *P*.

2. (a) Draw each of the following shapes accurately.

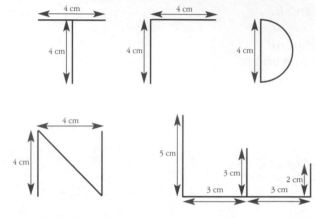

(b) A point *P* is 1 cm from each shape.
Draw the locus of all the possible positions of *P* for each diagram.

3. (a) Mark a point *X*.
Draw the locus of *P* so that the length of *XP* is 5 cm.
(b) Draw a line *AB* of length 5 cm.
Draw the locus of *P* so that *P* is 3 cm from *AB*.
(c) Draw a circle with centre *X* and of radius 4 cm.
Draw the locus of *P* so that *P* is 1 cm from the perimeter of the circle.
(d) Mark two points, *A* and *B*, where the length of *AB* is 7 cm.
Draw the locus of *P* so that *P* is equidistant from the points *A* and *B*.
(e) Mark a point *A*.
Draw two lines *AB* and *AC* each of length 5 cm such that angle *BAC* is 65°.
Draw the locus of *P* so that *P* is equidistant from the lines *AB* and *AC*.

4. *ABCD* is a rectangular field where
AB = 120 m and *BC* = 100 m.
Make a scale drawing of the field using a scale of 1 : 1000.

A point *P* is:
(a) Equidistant from *A* and *C*.
(b) Equidistant from *BC* and *CD*.
Construct loci **(a)** and **(b)** and mark the position of point *P*.
Use a ruler and compasses only and show your construction arcs.

2 5. Make another scale drawing of the rectangular field *ABCD* from question 4 using a scale of 1 : 2000.
A point *P* is:
(a) More than 50 m from *A*.
(b) More than 20 m from *BC*.
(c) Closer to *A* than *C*.
Construct loci **(a)**, **(b)** and **(c)** and shade the region in which *P* can be.
Use a ruler and compasses only and show your construction arcs.

2 6. Make accurate constructions of these triangles.

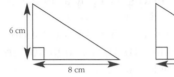

Use a ruler and pair of compasses only.
You **must not** use a protractor.
Show all your construction arcs.

2 7. (a) Construct an angle of 60°.
Use your construction to construct an angle of 30°.
(b) Repeat **(a)**.
Use your construction of 30° to construct an angle of 120°.
(c) Construct an angle of 150°.

---

8. # TRANSFORMATIONS, CONGRUENCE & SIMILARITY

3 ## *Reflections, rotations and translations*

When shapes are reflected, rotated or translated they change position.
A shape in a new position after a transformation is called the 'image' of the shape.
In the diagrams in this section images are shown in blue.

Reflection
Shapes are reflected in mirror lines.

Rotation
Shapes are rotated about a centre through an angle in a clockwise or anticlockwise direction.

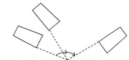

Translation
Shapes are translated by being moved so that all points on the shape move the same distance and direction.

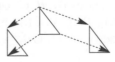

TRANSFORMATIONS, CONGRUENCE & SIMILARITY

Transformations on a graph

Reflections are described by: the equation of the mirror line.

Rotations are described by: the coordinates of the centre of rotation.
the angle and the direction of rotation.

Translations are described by: the distances moved in the directions of the x- and y-axes.
These could be described using a column vector (see p. 164).

EXAMPLES

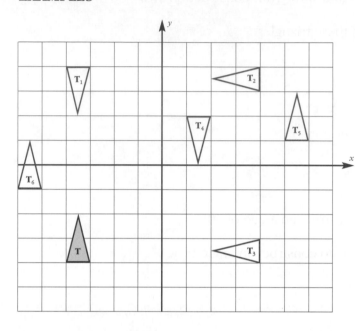

T moves to **T₁** by a reflection in the x-axis

T moves to **T₂** by a reflection in the line $x + y = 0$

T moves to **T₃** by a rotation with centre $(0, 0)$ through 90° anti-clockwise

T moves to **T₄** by a rotation with centre $(^-1, ^-1)$ through 180°

T moves to **T₅** by a translation of $\begin{pmatrix} 9 \\ 5 \end{pmatrix}$

9 units right (in the direction of the x-axis) and 5 units up (in the direction of the y-axis)

T moves to **T₆** by a translation of $\begin{pmatrix} ^-2 \\ 3 \end{pmatrix}$

2 units left and 3 units up

> ### Examiner's tips
> - *Learn how to use tracing paper to help you get the hang of transformations.*
> - *You could be asked to transform **given shapes** with given descriptions or to **describe** a transformation when both the original shape and the image are given.*

2 *Enlargement with a positive scale factor*

An enlargement transforms a shape in the following ways:

All lengths are multiplied by a scale factor.
All angles remain the same.
The position of the shape changes.

Enlargements are described by: a scale factor and a centre of enlargement.

To draw an enlargement draw construction 'rays' from the centre of enlargement, O, through the vertices (A, B, C) of the shape being enlarged.
The vertices (A_1, B_1, C_1) of the image lie on these rays.
OA_1 = scale factor $\times OA$, OB_1 = scale factor $\times OB$, OC_1 = scale factor $\times OC$, …

EXAMPLES

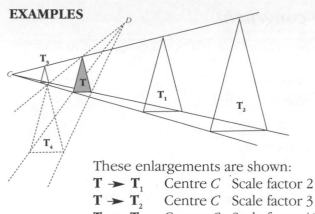

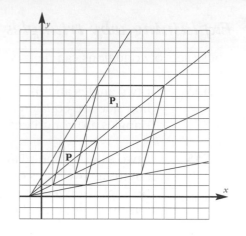

These enlargements are shown:

$\mathbf{T} \rightarrow \mathbf{T_1}$ Centre C Scale factor 2
$\mathbf{T} \rightarrow \mathbf{T_2}$ Centre C Scale factor 3
$\mathbf{T} \rightarrow \mathbf{T_3}$ Centre C Scale factor ½
$\mathbf{T} \rightarrow \mathbf{T_4}$ Centre D Scale factor 2

$\mathbf{P} \rightarrow \mathbf{P_1}$ Centre (⁻1, 0)   Scale factor 2

1 Enlargement with a negative scale factor

When an enlargement of a shape has a negative scale factor, the image is on the opposite side of the centre of enlargement.

EXAMPLES

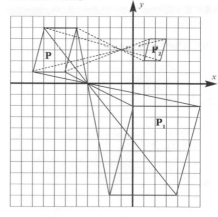

$\mathbf{P} \rightarrow \mathbf{P_1}$ enlargement
Centre (⁻4, 0)
Scale factor ⁻2

$\mathbf{P} \rightarrow \mathbf{P_2}$ enlargement
Centre (⁻1, 3)
Scale factor ⁻½

2 Congruence and congruent triangles

Two shapes that are identical in every way are said to be congruent.
Shapes transformed one to another by reflection, rotation or translation are congruent.

EXAMPLES

Which of the following triangles are congruent?

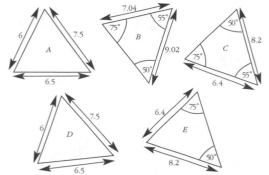

Triangle A is congruent to triangle D because all its lengths are the same.
Triangles C and E are congruent because they have equal angles and two equal lengths.
Although triangles B and C have equal angles they are not congruent because they are a **different size**.

TRANSFORMATIONS, CONGRUENCE & SIMILARITY

1   *Explaining why triangles are congruent*

These sets of conditions can be used to show whether one triangle is congruent to another:

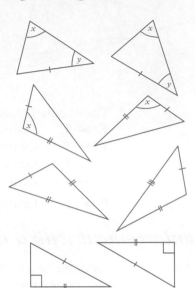

AAS   If two angles and the length of a corresponding side are equal in both triangles, then the triangles are congruent.

SAS   If two sides of one triangle have the same lengths as two sides of the second triangle and the angle **between** these two sides is equal in both triangles, then the triangles are congruent.

SSS   If all three sides of one triangle have the same lengths as the sides of the second triangle, then the triangles are congruent.

RHS   If both triangles contain a right angle and have equal hypotenuses and one other side equal in length, then the triangles are congruent.

Remember

To show that two triangles are congruent:
Use angle and length facts to show that one of the
above sets of conditions applies.
If you are asked to do so, explain
the reasons carefully.

e.g.1   Explain why triangles X and Y are congruent to triangle T.

$AB = DE$
$BC = EF$
$AC = DF$
SSS
So X is congruent to T.

$BC = HI$
Angle ABC = angle GHI
Angle ACB = angle GIH
AAS
So Y is congruent to T.

e.g.2

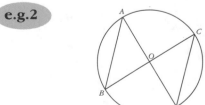

Angle AOB = angle COD
OA, OB, OC and OD are
radii so they are all equal.
So $OA = OD$ and $OB = OC$
SAS
So triangle OAB is
congruent to triangle OCD.

2 | Similar shapes

Similar shapes are **enlargements** of each other. This means that:
  Their lengths are connected by a scale factor (corresponding lengths are in the same ratio).
  Corresponding angles are equal.

The scale factor can be calculated from corresponding lengths in two similar shapes.
Use known lengths and the scale factor to find unknown lengths in a similar shape.

e.g.1

Triangles *ABC* and *XYZ* are similar.

$AB = 5$ cm and $XY = 12$ cm	
Scale factor = 2.4	$12 \div 5$
$YZ = 10.8$ cm	$\mathbf{2.4} \times 4.5$
$AC = 5.5$ cm	$13.2 \div \mathbf{2.4}$
Angle $x = 75°$	Corresponding angles are equal

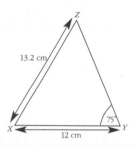

1 | Area and volume of similar solids

Solids are similar if corresponding lengths on
the solids are connected by a scale factor.
If the **length** scale factor = k, then: the **area** scale
factor = k^2 and the **volume** scale factor = k^3

This means that if the lengths of a solid are
enlarged by a scale factor, k.
Lengths are multiplied by k.
Surface areas are multiplied by k^2.
Volumes are multiplied by k^3.

Remember
To work out a larger from a smaller
value in a similar shape **multiply** by
the scale factor.
To work out a smaller from a larger
value in a similar shape **divide** by
the scale factor.

e.g.1

The diagram shows two similar cones. The volume of cone $A - 125$ cm³.

The height of cone $A = 4$ cm	
The height of cone $B = 8$ cm	
Length scale factor = 2	$8 \div 4$
Volume scale factor = 8	2^3
Volume of cone $B = 1000$ cm³	8×125

e.g.2

Two similar cylinders, X and Y, have volumes of 20 cm³ and 312.5 cm³.
The curved surface area of $Y = 250$ cm²

Volume scale factor = 15.625	$312.5 \div 20$
Length scale factor = 2.5	$\sqrt[3]{15.625}$
Area scale factor = 6.25	2.5^2
Curved surface area of $X = 40$ cm	$250 \div 6.25$

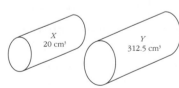

e.g.3

The areas of the bases of two similar bottles are 9.6 cm² and 21.6 cm².
The volume of the smaller bottle is 50 cm³.

Area scale factor = 2.25	$21.6 \div 9.6$
Length scale factor = 1.5	$\sqrt{2.25}$
Volume scale factor = 3.375	1.5^3
Volume of larger bottle = 168.75 cm³	3.375×50

🖩 Use a calculator for questions 8 and 9.

1. Make some copies of this diagram.

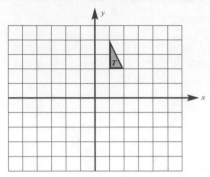

Draw the position of triangle **T** after:
- **(a)** Reflection in the *x*-axis
- **(b)** Reflection in the line $x = {}^-2$
- **(c)** Reflection in the line $x + y = 0$
- **(d)** Reflection in the line $x - y = 0$
- **(e)** Rotation of 90° anticlockwise about the origin
- **(f)** Rotation of 180° about the origin
- **(g)** Rotation of 90° clockwise about the point (1, 1)
- **(h)** Translation of 2 right and 4 down
- **(i)** Translation of 3 left and 1 up
- **(j)** Translation with vector $\begin{pmatrix} {}^-6 \\ {}^-7 \end{pmatrix}$

2. Describe each of the transformations that moves triangle **T** to each of triangles **T₁** to **T₁₀** in this diagram.

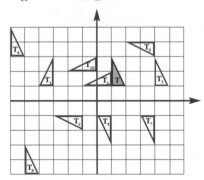

3. On axes with both *x* and *y* from ⁻8 to 12 draw the trapezium with vertices at (2, 2), (2, 4), (3, 2) and (3, 3).
Draw the following enlargements of this trapezium.
- **(a)** Centre (0, 0) and scale factor 2
- **(b)** Centre (0, 0) and scale factor ½
- **(c)** Centre (0, 0) and scale factor 3
- **(d)** Centre (0, 0) and scale factor ⁻2
- **(e)** Centre (2, 4) and scale factor ⁻2
- **(f)** Centre (3, 2) and scale factor ⁻½

2 4.

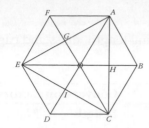

(a) Name a triangle that is congruent to triangle:
(i) *ABH*   (ii) *AOE*   (iii) *OCD*

(b) Name a shape that is congruent to shape:
(i) *ABCHO*   (ii) *AECO*

1 5. *ABDF* is a rhombus. *BC* = *EF*.

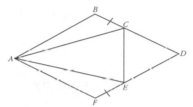

Explain why triangles *ABC* and *AFE* are congruent.

1 6. *AC* is the diameter
of the circle.
AB = *AD*.

Explain why triangles *ABC* and *ADC* are congruent.

2 7. These triangles are similar.

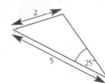
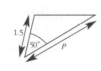
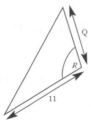

(a) Work out lengths *P* and *Q*.
(b) What is the value of angle *R*?

1 8. A can has height 10 cm and volume 200 cm³.
A similar can has height 15 cm.
What is the volume of the larger can?

1 9. A box has surface area 96 cm² and height 4 cm.
A similar box has volume 1728 cm³ and surface area 864 cm².
(a) Find the height of the larger box.
(b) Find the volume of the smaller box.

UNDERSTANDING AND USING MEASURES

4

Units of measurement

Two sets of units, **metric** and **imperial**, are used for measuring length, mass and capacity. Recently, metric units have replaced imperial units.

Metric units	Imperial units	Conversion factors
Length	**Length**	**Length**
1 kilometre (km) = 1000 metres (m)	1 mile = 1760 yards	5 miles is about 8 km
1 m = 100 centimetres (cm)	1 yard = 3 feet	1 inch is about 2.5 cm
1 m = 1000 millimetres (mm)	1 foot = 12 inches	1 foot is about 30 cm
1 cm = 10 mm		
Mass	**Mass**	**Mass**
1 tonne (t) = 1000 kilograms (kg)	1 ton = 20 stone	1 kg is about 2.2 pounds
1 kg = 1000 grams **(g)**	1 stone = 14 pounds	
	1 pound = 16 ounces	
Capacity	**Capacity**	**Capacity**
1 litre = 1000 millilitres (ml)	1 gallon = 8 pints	1 litre is about 1.75 pints
1 cm³ = 1 ml	1 pint = 20 fluid ounces	1 gallon is about 4.5 litres

Remember
kilo means thousand, 1000
centi means hundredth, $^1/_{100}$ and **milli**
means thousandth, $^1/_{1000}$.

Examiner's tip
In exam questions quantities are normally given in metric units.

4

Changing from one metric unit to another

EXAMPLES

To change ...	You ...	Example ...	
cm to mm	**multiply** by **10**	5.2 cm = 52 mm	(5.2 × 10)
mm to cm	**divide** by **10**	423 mm = 42.3 cm	(423 ÷ 10)
m to cm	**multiply** by **100**	5.2 m = 520 cm	(5.2 × 100)
cm to m	**divide** by **100**	963 cm = 9.63 m	(963 ÷ 100)
m to mm	**multiply** by **1000**	0.72 m = 720 mm	(0.72 × 1000)
mm to m	**divide** by **1000**	2635 mm = 2.635 m	(2635 ÷ 1000)
kg to g	**multiply** by **1000**	8.4 kg = 8400 g	(8.4 × 1000)
g to kg	**divide** by **1000**	3730 g = 3.73 kg	(2635 ÷ 1000)
litres to ml	**multiply** by **1000**	1.7 litres = 1700 ml	(1.7 × 1000)
ml to litres	**divide** by **1000**	420 ml = 0.42 litres	(420 ÷ 1000)

4

Changing to and from metric and imperial units

EXAMPLES

Change 40 cm to inches.	Change 2 litres to pints.	Change 8 kg to pounds.
1 inch is about 2.5 cm	1 litre is about 1.75 pints	1 kg is about 2.2 pounds
$40 \div 2.5$	2×1.75	8×2.2
40 cm is about 16 inches.	2 litres is about 3.5 pints.	8 kg is about 17.6 pounds.
Change 40 litres to gallons.	Change 45 miles to km.	Change 80 km to miles.
1 gallon is about 4.5 litres	5 miles is about 8 km	5 miles is about 8 km
$40 \div 4.5$	$45 \div 5 = 9 \qquad 9 \times 8 = 72$	$80 \div 8 = 10 \qquad 10 \times 5 = 50$
40 litres is about 8.9 gallons.	45 miles is about 72 km.	80 km is about 50 miles.

4

Choosing appropriate units

Remember
Work out the answers to questions using the units that are given on the answer line.
On **one** question units will **not** be given.
You will have to decide what the units are and write it on the answer line.
There will be a mark for doing this.

4

Units of area and volume

Area

There are 100 mm² in 1 cm²	10×10
There are 10 000 cm² in 1 m²	100×100
There are 1 000 000 mm² in 1 m²	1000×1000
There are 1 000 000 m² in 1 km²	1000×1000

Volume

There are 1000 mm³ in 1 cm³	$10 \times 10 \times 10$
There are 1 000 000 cm³ in 1 m³	$100 \times 100 \times 100$

2

Dimensions and formulae

Dimensions can be used to help distinguish between length, area and volume formulae.
Length has dimension 1 (L), area has dimension 2 (L^2), volume has dimension 3 (L^3).

EXAMPLES

a, b and c represent lengths. In each formula replace each of a, b and c with L.

$W = a + b + c$ $W = L + L + L = 3L$ dimension 1

$X = ab + c^2$ $X = L \times L + L^2 = 2L^2$ dimension 2

$Y = a^2b + b^2c$ $Y = L^2 \times L + L^2 \times L = 2L^3$ dimension 3

$Z = ab + c^3$ $Z = L \times L + L^3 = L^2 + L^3$ mixed dimensions

So: W represents a length formula

X represents an area formula

Y represents a volume formula

Z does not represent a length, area or volume formula

Test 33

Use a calculator for questions 5, 6 and 8.

1. Change each of these lengths to metres.
- **(a)** 2000 mm
- **(b)** 2350 mm
- **(c)** 300 cm
- **(d)** 323 cm
- **(e)** 734 mm
- **(f)** 70 mm
- **(g)** 2 cm
- **(h)** 23 cm
- **(i)** 4 km
- **(j)** 42.34 km

2. Change each of these lengths to mm.
- **(a)** 20 cm
- **(b)** 23 m
- **(c)** 3 km
- **(d)** 0.23 m

3. Change each of these lengths to km.
- **(a)** 200 m
- **(b)** 3562 m
- **(c)** 3000 cm
- **(d)** 42 300 cm
- **(e)** 5 000 000 mm
- **(f)** 632 000 mm

4. **(a)** How many grams in 2 kg?
- **(b)** How many kilograms in 346 g?
- **(c)** How many litres in 3478 ml?
- **(d)** How many ml in 32 litres?
- **(e)** How many grams in 0.6 kg?
- **(f)** How many ml in 0.05 litres?

5. Clare is 5 foot 3 inches tall.
Buki is 157 cm tall.
Who is taller and by how much?

6. (a) How many metres in 2000 feet?
   (b) How many kilometres in 3 miles?
   (c) How many feet in 170 cm?
   (d) How many miles in 7 km?
   (e) How many pounds in 1.25 kg?

7. Sam's weight is given as 63.2792 kg on an electronic scale.
   (a) Give Sam's weight to a suitable degree of accuracy.
   (b) Estimate Sam's weight in stones and pounds.

8. The dimensions of a cuboid are 0.6 m by 1.1 m by 1.95 m.
   Calculate the volume of the cuboid:
   (a) in cubic metres
   (b) in cubic centimetres
   In each case give your answer to a suitable degree of accuracy.

9. a, b, c and d represent lengths.
   Which of the following expressions represent lengths, areas or volumes?
   (a) cd **(b)** $a(b + c)$ **(c)** $2(a + b)$
   (d) $a^2 + b^2$ **(e)** $2(ab + bc + cd)$
   (f) $a^2b + cb^2$ **(g)** $a^3 + b^3 + c^3$

10. x, y and z are lengths.
   Which the following formula represent lengths, areas or volumes?
   (a) $2(x + y + z)$ **(b)** $xy + yz$
   (c) $2xyz$ **(d)** $x^2 + y^2 + z^2$
   (e) $2x + 3y + 4z$ **(f)** $(x + y + z)(x^2 + y^2 + z^2)$

10.   LENGTHS AND ANGLES IN TRIANGLES

Naming the sides of a right-angled triangle

The sides of a right-angled triangle are given special names.
The names depend on the angle you either use or want to work out.

For angle x

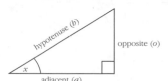

For angle y

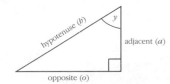

Remember

The longest side of a right-angled triangle is called the hypotenuse.

Shape, Space and Measures

2

Pythagoras' rule in 2-D

Pythagoras' rule is used to solve problems involving the lengths of right-angled triangles.

Pythagoras' rule
In any right-angled triangle the square of the length of the hypotenuse
(b) is equal to the sum of the squares on the two shorter sides (o and a).
$b^2 = o^2 + a^2$

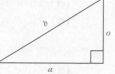

e.g.1

$b^2 = 4^2 + 6^2$
$b^2 = 52$ $16 + 36$
$b = 7.21$ cm $\sqrt{52}$

4 cm

6 cm

e.g.2

$9^2 = o^2 + 7^2$
$o^2 = 32$ $9^2 - 7^2$
$o = 5.66$ cm $\sqrt{32}$

9 cm

7 cm

Remember
When using Pythagoras' rule to find the
hypotenuse **add** the squares.
When using Pythagoras' rule to find a shorter
length **subtract** the squares.

Examiner's tip
*Pythagoras' rule is a fundamental
part of mathematics and is very
likely to come up at least once
in an exam.*

1

Pythagoras' rule in 3-D

e.g.1

The diagram shows a cuboid of width 3.5 cm, length 4.7 cm and height 2.8 cm.
  In triangle *ABC*, angle *ABC* is a right angle
  $AC^2 = 4.7^2 + 3.5^2$
  $AC^2 = 34.34$ $22.09 + 12.25$
In triangle *ACG*, angle *ACG* is a right angle
  $AG^2 = AC^2 + CG^2$
  $AG^2 = 42.18$ $34.34 + 2.8^2$
  $AG = 6.49$ $\sqrt{42.18}$

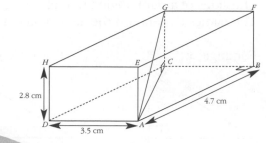

2.8 cm

3.5 cm

4.7 cm

Remember
Problems using Pythagoras' rule in 3D normally
involve more than one triangle.

2

Trigonometry in right-angled triangles

Trigonometry is used to find lengths and angles in triangles.

The sine (sin), cosine (cos) and tangent (tan) formulae

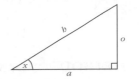

Trigonometry uses these formulae:

$$\sin \boldsymbol{x} = \frac{\text{opposite}}{\text{hypotenuse}} = \frac{\boldsymbol{o}}{\boldsymbol{b}}$$

$$\cos \boldsymbol{x} = \frac{\text{adjacent}}{\text{hypotenuse}} = \frac{\boldsymbol{a}}{\boldsymbol{b}}$$

$$\tan \boldsymbol{x} = \frac{\text{opposite}}{\text{adjacent}} = \frac{\boldsymbol{o}}{\boldsymbol{a}}$$

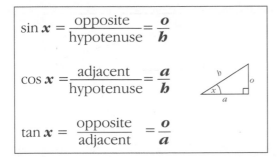

> ### *Remember*
> You need to remember the trig formulae; the mnemonic SOHCAHTOA might help with this.
> The sides labelled opposite or adjacent depend on the angle you are given or want to find.

Using the trig formulae

Step 1   Label the sides of the triangle.
      Choose the formula that includes:
      The two given values and the length or angle you need to find.

Step 2   Substitute the given values into the formula.

Step 3   Rearrange the formula and then calculate.

EXAMPLES

Finding the opposite or adjacent

Find the length of BC
in triangle ABC.

Step 1 $AB = \boldsymbol{b} = 7.2$ cm
      $BC = \boldsymbol{o}$
      $AC = \boldsymbol{a}$

      $\sin x = \dfrac{\boldsymbol{o}}{\boldsymbol{b}}$

Step 2 $\sin 40° = \dfrac{BC}{7.2}$

Step 3 $BC = 4.63$ $7.2 \times \sin 40°$

Finding the hypotenuse

Find the length of AB
in triangle ABC.

Step 1 $AB = \boldsymbol{b}$
      $BC = \boldsymbol{o}$
      $AC = \boldsymbol{a} = 5.6$ cm

      $\cos x = \dfrac{\boldsymbol{a}}{\boldsymbol{b}}$

Step 2 $\cos 52° = \dfrac{5.6}{AB}$

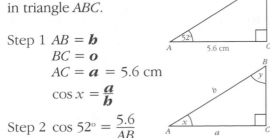

Step 3 $AB = 9.10$ $5.6 \div \cos 52°$

Finding an angle

Find angle y in triangle ABC.

Step 1 $AB = \boldsymbol{b}$
      $AC = \boldsymbol{o} = 8.1$ cm
      $BC = \boldsymbol{a} = 5.3$ cm

      $\tan y = \dfrac{\boldsymbol{o}}{\boldsymbol{a}}$

Step 2 $\tan y° = \dfrac{8.1}{5.3}$

Step 3 $\tan y° = 1.528 \dots$ $8.1 \div 5.3$
         $y = 56.8°$ $\tan^{-1} 1.528 \dots$

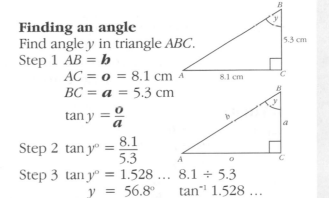

$\tan^{-1} 1.528\dots$ is the angle which has a tangent equal to $1.528\dots$ It can be calculated using the 2ndF button on a scientific calculator using this sequence…

2ndF	tan	1	.	5	2	8	=

> ### *Remember*
> Before doing a trigonometry problem:
> Make sure your angles are measured in degrees on your calculator. (You **must** see DEG on your calculator display).

Shape, Space and Measures

2

Practical trigonometry problems

e.g.1

A telescope on a pier is 5.3 m above sea level.
The angle of depression of a ship from the telescope is 2.2°.
How far is the ship from the pier?

METHOD

Step 1

$AB = \boldsymbol{h}$

$BC = \boldsymbol{o}$ $\qquad = 5.3$

$AC = \boldsymbol{a}$

$\tan x = \dfrac{\boldsymbol{o}}{\boldsymbol{a}}$

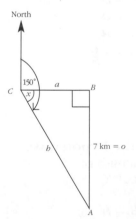

Step 2

$\tan 2.2° = \dfrac{5.3}{AC}$

Step 3

$AC = 138 \text{ m}$ $\qquad 5.3 \div \tan 2.2°$

ANSWER

The ship is 138 m from the pier.

Remember

Angles of **elevation** and **depression** are the angles
turned through when we look **up** and **down** from the
horizontal.

e.g.2

Tom walks 7 km north from A to B.
He then walks west to C.
He returns directly from C to A walking on a bearing of 150°.
What is the distance from C to A?

METHOD

Step 1

$AC = \boldsymbol{h}$

$AB = \boldsymbol{o} = 7$

$BC = \boldsymbol{a}$

$\sin x = \dfrac{\boldsymbol{o}}{\boldsymbol{h}}$

Step 2

$\sin 60° = \dfrac{7}{AC}$ $\qquad x = 150 - 90$

Step 3

$AC = 8.08$ $\qquad 7 \div \sin 60$

ANSWER

The distance from C to A is 8.1 m to 2 s.f.

Examiner's tip

*In practical questions you are
always given a clearly drawn
right-angled triangle.*

Shape, Space and Measures

Trigonometry in 3-D

e.g.1

The diagram shows a square-based pyramid *ABCDE*.
X is the centre of the base of the pyramid. *AB* = 5 cm and angle *EAX* = 70°.
Calculate the length *EA*, the slant height of the pyramid.

Using Pythagoras' rule in triangle *AXB*

$$AB^2 = AX^2 + BX^2 = 2AX^2 \qquad AX = BX$$
$$25 = 2AX^2$$
$$AX = 3.54 \qquad\qquad \sqrt{12.5}$$

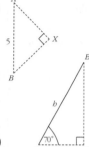

Using trigonometry in triangle *AXE*

$$\cos 70 = \frac{3.54}{EA}$$
$$EA = 10.35 \qquad\qquad 3.54 \div \cos 70$$

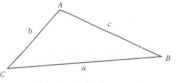

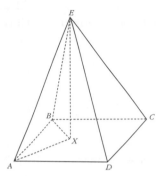

Trigonometry in triangles that are not right-angled

Naming sides and angles

In triangle *ABC*:   the side opposite angle *A* has length *a*
the side opposite angle *B* has length *b*
the side opposite angle *C* has length *c*

The sine rule

$$\frac{a}{\sin A} = \frac{b}{\sin B} = \frac{c}{\sin C}$$

The cosine rule

$$a^2 = b^2 + c^2 - 2bc\cos A$$
$$b^2 = c^2 + a^2 - 2ca\cos B$$
$$c^2 = a^2 + b^2 - 2ab\cos C$$

Finding the length of a side

If you are given …	Use …
Two angles and a side opposite one of the known angles	Sine rule
Two sides and the angle between the sides	Cosine rule

Finding an angle

If you are given …	Use …
The side opposite the angle you need **and** a side opposite a known angle	Sine rule
Three sides	Cosine rule

EXAMPLES

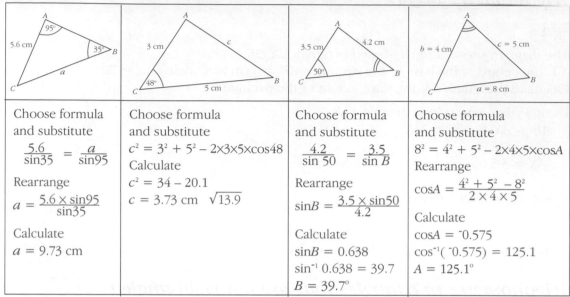

Choose formula and substitute $\dfrac{5.6}{\sin 35} = \dfrac{a}{\sin 95}$ Rearrange $a = \dfrac{5.6 \times \sin 95}{\sin 35}$ Calculate $a = 9.73$ cm	Choose formula and substitute $c^2 = 3^2 + 5^2 - 2 \times 3 \times 5 \times \cos 48$ Calculate $c^2 = 34 - 20.1$ $c = 3.73$ cm $\sqrt{13.9}$	Choose formula and substitute $\dfrac{4.2}{\sin 50} = \dfrac{3.5}{\sin B}$ Rearrange $\sin B = \dfrac{3.5 \times \sin 50}{4.2}$ Calculate $\sin B = 0.638$ $\sin^{-1} 0.638 = 39.7$ $B = 39.7°$	Choose formula and substitute $8^2 = 4^2 + 5^2 - 2 \times 4 \times 5 \times \cos A$ Rearrange $\cos A = \dfrac{4^2 + 5^2 - 8^2}{2 \times 4 \times 5}$ Calculate $\cos A = {}^-0.575$ $\cos^{-1}({}^-0.575) = 125.1$ $A = 125.1°$

1 Area of a triangle

Area = $\frac{1}{2} ab \sin C$
Area = $\frac{1}{2} ac \sin B$
Area = $\frac{1}{2} bc \sin A$

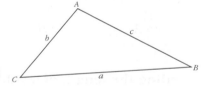

You can use this formula if you know two sides of a triangle
and the angle between them.

e.g.1

Area = 6.38 cm² $\qquad \frac{1}{2} \times 3.6 \times 5.1 \times \sin 44°$

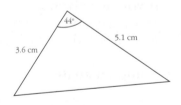

Remember
The formulae for the area of a triangle is also given on the
formulae sheet on your exam paper.

1 Area of the segment of a circle

The area of the shaded segment is the difference between the area of sector OAB and the
area of the triangle OAB.

e.g.1

Area of sector = 34.208 ... $\qquad {}^{80}/_{360} \times \pi \times 7^2$
Area of triangle = 24.127 ... $\qquad \frac{1}{2} \times 7^2 \times \sin 80°$
Area of segment = 10.1 cm² $\qquad 34.208 ... - 24.127 ...$

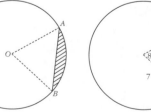

Use a calculator for questions 3 to 11.

1. Find the unknown lengths in these triangles. Then find their areas and perimeters.

(a)   **(b)**

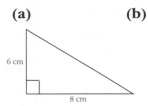

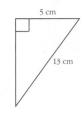

2. In the triangle $\sin x = {}^3/_5$

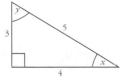

In a similar way write down:
(a) $\cos x$ **(b)** $\tan x$ **(c)** $\sin y$
(d) $\cos y$ **(e)** $\tan y$

3. The diagram shows a right-angled triangle.

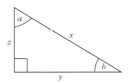

Calculate:
(a) x when $y = 18$ cm and $z = 15$ cm
(b) y when $z = 18$ cm and $a = 35°$
(c) z when $y = 1.8$ cm and $x = 3.5$ cm
(d) a when $z = 11$ cm and $x = 16$ cm
(e) z when $x = 14$ cm and $b = 42°$
(f) x when $y = 2.8$ cm and $a = 61°$
(g) b when $z = 16$ cm and $y = 10$ cm
(h) x when $z = 2.6$ cm and $a = 35°$

4. The diagram shows a ski slope.
$AB = 125$ m, $BC = 160$ m.

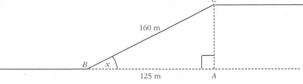

(a) Find the length of AC.
(b) Work out angle x.

Shape, Space and Measures

Shape, Space and Measures

5. A man starts at *A* and walks 5km due north and then 7km due east to *B*.
The man returns to *A* directly along the route *BA*.

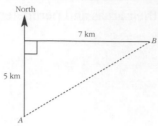

(a) How far does the man walk altogether?
(b) Work out the bearing of *A* from *B*.

6. The diagram shows a flagpole, *AB*, on horizontal ground.
The angle of elevation from *C* to the top of the flagpole is 12°.
AC = 120m.

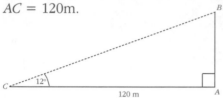

Work out the height of the flagpole.

7. Find the angles marked with letters in these triangles.

(a)
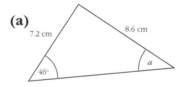

(b)
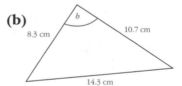

(c)

(d)
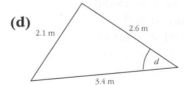

8. Find the lengths marked with letters in these triangles.

(a)
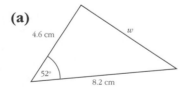

(b)
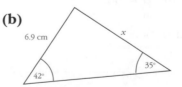

(c)
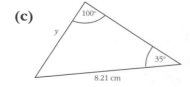

(d)
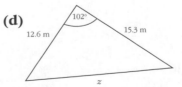

9. Find all the unknown lengths and angles in these triangles.
Then find their areas.

(a)

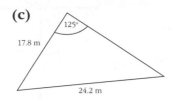

23.5 cm

55°   34°

(b)

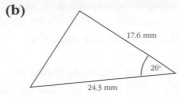

17.6 mm

26°

24.3 mm

(c)

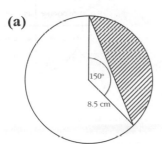

125°

17.8 m

24.2 m

(d)

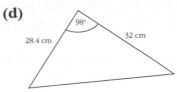

98°

28.4 cm   32 cm

10. Find the area of each of these shaded segments.

(a)

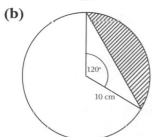

150°

8.5 cm

(b)

120°

10 cm

11. The diagram shows a cuboid.

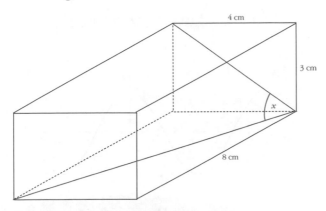

4 cm

3 cm

x

8 cm

Work out the angle marked x.

11. TRIGONOMETRIC FUNCTIONS FOR ANY ANGLE

1 Sine, cosine and tangent for any angle

The diagram shows the $x - y$ plane divided into four quadrants by the x-axis and the y-axis.
The point P, **where OP = 1**, rotates in an anticlockwise direction about O.
a is the angle between OP and the positive x-axis, Ox.

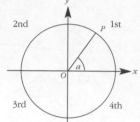

When a is between 0° and 90°, P is in the first quadrant.
When a is between 90° and 180°, P is in the second quadrant.
When a is between 180° and 270°, P is in the third quadrant.
When a is between 270° and 360°, P is in the fourth quadrant.

When P continues rotating after one turn a is greater than 360°.
When P rotates in a clockwise direction a is negative.

The trigonometric formulae for any angle are defined as follows:
  sin a is the y-coordinate of P
  cos a is the x-coordinate of P
  tan a is the gradient of OP

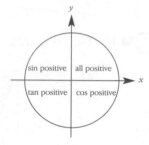

The diagram shows the signs of sin, cos and tan in each quadrant.

Quadrant	Angle	sin$a$	cos$a$	tan$a$
1ˢᵗ	30°	0.5	0.87	0.58
2ⁿᵈ	150°	0.5	⁻0.87	⁻0.58
3ʳᵈ	210°	⁻0.5	⁻0.87	0.58
4ᵗʰ	330°	⁻0.5	0.87	⁻0.58

1 Trigonometric graphs

The basic pattern of a trigonometric graph keeps repeating itself.
For this reason trigonometric graphs are called periodic graphs.

The graph of $y =$ sin$a$
The period is 360°.
Maximum value is 1.
Minimum value is ⁻1.
Passes through (0, 0).
Crosses the x-axis every 180°.

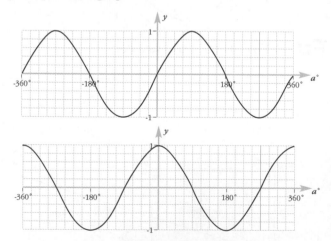

The graph of $y =$ cos$a$
The period is 360°.
Maximum value is 1.
Minimum value is ⁻1.
Passes through (90°, 0).
Crosses the x-axis every 180°.

Remember
You might be asked to sketch transformations
of $y =$ sin$x$ and $y =$ cos$x$.

The graph of $y = \tan a$
The period is $180°$.
Passes through $(0, 0)$.
Crosses the x-axis every $180°$.
The graph is not continuous.

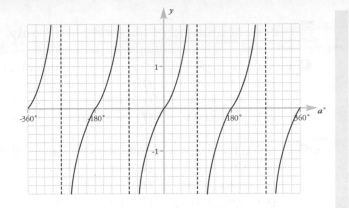

1

Solving trigonometric equations

Equations such as $\sin a = p$, $\cos a = q$ and $\tan a = r$ have **many** solutions.
A scientific calculator gives one of these solutions, e.g. $p = \sin^{-1} a$

For $\sin a = p$ and $\tan a = r$ the calculator gives the solution
between $-90°$ and $90°$.
For $\cos a = q$ the calculator gives the solution between $0°$ and $180°$.

Other solutions can be worked out using the trigonometric graphs.

> **Examiner's tips**
> *Trigonometric
> equations can occur
> on either the
> calculator or non-
> calculator paper.*
> *- Learn the basic shape
> of the trigonometric
> graphs.*

e.g.1

$\cos a = 0.5$
One value of a is $60°$ $\cos^{-1} 0.5$
Use the graph of $y = \cos x$ to find **other** values of a.
The solutions occur where the graph of $y = \cos a$ crosses the line $y = 0.5$
Use the symetry of the graph of $y = \cos a$ to find accurate values of a from the given
value.

Some other values are:
$300°$	$360 - 60$
$420°$	$360 + 60$
$660°$	$720 - 60$
$780°$	$720 + 60$

Negative values can be found by
subtracting multiples of $360°$.

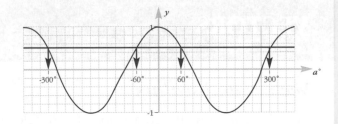

e.g.2

One solution of $\sin a = 0.6$ is $a = 36.9°$.
Use the graph of $y = \sin a$ to find the solutions of $\sin a = {}^-0.6$.
The solutions occur where the graph of $y = \sin a$ crosses the line $y = {}^-0.6$
Use the symetry of the graph of $y = \sin a$ to find accurate values of a from the given
value.

Some other solutions are:
$216.9°$	$180 + 36.9$
$323.1°$	$360 - 36.9$
$576.9°$	$540 + 36.9$
$683.1°$	$720 - 36.9$

Negative solutions can be found by
subtracting multiples of $360°$.

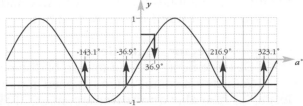

Test 35

🖩 Use your calculator for question 2 and 3 **only**.

1. Sketch the following graphs for values of x between $-360°$ and $360°$.
  (a) $y = \sin x$ **(b)** $y = 2\sin x$
  (c) $y = \sin 2x$ **(d)** $y = \cos x$
  (e) $y = \cos 3x$ **(f)** $y = \tan x$

🖩 **2.** Solve the following equations for values of x from $-360°$ to $360°$.
  (a) $\sin x = 0.3$ **(b)** $\sin x = {}^-0.3$
  (c) $\cos x = {}^-0.8$ **(d)** $\tan x = 0.4$
  (e) $\cos x = 0.35$ **(f)** $\tan x = {}^-0.3$

🖩 **3.** Find two solutions of $\cos p = 0.3$.

4. a satisfies the equation $\sin a = \sin 210°$.
  Find a value of a other than $210°$.

5. One solution of the equation $\sin a = 0.5$ is $a = 30°$.
  (a) Find the other solution of
    $\sin a = 0.5$ for values of x between $0°$ and $360°$.
  (b) Find the solutions of $\sin x = {}^-0.5$ for values of a between $-360°$ and $360°$.

6. One solution of the equation $\tan x = 1.5$ is $x = 56.3°$.
  (a) Find the other solution of $\tan x = 1.5$ for values of x between $0°$ and $360°$.
  (b) Find the solutions $\tan x = {}^-1.5$ for values of x between $-360°$ and $360°$.

12. VECTORS

1 · Vectors and scalars

The diagram shows the translation of a triangle.
The column vector describes the translation.

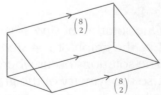

The column vector describes both the **distance** and
the **direction** that the triangle moves.

Vectors are quantities that have both **size** and **direction**.
Quantities that do **not** have direction but only size are called **scalar** quantities.

Examples of **vector quantities** are:
    Displacement – a combination of distance and direction
    Velocity – a combination of speed and direction
Examples of **scalar quantities** are: mass, distance, speed, …

1

Representing vectors

Column vectors

The top number represents the distance moved **horizontally**
(+ to the right, – to the left).
The bottom number represents the distance moved **vertically**
(+ upwards, – downwards).

Directed line segments

Line segments can be used to represent vectors.
The length of the line represents the **distance** moved.
The arrow shows the direction moved.

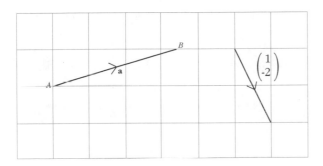

Labelling vectors

The two ways of labelling vectors are shown in the diagram.

A single lower case bold letter such as **a** is often used.

(In handwritten work this is replaced with a wavy line beneath the letter).

Upper case letters such as AB with an arrow over the $\overrightarrow{AB}$ are also used.

$\overrightarrow{AB}$ represents the displacement from A to B.

EXAMPLES

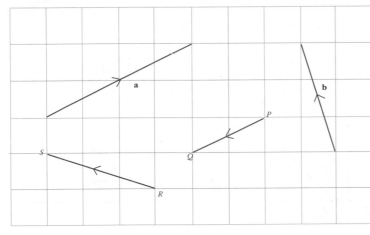

$$\mathbf{a} = \begin{pmatrix} 4 \\ 2 \end{pmatrix}$$

$$\mathbf{b} = \begin{pmatrix} -1 \\ 3 \end{pmatrix}$$

$$\overrightarrow{PQ} = \begin{pmatrix} -2 \\ -1 \end{pmatrix}$$

$$\overrightarrow{RS} = \begin{pmatrix} -3 \\ 1 \end{pmatrix}$$

1

Relationships between vectors

Equal vectors

Vectors are equal if they move through
the same distance in the same direction.
They do **not** have to be in the same position.

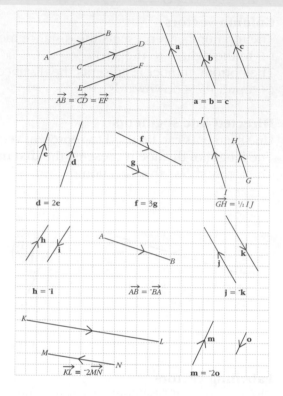

Vectors multiplied by a scalar (n)

a and **na** are vectors in the same direction
(they are parallel).
The length of **na** is **n** × the length of **a**.

Vectors in opposite directions

a and **⁻a** have the same length.
They are in the opposite direction.

a and **⁻na** are in the opposite direction.
The length of **⁻na** is **n** × the length of **a**.

1

Vector addition and subtraction

To add or subtract vectors combine the displacements represented by the vectors.
This combination of displacements gives a single resultant vector.

EXAMPLES

The table shows examples of vector addition using vectors **a**, **b** and **c**.
The resultant vector is shown in blue.

a + b	**b + c**	**a − b**	**b + 2c**	**a − 2c**
Draw **a** Then draw **b** from the end of **a**.	Draw **b** Then draw **c** from the end of **b**.	Draw **a** Then draw **-b** from the end of **a**.	Draw **b** Then draw 2**c** from the end of **b**.	Draw **a** Then draw -2**c** from the end of **a**.

This diagram shows that $\overrightarrow{AB} + \overrightarrow{BC} + \overrightarrow{CD} = \overrightarrow{AD}$

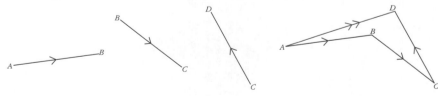

1 *Using vectors*

Describing position

Vectors can be used to describe the positions of points.

e.g.1

The diagram shows a tessellation of parallelograms.
$\overrightarrow{AB} = \mathbf{a}$ and $\overrightarrow{AE} = \mathbf{b}$

In terms of $\mathbf{a}$ and $\mathbf{b}$

$\overrightarrow{AD} = 3\mathbf{a}$ $\overrightarrow{CK} = 2\mathbf{b}$
$\overrightarrow{AG} = 2\mathbf{a} + \mathbf{b}$ $\overrightarrow{BK} = \mathbf{a} + 2\mathbf{b}$
$\overrightarrow{LE} = {}^-3\mathbf{a} - \mathbf{b}$ $\overrightarrow{DE} = {}^-3\mathbf{a} + \mathbf{b}$

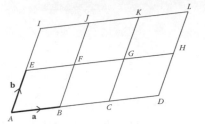

> **Remember**
> AD means the <u>line</u> joining A to D.
> $\overrightarrow{AD}$ means 'vector AD'

Geometrical problems

Relationships between vectors can be used to solve simple geometric problems.

e.g.2

$ABEF$ and $BCDE$ are identical parallelograms.
M is the midpoint of CD.
$\overrightarrow{AB} = \mathbf{x}$ and $\overrightarrow{AF} = \mathbf{y}$.
Show that $ADMB$ is a trapezium.

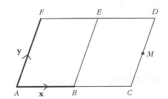

In terms of $\mathbf{x}$ and $\mathbf{y}$

$\overrightarrow{AD} = \overrightarrow{AC} + \overrightarrow{CD}$ $\overrightarrow{BM} = \overrightarrow{BC} + \overrightarrow{CM}$
$\overrightarrow{AD} = 2\overrightarrow{AB} + \overrightarrow{AF}$ $\overrightarrow{BM} = \overrightarrow{AB} + \frac{1}{2}\overrightarrow{CD}$
                          $\overrightarrow{BM} = \overrightarrow{AB} + \frac{1}{2}\overrightarrow{AF}$
$\overrightarrow{AD} = 2\mathbf{x} + \mathbf{y}$ $\overrightarrow{BM} = \mathbf{x} + \frac{1}{2}\mathbf{y}$

So $\overrightarrow{AD} = 2\overrightarrow{BM}$. This means that the lines AD and BM are parallel and AD is twice the length of BM. So $ADMB$ is a trapezium.

e.g.3

$OABC$ is a parallelogram.
$\overrightarrow{OA} = 3\mathbf{a} - 2\mathbf{b}$ and $\overrightarrow{OC} = 5\mathbf{a} + 6\mathbf{b}$.
D is the point such that $\overrightarrow{BD} = {}^-2\mathbf{a} + 6\mathbf{b}$.
Show that ACD is a straight line.

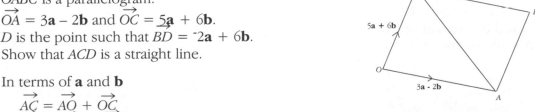

In terms of $\mathbf{a}$ and $\mathbf{b}$

$\overrightarrow{AC} = \overrightarrow{AO} + \overrightarrow{OC}$
$\overrightarrow{AC} = {}^-\overrightarrow{OA} + \overrightarrow{OC}$
$\overrightarrow{AC} = 2\mathbf{a} + 8\mathbf{b}$ ${}^-3\mathbf{a} + 2\mathbf{b} + 5\mathbf{a} + 6\mathbf{b}$

$\overrightarrow{AD} = \overrightarrow{AB} + \overrightarrow{BD}$
$\overrightarrow{AD} = \overrightarrow{OC} + \overrightarrow{BD}$
$\overrightarrow{AD} = 3\mathbf{a} + 12\mathbf{b}$ $5\mathbf{a} + 6\mathbf{b}\ {}^-2\mathbf{a} + 6\mathbf{b}$

So $\overrightarrow{AD} = \frac{3}{2}\overrightarrow{AC}$
This means that the lines AD and AC are parallel and have the point A in common.
So ACD must be a straight line (collinear).

> **Remember**
> If a vector is a multiple of another vector then the two vectors are parallel.
> If, **in addition**, the vectors have one point in common, they are collinear.

1. (a) Write column vectors for each vector in this diagram.

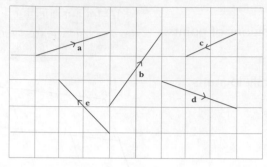

(b) Draw vector diagrams to show:
    (i) $\mathbf{a} + \mathbf{b}$ **(ii)** $\mathbf{c} - 2\mathbf{d}$
    (iii) $2\mathbf{a}$ **(iv)** $2\mathbf{a} + 3\mathbf{e}$
    (v) $2\mathbf{d} - \mathbf{e}$ **(vi)** $\mathbf{a} - \mathbf{b} + \mathbf{c}$

2. The diagram shows a tessellation of congruent parallelograms.
$\overrightarrow{AB} = \mathbf{a}$ and $\overrightarrow{AF} = \mathbf{b}$.

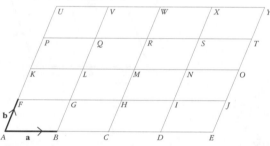

Write down the following in terms of $\mathbf{a}$ and $\mathbf{b}$.
(a) $\overrightarrow{AD}$ **(b)** $\overrightarrow{AK}$ **(c)** $\overrightarrow{AG}$
(d) $\overrightarrow{GU}$ **(e)** $\overrightarrow{TF}$ **(f)** $\overrightarrow{KY}$
(g) $\overrightarrow{YB}$ **(h)** $\overrightarrow{VC}$ **(i)** $\overrightarrow{BW}$

3. *OACB* is a parallelogram.
$\overrightarrow{OA} = \mathbf{a}$ and $\overrightarrow{OB} = \mathbf{b}$.
M is the midpoint of *OC*.
N is the midpoint of *AB*.

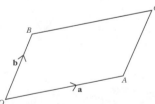

(a) Find the following vectors in terms of $\mathbf{a}$ and $\mathbf{b}$.
    (i) $\overrightarrow{OM}$ **(ii)** $\overrightarrow{ON}$
(b) Comment on your answers to **(a)**.

4. $\overrightarrow{OP} = {}^-3\mathbf{a} + 4\mathbf{b}$, $\overrightarrow{OQ} = 3\mathbf{a} + 6\mathbf{b}$
and $\overrightarrow{OR} = 12\mathbf{a} + 9\mathbf{b}$

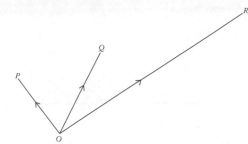

(a) Find the following vectors in terms of **a** and **b**.
  (i) $\overrightarrow{PQ}$ (ii) $\overrightarrow{PR}$
(b) Use your answer to **(a)** to explain why P, Q and R lie on a straight line.
(c) What is the ratio of the length of PQ to the length of QR?

5. $OPQR$ is a parallelogram.
$\overrightarrow{OP} = \mathbf{p}$ and $\overrightarrow{OR} = \mathbf{r}$.
A is a point on PQ.
$\overrightarrow{PA} = 2\overrightarrow{AQ}$.
PQ is extended to B such that $OABR$ is a parallelogram.
$\overrightarrow{OB} = x\mathbf{p} + y\mathbf{r}$.

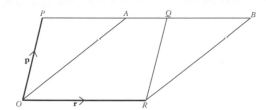

Find the values of x and y.

6. $OACB$ is a quadrilateral.
$\overrightarrow{OA} = \mathbf{a}$ and $\overrightarrow{OB} = \mathbf{b}$ and $\overrightarrow{AC} = 2OB$.
P is a point on AB such that $AP = 2PB$.

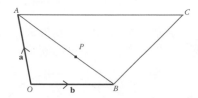

(a) Find the following vectors in terms of **a** and **b**.
  (i) $\overrightarrow{AB}$ (ii) $\overrightarrow{OC}$ (iii) $\overrightarrow{OP}$
(b) Explain why vectors $\overrightarrow{OC}$ and $\overrightarrow{OP}$ show that the points O, P and C lie on a straight line.
(c) Find $\overrightarrow{OQ}$ such that $OQPB$ is a trapezium.

GEOMETRICAL PROOFS

4

The angle sum of a triangle

The diagram shows a triangle *ABC* with the side *AB* extended.
A line is drawn at *B* parallel to *AC*.

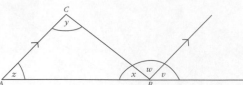

$x + w + v = 180°$ angles on a straight line
Angle v = angle z corresponding angles
Angle w = angle y alternate angles
So $x + y + z = 180°$

This means that the sum of the interior angles of **any** triangle (v, w and x) is 180°.

4

The angles of a quadrilateral

All quadrilaterals can be divided into two triangles by drawing a diagonal.
The sum of the interior angles of the quadrilateral $= a + b + c + d + e + f$

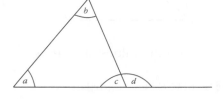

$a + b + c = 180°$ angle sum of triangle
$d + e + f = 180°$ angle sum of triangle

So $a + b + c + d + e + f = 360°$ $2 \times 180°$

This means that the sum of the interior angles of **any** quadrilateral is 360°.

4

Exterior angle of a triangle

The diagram shows a triangle with the side extended.

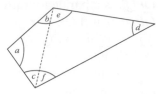

$a + b + c = 180°$ angle sum of triangle
$c + d = 180°$ angles on a straight line

So $a + b + c = c + d$
So $a + b = d$ taking c from both sides

This means that in any triangle, the exterior angle (d) is always equal to the sum of the two opposite interior angles (a and b).

2

The perpendicular bisector of a chord

The diagram shows a circle centre *O*.
AB is a chord.
OC is the perpendicular from the centre to the chord.

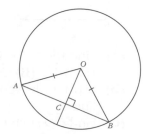

OA and *OB* are equal radii, so triangle *OAB* is isosceles.
Because *OC* is perpendicular to *AB*, *OC* is the line of symmetry
of triangle *OAB*.
So *AC* = *BC*

This explains why the perpendicular from the centre of a circle to a chord bisects the chord.

1

Angles in a semi-circle

The diagram shows a circle centre O and diameter AOB.
P is a point on the circumference.

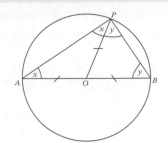

OA and OP are equal radii, so triangle OAP is isosceles.
So   angle APO = angle $OAP = x°$

Similarly, triangle BPO is isosceles.
So   angle BPO = angle $OBP = y°$

So $y + (y + x) + x = 180°$ angle sum of triangle APB
So $2x + 2y = 180°$ collecting terms
So $x + y = 90°$ dividing both sides by 2

So angle $APB = 90°$

This means that the angle at the circumference of a circle drawn from a diameter is **always** a right angle.

1

Angles from an arc to the centre and the circumference

The diagram shows a circle centre O.
P, Q and R are points on the circumference.
POS is a diameter.

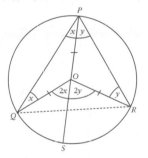

OP and OQ are equal radii, so triangle OPQ is isosceles.
So   angle OPQ = angle $OQP = x°$
Angle SOQ is the exterior angle of triangle OPQ
So   angle $SOQ = 2x$ the exterior angle equals the sum
                       of the two opposite interior angles
Similarly, angle SOR is the external angle of isosceles triangle OPR
So   angle $SOR = 2y°$

So   angle $QOR = 2x + 2y$
              $= 2(x + y)$
              $= 2 \times$ angle QPR

This means that the angle at the centre drawn from an arc is twice the angle at the circumference drawn from the same arc.

The diagram shows a circle centre O.
P, Q, R and S are points on the circumference.

    Angle $POS = 2a$
So   angle $PQS = a$ angle at centre = $2 \times$ angle at circumference
and angle $PRS = a$ angle at centre = $2 \times$ angle at circumference

So   angle PQS = angle PRS

This means that angles drawn at the circumference from the same arc are equal.

GEOMETRICAL PROOFS

1 Angles in a cyclic quadrilateral

A, B, C and D are points on the circumference of a circle.
AC and BD are the diagonals of the cyclic quadrilateral $ABCD$.

BDA and BCA are angles on the circumference from the arc AB
So   angle BDA = angle BCA = $w°$
Similarly
   angle BAC = angle BDC = $x°$
   angle DAC = angle DBC = $y°$
   angle DBA = angle DCA = $z°$

In triangle ABD
   $w + z + (x + y) = 180°$ angle sum of a triangle

So $(x + w) + (y + z) = 180°$ rearranging

So   angle CDA + angle ABC = $180°$

This means that the sum of the opposite angles of a cyclic quadrilateral equals 180°.

1 The angle between a tangent and a chord

PT is a tangent to a circle with diameter PR.
Q and S are points on the circumference of the circle.
PS is a chord.

   Angle PSR = $90°$ PR is a diameter
   Angle PRS = $x°$

So   angle RPS = $90 - x°$ angle sum of a triangle

   Angle RPT = $90°$ the tangent is perpendicular to the diameter
So   angle SPT = $x°$

So   angle SPT = angle PRS

   Angle PRS = angle PQS = $x°$ angles on the circumference from arc PS

So   angle PQS = angle SPT

This means that the angle between a tangent and a chord is equal to any angle at the circumference drawn from the chord.

Test 37

1. Reproduce each of the geometric proofs in this section.
   Then check your attempts.

Section 4: Handling Data
COLLECTING AND ORGANISING DATA

1.

4

Types of data

Qualitative (or categorical) data is data described in words such as colour, size or taste.
Quantitative data has a numerical value. There are two sorts:
    Discrete data has only particular values, e.g. any data obtained by counting.
    Continuous data does not have an exact value, e.g. any data obtained by measurement.
Primary data is collected as part of a statistical investigation.
Raw data is primary data that has not been organised in any way.
Secondary data is data that already exists.

4

Collecting data

Primary data can be collected by observation, by interview, or by recording the results of experiments. There are a number of ways of recording the data.

> ### Examiner's tip
> *In your exam, you might be asked to:*
>   *Design a data collection sheet.*
>   *Interpret a two-way table.*
>   *Write a question for a questionnaire.*
>   *Criticise or improve a question in a questionnaire.*

Data collection sheets
A data collection sheet can be used to record data involving one variable.
For example: The sorts of food eaten in the school canteen

Food	Tally	Frequency
Chips	ⵏⵏⵏ ⵏⵏⵏ III	13
Salad	ⵏⵏⵏ III	8
Fruit	IIII	4

COLLECTING AND ORGANISING DATA

A data collection sheet also can be used to collect large amounts of quantitative data.
For example: The heights of 30 seedlings two weeks after planting

Height, h, mm	Tally	Frequency
$0 \le h < 10$	IIII IIII II	12
$10 \le h < 20$	IIII IIII I	11
$20 \le h < 30$	IIII II	7

In this case the data is collected in groups (or classes).
The groups that the data is put into are called class intervals.

Two-way tables

Two-way tables are used to collect (or summarise) data involving two variables.
For example: The favourite sports of boys and girls in a class of 30 pupils.

	Football	Hockey	Netball	Basketball
Boys	IIII IIII IIII			II
Girls	II	III	IIII III	I

Databases

A database can be used to collect data involving more than two variables.
For example: The gender, height and shoe size of students in a class

Gender	Height, cm	Shoe size
Male	145	8
Female	140	6
Male	150	7

4   *Questionnaires*

A questionnaire is a set of questions used for collecting data in a survey.
Questionnaires should:
   Use simple language and short questions with concise answers.
   Include response sections such as tick boxes.
   Avoid open or leading questions.

An example of a leading question: 'What do you think of our new improved layout?'

A better question:
   Tick one of the following to show what you think of the new layout.
   Easier to follow ☐   Harder to follow ☐   No difference ☐

An example of an open question: 'How many hours of TV do you watch?'

A better question:
   Tick one of the boxes to show how long you watched TV last night.
   0 hours ☐   1 to 2 hours ☐   3 to 4 hours ☐   More than 4 hours ☐

4 *Hypotheses*

A hypothesis is a statement that may or may not be true.
It normally compares one variable with another.
Data collected should focus on the hypothesis.

e.g.1

This two-way table shows information about a class of students.

	Like sport	Don't like sport
Boys	14	6
Girls	8	2

Does the data in the table prove or
disprove the hypothesis
'More boys like sport than girls'?

$^{14}/_{20}$ boys like sport.
This is 70% of the boys in the class.
$^{14}/_{20} \times 100 = 70$
$^{8}/_{10}$ girls like sport.
This is 80% of the girls in the class.
$^{8}/_{10} \times 100 = 80$
So the data disproves the
hypothesis.

2 *Sampling*

A population is a group about which information is required.
To find the information, a sample taken from the population is usually investigated.
Examples of populations and possible samples are shown in the table.

Population	Sample
The students in a school	One student from each form class in the school
The leaves on a tree	One leaf from every branch on the tree

Samples should represent populations.
A sample that is not representative is called a biased sample.

e.g.1

Investigation   Survey of reading habits of students in a school
Sample   Students who visit the school library at lunchtime
This is a biased sample because it does not include those students who do not use the
school library or those students who do other things at lunchtime

COLLECTING AND ORGANISING DATA

1

Sampling methods

There are a number of different ways of obtaining a representative sample. For example:

Simple random sampling
Every member of the population has the same chance of being chosen.

Systematic sampling
Members of the population are selected at regular intervals.

Stratified random sampling
The population is divided into groups.
A simple random sample is taken from each group in proportion to the size of the group.

Examiner's tip
In your exam, you will probably be asked about stratified random sampling. You could decide on a different sampling method in your coursework.

e.g.1

In a school there are: 420 students in Key Stage 3
310 students in Key Stage 4
130 students in the 6th form
The school wants to survey opinion about after-school clubs.
They decide to ask a stratified random sample of size 100 to complete a questionnaire.

To find the numbers of each group in the sample, divide 100 in the ratio 420 : 310 : 130
420 : 310 : 130 = 42 : 31 : 13
42 + 31 + 13 = 86
For every 86 students in the sample, there are:
42 in Key Stage 3
31 in Key Stage 4
13 in the 6th form
100 ÷ 86 = 1.163
42 × 1.163 = 48.846 …
31 × 1.163 = 36.053 …
13 × 1.163 = 15.119 …
This gives a sample size of:
49 in Key Stage 3
36 in Key Stage 4
15 in the 6th form

DO THIS
Explain why this sample might not be representative in a **mixed** school.

ANSWER TO THE DO THIS
The proportion of boys and girls in the sample might not reflect the proportion of boys and girls in the population.

Use a calculator for questions 9 and 10 only.

1. The days of the week on which 20 students were born is shown below.

Mon	Tue	Sat	Mon
Tue	Wed	Fri	Sun
Fri	Mon	Thu	Sun
Wed	Mon	Sat	Sat
Thu	Tue	Mon	Mon

Design and complete a data collection sheet to record this data.

2. The heights of 30 plants given to the nearest centimetre are shown below.

8	12	10	18	9	11
12	7	13	18	14	21
7	16	19	21	9	10
8	23	8	14	18	17
24	12	17	7	14	26

Design and complete a grouped data collection sheet to record this data.

3. 'Boys eat more crisps than girls'.
Design a two-way table to help collect data to investigate this hypothesis.

4. James is designing a questionnaire to investigate the hypothesis 'Boys read for pleasure more than girls'.
Suggest four questions that James might use.

5. The following questions were found on a questionnaire.
(a) How much sport do you watch on TV?
(b) Do you or do you not read comics?
(c) What is your age?
(d) I think R and B music is great. What do you think?
What is wrong with each of these questions?
Write an improved version of each question.

6. This two-way table shows the results of a survey.

	Blonde hair	Brown hair
Blue eyes	5	15
Green eyes	3	7

Do the results of the survey show that the hypothesis 'There are more blondes with blue eyes than with green eyes' is true or false?

7. Joe is investigating shopping habits.
He plans to ask 50 people at his local newsagent to complete a short questionnaire on a Monday morning.
Give three reasons why Joe's results might be biased.

8. Describe the sample you would use to investigate the hypothesis 'Students at school like Maths more than English'.

9. The table shows the number of students in each year of a school.

Year 7	164
Year 8	200
Year 9	155
Year 10	221
Year 11	246

How many pupils in each year group would there be in a stratified random sample of size 100?

10. The table shows the number of boys and girls in each year of a school.

	Boys	**Girls**
Year 7	80	73
Year 8	55	70
Year 9	98	112
Year 10	101	114
Year 11	110	130

(a) How many boys would there be in a stratified random sample of size 50?
(b) How many pupils in Year 7 would there be in a stratified random sample of size 50?

2. PRESENTING DATA

Bar charts and bar line graphs

A bar chart is a frequency diagram used for qualitative or discrete data.
Bar line graphs are similar to bar charts and show the frequencies of discrete data.

e.g.1

This bar chart compares the favourite colours of boys and girls in class 8A.

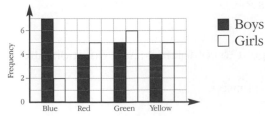

Examiner's tip
Questions are usually about interpreting a given bar chart.

There are 20 boys in 8A $7 + 4 + 5 + 4$
5 more boys than girls chose blue $7 - 2$

e.g.2

The bar line graph shows the shoe sizes of a group of people.

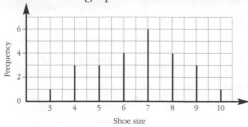

The most common shoe size is 7.
The smallest shoe size is 3.
4 people out of 25 wear shoe size 6.
16% wear shoe size 6. $^4/_{25} \times 100$

Remember
There are gaps between the bars or lines because the data has no intermediate values.

4   Drawing and interpreting pie charts

A pie chart is a diagram used for qualitative data.
In a pie chart frequencies are proportional to the angles of sectors of circles.

e.g.1

Daily weather in November

Snow	Rain	Cloud
6 days	11 days	13 days

Angles in the sectors of a pie chart are in the ratio 6 : 11 : 13.
Divide 360° in the ratio 6 : 11 : 13.
6 + 11 + 13 = 30   360 ÷ 30 = 12
Snow   72°   6 × 12
Rain   132°   11 × 12
Cloud   156°   13 × 12

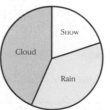

e.g.2

This pie chart shows the distribution of 1800 people at a concert.

The angle for men is 120°   120 : 360 = 1 : 3
So the number of men is 600   1 : 3 = 600 : 1800

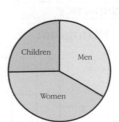

Examiner's tip
When drawing a pie chart, show how you work out the angles, and label each of the sectors.

Stem and leaf diagrams

A stem and leaf diagram shows raw quantitative data in order.
Back-to-back stem and leaf diagrams can be used to compare two
sets of data.

e.g.1

The stem and leaf diagram shows scores for 15 boys in a
maths test.

12	22	43	29	37
38	41	7	48	36
38	27	31	24	18

```
0 | 7
1 | 2 8
2 | 2 4 7 9
3 | 1 6 7 8 8
4 | 1 3 8
```

> **Examiner's tip**
> When drawing a
> stem and leaf
> diagram you must
> remember to
> explain the stem
> with a key.

| 2 | 7   means 27 |

e.g.2

This back-to-back stem and leaf diagram
compares boys' and girls' scores in the test.

The diagram shows:
  The girls obtained more high scores
  than the boys.
  The spread of the girls' scores
  is less than the boys.

```
              Girls   Boys
                 | 0 | 7
               8 | 1 | 2 8
           8 4 2 | 2 | 2 4 7 9
       9 9 8 6 4 | 0 3 | 6 7 8 8 9
         9 9 6 5 2 | 4 | 1 3 8
```

| **Girls** |
| 8 | 1 means 18 |
| **Boys** |
| 1 | 2 means 12 |

Diagrams for grouped frequency distributions

Histogram

A histogram looks like a bar chart without gaps.
When the bars have equal width, the height of each bar is
equal to the frequency.
The width of each bar is **equal** to the width of each class interval.

Frequency polygon

In a frequency polygon, frequencies are plotted at the **midpoints**
of each class interval and points are joined with **straight lines**.

e.g.1

A frequency distribution for the heights of 50 plants

Height, h, cm	$0 \leq h < 10$	$10 \leq h < 20$	$20 \leq h < 30$	$30 \leq h < 40$	$40 \leq h < 50$
Frequency	2	12	18	14	4

Histogram

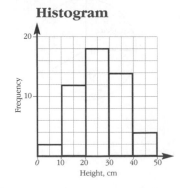

Frequency polygon

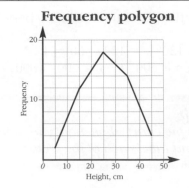

2

Cumulative frequency diagrams

To draw a cumulative frequency graph, work out cumulative frequencies from a grouped frequency table and use them to draw a cumulative frequency graph.

e.g.1

A cumulative frequency table and graph, for the heights of 50 plants.

Height h, cm	Frequency	Height h, cm	Cumulative Frequency
$0 \leq h < 10$	1	< 10	1
$10 \leq h < 20$	12	< 20	13 (1 + 12)
$20 \leq h < 30$	19	< 30	32 (13 + 19)
$30 \leq h < 40$	14	< 40	46 (32 + 14)
$40 \leq h < 50$	4	< 50	50 (46 + 4)

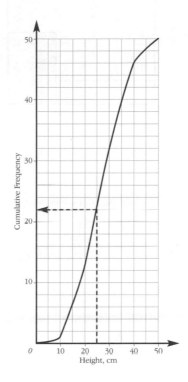

The cumulative frequency graph shows that 22 plants have a height less than 25 cm.

> ### Examiner's tips
> - *A cumulative frequency graph should be roughly S-shaped.*
> - *Always plot cumulative frequency against the upper boundary of each class interval.*

1

Histograms with unequal class intervals

A histogram with unequal class intervals is drawn using the idea of frequency density.

Frequency density = Frequency ÷ Class width

e.g.1

Times taken for 50 people to complete a 2-mile walk

Time, t, min	$0 \leq t < 20$	$20 \leq t < 30$	$30 \leq t < 35$	$35 \leq t < 40$	$40 \leq t < 55$
Frequency	8	12	12	9	9
Frequency density	0.4 (8 ÷ 20)	1.2 (12 ÷ 10)	2.4 (12 ÷ 5)	1.8 (9 ÷ 5)	0.6 (9 ÷ 15)

> ### Examiner's tips
> - *You will be given graph paper to **draw** a histogram but the axes will **not** be labelled.*
> - *You could be asked to **interpret** frequency density on a given histogram.*

> ### Remember
> Using frequency density for a histogram means that the area of bars equals the frequency.

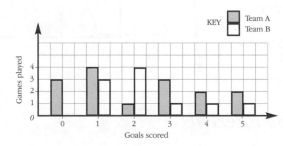

An estimate of the number who took between 15 and 25 minutes is obtained from the shaded area on the histogram.

Shaded area = 8 $0.4 \times 5 + 1.2 \times 5$

So 8 people took between 15 and 25 minutes to complete the walk.

Test 39

Use a calculator for question 7 only.

1. The bar chart shows the goals scored in games played by two football teams, *A* and *B*.

KEY — Team A / Team B

Games played vs Goals scored

(a) How many games did each team play?

(b) What is the percentage of games in which team *A* scored no goals?

(c) Emma thinks that team *A* scored more.
Does the diagram prove or disprove this hypothesis?

2. The table shows how 180 students travel to school.

Method of travel	Bus	Train	Walk
Frequency	50	30	100

Draw a pie chart to show this information.

3. A student earns £72 a week working in a shop.
The pie chart shows what she does with this money.
How much does she save each week?

4. The weights in kg of 12 children at birth are shown below.
3.6   4.2   3.2   2.8   4.4   5.1
4.5   4.3   3.7   2.9   4.0   3.8
Draw a stem and leaf diagram to show this information.

5. The back-to-back stem and leaf diagram compares the lengths of leaves from two plants.

				A				B				

3 | 4   means 34 mm

```
                9 8 | 0 | 5 8 9
            4 4 2 | 1 | 2 6 8
        9 8 6 4 0 | 2 | 6 7 8 9
        3 2 1 1 0 | 3 | 4 6 8 9 9
```

Comment on the lengths of the leaves from these two plants.

6. The table shows the time taken for 50 students to complete a puzzle.

Time, t, seconds	$0 \leq t < 20$	$20 \leq t < 40$	$40 \leq t < 60$	$60 \leq t < 80$
Frequency	4	22	18	6

(a) Draw a frequency polygon to show this information.
(b) Draw up a cumulative frequency table and use it to draw a cumulative frequency graph.
(c) Use the cumulative frequency graph to estimate the number of students who took less than 30 seconds to complete the puzzle.

7. The table shows the time taken for 50 students to travel to school.

Time, t, minutes	$0 \leq t < 10$	$10 \leq t < 15$	$15 \leq t < 25$	$25 \leq t < 50$
Frequency	8	14	18	10

(a) Calculate the frequency densities for each class interval.
(b) Use the frequency densities to draw a histogram to show the information.
(c) Use the histogram to work out how many students took between 20 and 30 minutes to travel to school.

3. MEASURES OF AVERAGE AND SPREAD

4 Mean, median and mode

A single value that is used to represent a set of data is called an average.
There are three ways to measure an average.

Mean   The sum of the values divided by the number of values.
Median The middle value when the values are arranged in order.
         For an even number of values, the median is the mean of the middle two.
Mode   The most frequently occurring value.

MEASURES OF AVERAGE AND SPREAD

e.g.1

Eight workers are paid the following hourly rates: &3, &16, &6, &5, &4, &5, &4, &5
The mean wage is &6. $(3 + 16 + 6 + 5 + 4 + 5 + 4 + 5) \div 8 = 6$
The median wage is &5. 3   4   4   **5**   **5**   5   6   16
The mode is &5.

The range

Sets of data with the same averages can contain different values.
For example:

Set *A*   0   1   5   5   5   6   13
Set *B*   5   5   5   5   5   5   5

Both of these sets of data have a mean, median and mode of 5
These sets of data differ in how the values are **spread** out.
The **range** is a simple way of measuring this.

> Range = highest value – lowest value

Set *A*   Range = 13   (13 – 0)
Set *B*   Range = 0   (5 – 5)

Measures of **average** and **spread** are used to **compare** two sets of data.

e.g.1

The mean and range of the heights of plants fed with different brands of fertilizer are shown.

	Mean, cm	Range, cm
Brand *X*	24	18
Brand *Y*	23	5

There is little difference between the mean heights.
The range for brand *X* is large compared with the range for brand *Y*.
So the heights of plants grown using brand *X* are more **variable**.
The heights of plants grown using brand *Y* are more **consistent**.

Averages and range from diagrams

e.g.1

The stem and leaf diagram shows the ages of 15 members of a sports club in order.

$\frac{1}{2}$ of (15 + 1) = 8, so the **median** is the 8th value
The **median** age is 23.

The most frequently occurring age is 18.
So the **modal** age is 18.

The **range** = 16 years   31 – 15

```
1 | 5 6 7 8 8 8
2 | 0 3 5 5 7 8 8
3 | 0 1
```

> 2 | 5 means 25 years

e.g.2 The diagram shows the number of peas in 20 pea pods.

The most frequently occurring
number of peas is 8.
The **mode** = 8

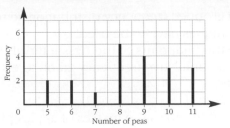

The first 11 values are
5 5 6 6 7 8 8 8 8 **8** **9** …
The number of values is even, so there are two middle values.
The **median** = 8½   ½ of 20 = 10;
The median is the mean of the 10th and 11th values.

To find the mean, first find the total number of peas in all 20 pods.
$(2 \times 5) + (2 \times 6) + (1 \times 7) + (5 \times 8) + (4 \times 9) + (3 \times 10) + (3 \times 11) = 168$
So the total number of peas in the 20 pods is 168
The **mean** is 8.4.   168 ÷ 20

The **range** = 6   11 – 5

Averages and range from a frequency table

e.g.1

The table shows the number of people in 40 houses.

Number of people	Frequency	Number x Frequency
2	7	$2 \times 7 = 14$
3	12	$3 \times 12 = 36$
4	8	$4 \times 8 = 32$
5	5	$5 \times 5 = 25$
6	4	$6 \times 4 = 24$
7	3	$7 \times 3 = 21$
8	1	$8 \times 1 = 8$

The **mode** is 3 people per house.

The first 7 values are 2, the 8th to the 19th values are 3 and the 20th to 27th values are 4, …
The number of values is even, so there are two middle values.
The **median** is 4.   ½ of 40 = 20; the median is the mean of the 20th and 21st values

The total number of people in all 40 houses = 160   14 + 36 + 32 + 25 + 24 + 21 + 8
So the **mean** is 4.   160 ÷ 40

The **range** = 6   8 – 2

MEASURES OF AVERAGE AND SPREAD

The average and spread of a grouped frequency distribution

In a grouped frequency distribution actual data values are not known so different techniques have to be used.
Use the midpoints of the class intervals to calculate an estimate of the mean.
Use a cumulative frequency graph to estimate the median and the interquartile range.

e.g.1

The table shows the masses of apples picked from 60 trees.

Mass, m, kg	$0 \le m < 10$	$10 \le m < 20$	$20 \le m < 30$	$30 \le m < 40$	$40 \le m < 50$
Frequency	1	13	28	15	3

Calculating an estimate of the mean

To find the mean, first estimate the total mass of apples picked from all 60 trees.
Use the midpoints of the class intervals to help make this estimate.

Midpoint of class interval, kg	Frequency	Midpoint x Frequency
5	1	$5 \times 1 = 5$
15	13	$15 \times 13 = 195$
25	28	$25 \times 28 = 700$
35	15	$35 \times 15 = 525$
45	3	$3 \times 45 = 135$

Estimate of mass of apples = 1560 kg $5 + 195 + 700 + 525 + 135$
So the estimate of the mean is 26 kg $1560 \div 60$

Examiner's tips

- You **could** be **told** to use midpoints; however, remember the method in case you are not!
- Check that the estimated mean is roughly in the middle of the distribution.

Using a cumulative frequency graph

Mass, m, kg	Cumulative Frequency
< 10	1
< 20	14 (1 + 13)
< 30	42 (14 + 28)
< 40	57 (42 + 15)
< 50	60 (57 + 3)

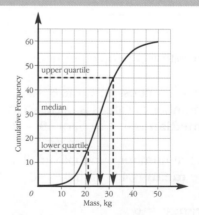

The cumulative frequency graph can be used to:
Read off the middle value to estimate the median.
Read off the value at $\frac{1}{4}$ of the total frequency; this is called the lower quartile.
Read off the value at $\frac{3}{4}$ of the total frequency; this is called the upper quartile.
Find the interquartile range.

Interquartile range = upper quartile – lower quartile

The median mass of apples per tree = 26 kg
The interquartile range = 12 kg   33 (UQ) – 21 (LQ)

Remember
The interquartile range measures the **spread** of
the middle ½ of a set of data.
It is a better measure of spread than the range
because extreme values are excluded.

2   *Box plots*

A box plot is a diagram that shows:
  the median
  the upper and lower quartiles
  the highest and lowest values.

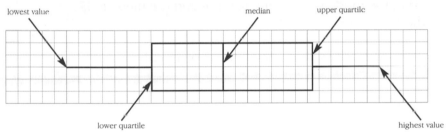

A box plot is sometimes called a box and whisker plot.
Box plots can be used to compare two sets of data.

e.g.1

The box plots show the times some 12-year-old boys and girls took to run a mile.

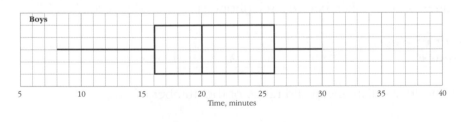

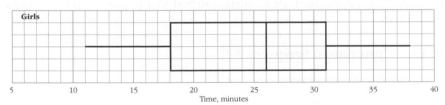

The fastest boy took 8 minutes; the slowest took 30 minutes.
The fastest girl took 11 minutes; the slowest took 38 minutes.
The range of times taken by the boys was 22 minutes.   30 – 8
The range of times taken by the girls was 27 minutes.   38 – 11

The median time of the boys was 20 minutes.
The median time of the girls was 26 minutes.
The interquartile range of the boys times was 10 minutes.   26 – 16
The interquartile range of the girls times was 13 minutes.   31 – 18

So, on average, the boys ran the mile faster and with more consistent times than the girls.

Test 40

Use a calculator in question 5 only.

1. There are five values in a set of data.
The mean is 8, the mode is 3, the median is 4 and the range is 17
What are the five values?

2. The stem and leaf diagram shows the heights of 15 girls.

```
13 | 4 6 8
14 | 2 3 3 3 5 8 9
15 | 0 4 7 8
16 | 1
```
| 15|4 means 154 cm |

(a) What is the range of the heights?
(b) What is the median height?
(c) Which height is the mode?

3. The number of rings taken before a telephone is answered is recorded.

Number of rings	1	2	3	4	5
Frequency	3	7	6	3	1

Find the mode, median, mean and range of the number of rings.

4. The table shows the distribution of lengths jumped in a triple jump competition by 60 competitors.

Length, m	Cumulative Frequency
< 4	5
< 8	15
< 12	40
< 16	60

(a) Draw a cumulative frequency graph to illustrate the data.
(b) Use the cumulative frequency graph to find:
    (i) the median
    (ii) the interquartile range.
(c) The shortest and longest lengths jumped were 2.6 m and 15.2 m.
    Draw a box plot to represent the data.

5. The table shows the hourly wage paid to 50 workers in company A.

Wage, w, £	$0 \leq w < 5$	$5 \leq w < 10$	$10 \leq w < 15$	$15 \leq w < 20$	$20 \leq w < 25$
Frequency	12	18	10	7	3

(a) Calculate an estimate of the mean wage.
(b) Draw a cumulative frequency table and graph to show the data.
(c) Use the cumulative frequency graph to estimate the median and interquartile range.
(d) The lowest wage paid by company A is £3.50 per hour.
    The highest wage paid is £24.50 per hour.
    Draw a box plot to show the hourly wages paid by company A.
(e) This box plot shows the hourly wages paid by company B.

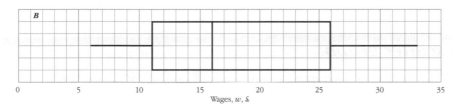

Wages, w, £

Compare the wages paid by companies A and B.

4. CORRELATION

Scatter graphs and lines of best fit

A scatter graph shows the relationship between two sets of data.
This relationship is called **correlation**.
Correlation can be positive or negative.

A **line of best fit** can be used to show the strength of any correlation.
To draw a line of best fit:
    Draw a straight line that passes through as many of the points as possible.
    Make sure that there is roughly the same number of points on each side of the line.
The closer the points are to the line of best fit the better the correlation.
If the points lie on a straight line the correlation is said to be perfect.

189

CORRELATION

EXAMPLES

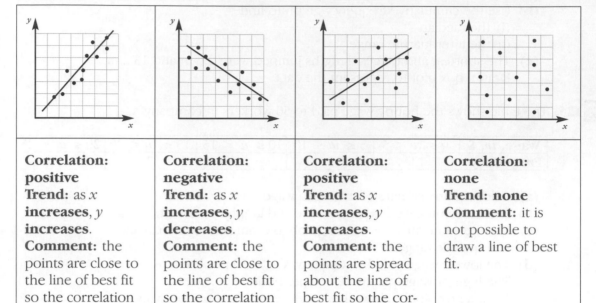

Correlation: positive Trend: as *x* increases, *y* increases. Comment: the points are close to the line of best fit so the correlation is **good**.	**Correlation: negative** Trend: as *x* increases, *y* decreases. Comment: the points are close to the line of best fit so the correlation is **good**.	**Correlation: positive** Trend: as *x* increases, *y* increases. Comment: the points are spread about the line of best fit so the correlation is **poor**.	**Correlation: none** Trend: **none** Comment: it is not possible to draw a line of best fit.

Using a scatter graph

The line of best fit can be used to estimate values of one set of data when a value from the other set is known.

e.g.1

Some students took a French test and a German test.
The results are shown in the table.

French	14	20	22	26	30	30	32	36	38	40	44	45	54
German	10	16	24	28	25	32	38	36	46	38	42	53	52

The scatter graph shows the results.

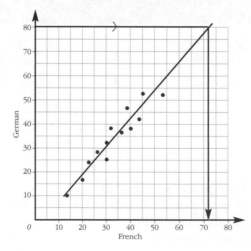

The line of best fit shows a good positive correlation between the scores.
Jenny scored 80% in the German test but missed the French test.
The line of best fit suggests that a good estimate for Jenny's French score is 72%.
This might **not** be reliable because all scores shown on the scatter graph are below 60%.

Test 41

Do not use a calculator.

1. The table shows lengths and weights of ten cucumbers.

Length, cm	40	42	42	45	48	50	54	55	56	57
Weight, g	95	125	85	135	175	180	155	195	188	225

(a) Draw a scatter graph for this data.
(b) Draw a line of best fit.
(c) Describe the relationship between the length and weight of these cucumbers.
(d) Estimate the length of a cucumber that weighs 150 g.

2. The table shows the marks given by two different judges in a competition.

Judge X	29	31	34	34	40	42	42	44	48	46
Judge Y	33	30	29	38	43	40	45	50	44	52

(a) Draw a scatter graph for this data.
(b) Draw a line of best fit.
(c) Use your line of best fit to decide which judge gave the better marks.
(d) A late entry was awarded 60 marks by Judge X.
   Estimate the mark that might have been given by Judge Y.
   Is this a reliable estimate?
   Explain your answer.

3. Describe the correlation you would expect there to be between each of these pairs of quantities.
   (a) Ice cream sales and temperature.
   (b) Age of car and second-hand car price.
   (c) Shoe size and scores in a maths test.
   (d) Average speed on a journey and the time the journey takes.
   (e) Weight and height of adults.
   (f) Weight and height of children.

5. TIME SERIES

Time series graphs and seasonal variation

Time series data is data that is recorded at intervals of time.
A graph showing how data changes with time is called a **time series graph**.
Seasonal variations are changes in time series data that occur with the seasons of the year.

e.g.1

The table shows the quarterly number of absences in a factory over a period of 3 years.
The absences are plotted on a time series graph.

Year	Quarter	Absences
2009	1	44
	2	36
	3	30
	4	62
2010	1	52
	2	48
	3	30
	4	66
2011	1	56
	2	48
	3	38
	4	58

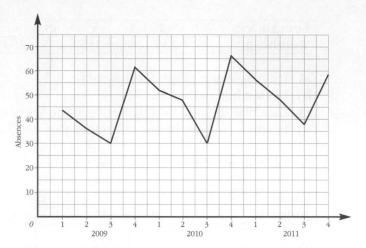

Only points plotted on the graph represent data values.
The lines are drawn only to show the trend.
There is a clear seasonal variation with absences increasing in the 4th quarter of each year.

Moving averages

Moving averages are used to smooth out changes in time series data.
They can be plotted on a time series graph to show any trend more clearly.

e.g.1

Calculate the 3-point moving averages for: 14   24   19   23   30   13
1st average = 19 $(14 + 24 + 19) \div 3$
2nd average = 22 $(24 + 19 + 23) \div 3$
3rd average = 24 $(19 + 23 + 30) \div 3$
4th average = 22 $(23 + 30 + 13) \div 3$

The 4-point moving averages for the absences in the example above are calculated below
and plotted on the graph.

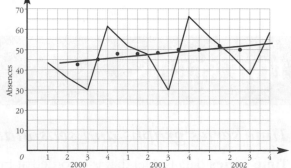

1st average = 43 $(44 + 36 + 30 + 62) \div 4$
2nd average = 45 $(36 + 30 + 62 + 52) \div 4$
3rd average = 48 $(30 + 62 + 52 + 48) \div 4$
4th average = 48 $(62 + 52 + 48 + 30) \div 4$
5th average = 49 $(52 + 48 + 30 + 66) \div 4$
6th average = 50 $(48 + 30 + 66 + 56) \div 4$
7th average = 50 $(30 + 66 + 56 + 48) \div 4$
8th average = 52 $(66 + 56 + 48 + 38) \div 4$
9th average = 50 $(56 + 48 + 38 + 58) \div 4$

The 4-point moving averages are plotted at the centre of each set of 4 points.
A line of best fit drawn for the moving averages shows the general trend in absence.

Test 42

📱 Use a calculator.

📱 **1.** Calculate the first three 4-point moving averages for this set of data.
12   21   13   26   14   23   14   28   17

📱 **2.** The table shows the number of units of electricity used each quarter by a school over a period of three years.

	2009				**2010**				**2011**		
Quarter	1	2	3	4	1	2	3	4	1	2	3	4
Units	2100	2400	1400	2200	1900	2600	1300	2200	2900	2800	1500	2300

(a) Show the data in a time series graph.
(b) Calculate the 4-point moving averages.
(c) Plot the moving averages on the time series graph.
(d) Comment on the trend in the amount of electricity used.

6.   PROBABILITY

4

Probability from equally likely outcomes

In a probability situation the possible things that can occur are called outcomes.
A particular outcome is called an event.
Probability describes how likely or unlikely it is that an event will occur.
Probabilities range between 0 (impossible) and 1 (certain).

When all outcomes are **equally likely**:

> The probability of an event = $\dfrac{\text{Number of outcomes in the event}}{\text{Total number of equally likely outcomes}}$

e.g.1

A bag contains 6 red counters and 4 yellow counters.
A counter is taken from the bag at random.
  There are 10 (6 + 4) equally likely outcomes.
  The number of outcomes in the event 'picking a red counter' is 6
  So p(red) = $^6/_{10}$ p(red) means the probability of picking a red counter

> **Examiner's tips**
> *- Make sure you write a probability either as a fraction, a decimal or a percentage and do not simplify your answer unless you are told to do so.*
> *- The phrases 'at random' and 'fair' are often used in probability questions; they are just ways of saying that outcomes are equally likely.*

Relative frequency

Probabilities cannot always be calculated using equally likely outcomes.
In some cases, they have to be estimated using the results of experiments or surveys.
In this case, the idea of **relative frequency** is used.

> Relative frequency = $\dfrac{\text{The number of times an event occurs in an experiment (or a survey)}}{\text{Total number of trials in the experiment (or observations in the survey)}}$

Relative frequency is a good estimate of probability when the number of
trials/observations is large; the more trials/observations the better the estimate.

e.g.1

10 000 drivers take part in a survey.
6300 of the drivers passed their driving test first
time.
From the survey:

The relative frequency of passing the test
first time = $^{6300}/_{10\,000} = 0.63$
The best estimate of the probability of a
learner driver passing the test first time is
0.63.
The number taking part in the survey is
large enough for this to be a good estimate.

Estimating outcomes and bias

The connection between relative frequency and probability can be used to:
Estimate how many times an event will occur in an experiment or survey.
Help decide whether a probability situation is fair or biased (not fair).

e.g.1

In an experiment Tim throws a fair dice 1200 times.
Estimate how many times he throws a 'six'.

There are a large number of trials and the dice is fair.
So, the relative frequency of throwing a six should
approximately equal p(six).
p(six) = $^1/_6$ p(six) means the probability of throwing a six
So Tim should throw about 200 sixes. $^1/_6 = {}^{200}/_{1200}$

e.g.2

Sam throws a different dice 20 times and gets a 'six' once.
He says that this means the dice is biased.

The relative frequency of getting a six = $^1/_{20}$ = 0.05
p(six) = 0.167   1 ÷ 6
The relative frequency is **not** approximately equal to the probability.
This means that Sam **could** be right.
However, the number of trials is **too small** to be sure.

The addition rule for probability

Events that cannot happen at the same time are called **mutually exclusive events**, e.g.
Throwing a '2' and throwing a '6' with a single throw of a dice are mutually exclusive.
Having blue eyes and blonde hair are **not** mutually exclusive.

The addition rule for probability is that if *(A)* and *(B)* are mutually exclusive events:

$$p(A \textbf{ or } B) = p(A) + p(B)$$

(A) and **(not** *A*) are mutually exclusive events.
So p(*A* **or** not A) = p(*A*) + p(**not** A)
The event (*A* **or** not A) is certain to occur.
This means that:

The probability of an event *A* **not** happening, $p(\textbf{not } A) = 1 - p(A)$

e.g.1

A spinner is divided into sectors each painted a different colour.
The spinner is spun.
The table shows the probabilities of getting each colour.

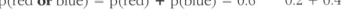

Red	Blue	Yellow	Green
0.2	0.4	0.3	0.1

p(red **or** blue) = p(red) **+** p(blue) = 0.6   0.2 + 0.4

A different coloured spinner is spun. The probability of getting a blue is 0.3
p(**not** blue) = 0.7   1 – 0.3

Combining two events

You can find all the possible outcomes when two events are combined by:
Listing the outcomes systematically
Completing a **probability space diagram**
Using a **tree diagram.**

e.g.1

Box *X* contains two red counters *(R)* and a blue counter *(B)*.
Box Y contains one red counter *(R)* and a green counter *(G)*.
One counter is taken from each box.

List

RR   RR   BR   RG   RG   BG

Probability space diagram

	R	R	B
R	RR	RR	BR
G	RG	RG	BG

Tree diagram

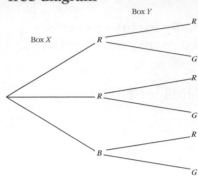

2   *The multiplication rule for probability*

If event A has no influence on whether event B occurs then events A and B are
independent.

The multiplication rule for probability is that if A and B are independent events:

$$p(A \textbf{ and } B) = p(\textbf{a}) \times p(\textbf{b})$$

Using a tree diagram

A tree diagram can be used to help calculate the probability of two or more events
happening.

e.g.1

A school has 10 maths teachers of whom 4 are male and 5 PE
teachers of whom 3 are male.

A maths teacher and a PE teacher are chosen at random.

A tree diagram can be drawn for this situation.
The probabilities can be written on the branches.

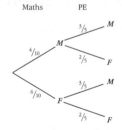

The teachers can be chosen in four possible ways.

    Maths male and PE male

    Maths male and PE female

    Maths female and PE male

    Maths female and PE female

Each of these possible outcomes corresponds to a branch of the tree diagram.

To find the probability of each outcome **multiply the probabilities** along the branches.

    So p(maths male **and** PE female) = $^8/_{50}$ $^4/_{10} \times ^2/_5$

    So p(maths female **and** PE male) = $^{18}/_{50}$ $^6/_{10} \times ^3/_5$

    So p(one teacher is male **and** the other is female) = $^{26}/_{50}$ $^8/_{50} + ^{18}/_{50}$

1 Conditional probability

Probabilities that change depending upon previous events are called **conditional** probabilities.

e.g.1

A bag contains 3 red counters and 7 blue counters.
One of the counters is taken at random and **not replaced**.
Another counter is then taken at random.

1st counter red:	$p(R)$	$= \frac{3}{10}$
2nd counter red:	$p(R)$	$= \frac{2}{9}$ one less **red** counter
So $p(R$ **and** $R) = \frac{6}{90}$	$\frac{3}{10} \times \frac{2}{9}$	

1st counter red:	$p(R)$	$= \frac{3}{10}$
2nd counter blue:	$p(\mathbf{B})$	$= \frac{7}{9}$ one less **red** counter
So $p(R$ **and** $B) = \frac{21}{90}$	$\frac{3}{10} \times \frac{7}{9}$	

1st counter blue:	$p(\mathbf{B})$	$= \frac{7}{10}$
2nd counter red:	$p(R)$	$= \frac{3}{9}$ one less **blue** counter
$p(B$ **and** $R) = \frac{21}{90}$	$\frac{7}{10} \times \frac{3}{9}$	

So p(one counter is red **and** the other is blue $= \frac{42}{90}$ $\frac{21}{90} + \frac{21}{90}$

> **Examiner's tip**
> *A tree diagram might not be given to you. However, you can use one if you think it will help.*

Test 43

Do not use a calculator.

1. Red tickets numbered 1 to 50 and blue tickets numbered 1 to 125 are sold in a raffle.
The winning ticket is picked at random.
Work out the probability that the winning ticket is:
(a) Red
(b) Numbered 2
(c) Red and numbered 2.

2. This table gives some information about the members of a club.

	Men	Women
Wears glasses	12	8
Does not wear glasses	48	12

(a) A member of the club is chosen at random.
What is the probability that this member is a woman?
(b) A man from the club is chosen at random.
What is the probability that he wears glasses?

3. A dice is thrown 600 times.
A six is obtained 42 times.
(a) What is the relative frequency of the dice landing on a six?
(b) Is the dice fair?
Explain your answer.

4. In an experiment a bead is taken from a bag and its colour is recorded.
The bead is then put back in the bag.
This trial is repeated a number of times.
The table shows the results.

Trials	100	200	300	400	500
Red beads	42	108	138	176	230

(a) Draw a graph to show how the relative frequency of picking a red bead changes as the number of trials increases.
(b) The bag contains 1000 beads.
Estimate the number of red beads in the bag.

5. The probability that a boy is born with blue eyes is 0.55.
What is the probability that a boy is born with eyes that are not blue?

6. A cafe offers a special lunch consisting of a starter of soup or melon and a main course of fish, chicken or pasta.
List all the possible combinations of starter and main course.

7. The probability that a girl picked at random is left-handed is 0.2 and the probability that she wears glasses is 0.3.
(a) Billy says that the probability that the girl is left-handed **or** wears glasses is 0.5.
Explain why Billy is wrong.
(b) Find the probability that the girl is right-handed **and** wears glasses.

8. A company uses two machines to make light bulbs.
The probability that machine A is working is 0.9.
The probability that machine B is working is 0.8.
(a) Copy and complete this tree diagram.

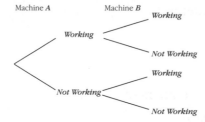

(b) What is the probability that both machines are working?
(c) What is the probability that exactly one machine is working?

9. A bag contains 7 red counters and 3 blue counters.
A counter is taken from the bag at random and is then replaced.
Another counter is then taken from the bag at random.
Work out the probability that:
(a) Both counters taken from the bag are red.
(b) The counters are a different colour.

10. Repeat question 9 with the first counter **not** being replaced.

NUMBER

TEST 1

1. **(a)** 11 988   **(b)** 17 442
   (c) 21 r 21   **(d)** 24 r 19
2. 990
3. 26
4. **(a)** 31 **(b)** 49 **(c)** 18
   (d) 120 **(e)** 5 **(f)** 5
5. See question 4
6. £1.91
7. **(a)** 23 **(b)** 0.37 **(c)** 300
   (d) 620 **(e)** 3.24 **(f)** 0.753
   (g) 0.725 **(h)** 0.076
8. **(a)** 8 **(b)** 0.04 **(c)** 0.005
   (d) 120 **(e)** 200 **(f)** 2.4
   (g) 50 **(h)** 120 **(i)** 125
   (j) 0.08 **(k)** 5 **(l)** 0.2
9. **(a)** Both numbers have been multiplied by 100
   (b) $20 \times 0.3 = 2 \times 10 \times 0.3 = 2 \times 3$
10. **(a)** 200 **(b)** 48
11. See question 10
12. **(a)** 123.54 **(b)** 1.2354 **(c)** 123.54
    (d) 0.58 **(e)** 5800 **(f)** 21.3
13. **(a)** 2400 **(b)** 48 cm

TEST 2

1. **(a)** 2.7 (2)   **(b)** 13.4 (3)
   (c) 0.7 (1)   **(d)** 3.7 (2)
   (e) 123.6 (4) **(f)** 0.7 (1)
2. **(a)** 13.54 (4) **(b)** 2.75 (3)
   (c) 123.56 (5) **(d)** 0.68 (2)
   (e) 12.65 (4) **(f)** 0.56 (2)
3. **(a)** 3, 10, 0.7, 4, 100, 0.7
   (b) 13.5, 2.75, 124, 0.675, 12.6, 0.556
4. **(a)** 10   **(b)** 400
5. **(a)** 50   **(b)** 60
   (c) 30   **(d)** 2000
6. **(a)** 119.5 g   **(b)** 3950 m
7. **(a)** Upper 4.375, Lower 4.265
   (b) Upper 2.935, Lower 2.825
   (c) Upper 2.64625, Lower 2.53825
   (d) Upper 5.10489 …, Lower 4.89655 …
8. **(a)** Upper bound = 90 900 mm²
   (b) Lower bound = 89 100 mm²

TEST 3

1. **(a)** 3 **(b)** ⁻7 **(c)** ⁻3
   (d) 3 **(e)** ⁻25 **(f)** 35
   (g) ⁻16 **(h)** 35
2. **(a)** ⁻10 **(b)** 10 **(c)** ⁻10
   (d) 36 **(e)** ⁻6 **(f)** ⁻4
   (g) 6 **(h)** ⁻3
3. **(a)** ⁻22 **(b)** ⁻10 **(c)** 18
   (d) ⁻6 **(e)** 3 **(f)** ⁻100
4. See question 3

TEST 4

1. **(a)** 6, 12, 15 and 24 **(b)** 2, 6, 12 and 24
   (c) 2 and 17
2. **(a)** 1, 2, 3, 4, 5, 6, 8, 10, 12, 15, 20, 24, 25, 30, 40, 50, 60, 75, 100, 120, 125, 150, 200, 250, 300, 375, 500, 600, 750, 1000, 1500, 3000
   (b) 42
3. **(a)** All even numbers apart from 2 have 2 as a factor as well as 1 and themselves.
   (b) No because $13 \times 17 = 221$, so 13 and 17 are factors of 221.
4. **(a)** $2^3 \times 3$ **(b)** $2^3 \times 3^2$
   (c) $2^2 \times 3^3$ **(d)** $2^2 \times 3 \times 5$
5. **(a)** 2 and 5 **(b)** 2, 3 and 5
   (c) $2^4 \times 5$ **(d)** $2^3 \times 3 \times 5$
   (e) 240 **(f)** 40
6. **(a)** LCM = 36, HCF = 6
   (b) LCM = 216, HCF = 18
7. The sum of any even multiple of 3 and any multiple of 2, e.g. 6 + 4, 12 + 10, …

TEST 5

1. **(a)** 8 **(b)** 625 **(c)** 81
   (d) 216 **(e)** 2401 **(f)** 128
2. **(a)** 144 **(b)** 2000 **(c)** 200
   (d) 49 000
3. **(a)** 7 **(b)** 6 **(c)** 15
   (d) 2 **(e)** 5 **(f)** 3
4. **(a)** Not true for 1 and 4
   $2 + 7 = 9, 11 + 5 = 16, 23 + 2 = 25$, $31 + 5 = 36, 47 + 2 = 49, 61 + 3 = 64$, $79 + 2 = 81, 97 + 3 = 100$
   (b) All square numbers > 4 are the sum of 2 different prime numbers
5. **(a)** ¼ or 0.25 **(b)** ⅕ or 0.2
   (c) 3 **(d)** 8
   (e) ⁵⁄₄ or 1.25 **(f)** ⅘ or 0.8

(g) $5/7$ or 0.714285 **(h)** $10/7$ or 1.428571
(i) $2/5$ or 0.4

6. **(a)** 5 **(b)** ⁻2 **(c)** 2
(d) 11 **(e)** 8 **(f)** 8
7. **(a)** 64.125 **(b)** 1.1 **(c)** 1.04
(d) 9 **(e)** 5.2 **(f)** 0.25
(g) 8 **(h)** 0.04 **(i)** 0.25
(j) 0.25
8. **(a)** $10^2 + 10^1 + 10^0 + 10^{-1} + 10^{-2}$
(b) $2^2 + 2^1 + 2^0 + 2^{-1}$
9. **(a)** $1/8$ **(b)** $1/25$ **(c)** $1/1000$
(d) 2 **(e)** 2 **(f)** 8
(g) $1/2$ **(h)** $1/2$ **(i)** $1/8$
(j) 8 **(k)** 125 **(l)** 25
(m) $1/9$ **(n)** $1/8$ **(o)** $1/32$

TEST 6
1. **(a)** 2.4×10^3 **(b)** 1.367×10^6
(c) 8.23×10^5 **(d)** 1.213×10^9
(e) 3.4×10^{-1} **(f)** 2×10^{-4}
(g) 5.46×10^{-6} **(h)** 7.6×10^{-7}
2. **(a)** 600 000 **(b)** 36 000 000
(c) 42 300 **(d)** 1 234 000 000
(e) 0.000 07 **(f)** 0.008 61
(g) 0.000 176 **(h)** 0.000 000 009 034
3. **(a)** 1.4×10^{-1} **(b)** 5×10^9
(c) 2.5×10^7
4. **(a)** 8×10^2 **(b)** 2×10^{-4}
(c) 4×10^0 **(d)** 8×10^0
(e) 2×10^{-6} **(f)** 2.5×10^{-5}
5. Largest 6000, smallest 0.007
6. 1.525965×10^{19}
7. **(a)** 9 600 000 000 000, 9.6×10^{12}
(b) 0.000 000 000 000 028, 2.8×10^{-14}
(c) 0.000 000 000 000 125, 1.25×10^{-13}
8. **(a)** 1.87×10^8 **(b)** 7.14×10^{-10}
(c) 5.51×10^{18} **(d)** 1.46×10^7
(e) 6.85×10^2 **(f)** 1.08×10^4

TEST 7
1. **(a)** $2/3$ **(b)** $2/5$ **(c)** $3/4$
2. **(a)** 10 **(b)** 16 **(c)** 48
(d) $13\frac{1}{3}$ **(e)** $14\frac{1}{4}$ **(f)** $7\frac{1}{2}$
3. **(a)** $11/50$ **(b)** $2/5$ **(c)** $2/15$
(d) $3/16$
4. $11/18\,(44/72),\ 15/24\,(45/72),\ 23/36\,(46/72),\ 2/3\,(48/72)$
5. **(a)** $13/15$ **(b)** $7/15$ **(c)** $2/15$
(d) $1\frac{9}{40}$ **(e)** $1/24$ **(f)** $1/2$
(g) $1/30$ **(h)** $1\frac{19}{30}$ **(i)** $7/1$
6. **(a)** $1\frac{7}{8}$ **(b)** $5/6$ **(c)** $2/9$

(d) $1\frac{3}{25}$ **(e)** $1\frac{1}{24}$ **(f)** $5\frac{7}{20}$
(g) $2\frac{1}{5}$ **(h)** $2/5$
7. **(a)** 0.8 **(b)** 0.35 **(c)** 0.36
(d) 0.06 **(e)** 0.6 **(f)** 0.175
8. **(a)** $7/10$ **(b)** $3/25$ **(c)** $81/250$
(d) $3/40$ **(e)** $1/2000$ **(f)** $13/200$
9. **(a)** $4/9$ **(b)** $5/33$ **(c)** $25/111$
(d) $7/45$ **(e)** $5/66$ **(f)** $1606/4995$
10. See questions 5 to 9

TEST 8
1. **(a)** 70% **(b)** 45% **(c)** 32.5%
(d) 43.5% **(e)** 36% **(f)** 26.6%
(g) 21% **(h)** 7% **(i)** 12.5%
2. **(a)** $3/20$ **(b)** $9/25$ **(c)** $3/5$
(d) $1/8$ **(e)** $5/8$ **(f)** $3/40$
3. **(a)** 0.15 **(b)** 0.36 **(c)** 0.6
(d) 0.125 **(e)** 0.625 **(f)** 0.075
4. 1.5%
5. **(a)** 85% **(b)** 8% **(c)** 3.75%
6. **(a)** 20 **(b)** 60 **(c)** £15.40
(d) £8.75 **(e)** 42 **(f)** 27 pence
7. **(a)** £18 **(b)** £255 **(c)** £252
(d) £154
8. 74.1kg
9. 34 pence
10. **(a)** £147.50 **(b)** 12% **(c)** £140
11. **(a)** £11.05 **(b)** 20% **(c)** £14
12. **(a)** $216/1.08 = 200$
(b) $135/0.9 = 150$ cm
13. **(a)** 9×10^4 **(b)** 3.68×10^{-1}
14. **(a)** 16.4 …cm **(b)** 18 days
15. **(a)** 70.91 … million **(b)** 31 years

TEST 9
1. £1662
2. £1457
3. Small: 0.357 … pence per g
Large: 0.36 pence per g
So small bar is the better buy
4. £150
5. £874.18
6. **(a)** £460.13 **(b)** £220.11

TEST 10
1. **(a)** 5 : 8 5 : 6 2 : 3
(b) $1 : 8/5$ $1 : 6/5$ $1 : 3/2$
(c) $5/8 : 1$ $5/6 : 1$ $2/3 : 1$
2. £20
3. **(a)** 84 **(b)** 32

4. 400 ml
5. 75 g
6. (a) 14, 21   (b) James: £35, Sue: £20
7. (a) 48 black, 80 red   (b) 12 : 25
8. 78 degrees (angle sum of triangle = 180°)
9. £160, £240, £280 and £320
10. (a) 2   (b) 4
11. (a) 25   (b) ⅓

TEST 11

1. (a) 12 min   (b) 5 hours 18 min
   (c) 3 hours 45 min   (d) 2 hours 21 min
2. (a) 0.4 hours   (b) 5.8 hours
   (c) 3.25 hours   (d) 6.95 hours
3. (a) 315 km   (b) 5 hours 48 min
   (c) 54.3 … km/h
4. 60 km/h
5. 140 km
6. 0846
7. (a) 105.3 km/h   (b) 1135
   (c) 77 km
8. (a) 0.579 m³   (b) 11 655 kg

TEST 12

1. (a) $2\sqrt{3}$ (b) $2\sqrt{5}$ (c) $3\sqrt{5}$
   (d) $4\sqrt{5}$ (e) $3\sqrt{3}$ (f) $5\sqrt{2}$
2. (a) 6   (b) 9   (c) $2\sqrt{10}$
   (d) $16\sqrt{3}$ (e) $6\sqrt{2}$ (f) $6\sqrt{5}$
3. (a) $4\sqrt{3}$ (b) 36   (c) $3\sqrt{2}$
   (d) $5\sqrt{6}$ (e) $10\sqrt{2}$ (f) $\sqrt{10}$
4. (a) $11 - 6\sqrt{2}$ (b) $6 + 2\sqrt{5}$
   (c) $5 - 2\sqrt{6}$ (d) 48
   (e) 7   (f) $15 + 9\sqrt{3}$
5. (a) $\sqrt{3}/3$ (b) $\sqrt{10}/2$
   (c) $2\sqrt{5}$ (d) $4\sqrt{2}$
   (e) $3\sqrt{3}$ (f) $2\sqrt{2}$

ALGEBRA

TEST 13

1. (a) $9t$ (b) $5x - 4$ (c) $3p - 2q$
   (d) $3x - 6y$ (e) $6a - 3b - 2ab$
2. (a) $x + 5$ (b) $x + y$ (c) $2x$
3. $10b - a$
4. $1000 - 5x$
5. $y \times y$, y^2 and $y^5 \div y^3$
   $y + y + y$ and $2y + y$
   $y^2 + y$, $y \times y + y$ and $y(y + 1)$
6. (a) t^6 (b) x^5 (c) $12x^5$

(d) y^3 (e) y^5 (f) $5y^2$
(g) x^3y^7 (h) a^2b^2 (i) $8x^6$
(j) $4p^7$
7. (a) $3a + 15$ (b) $5x - 20$
   (c) $p^2 - 4p$ (d) $6x^2 + 12x$
   (e) $5a^2b - 15ab^2 + 10ab$
8. (a) $5t - 5$ (b) $9q - 14$
   (c) $7a + 14b$
9. (a) $3(2a + 1)$ (b) $5(2x - 3)$
   (c) $r(3r - 4)$ (d) $x(x - 1)$
   (e) $5a(a + 2)$ (f) $2ab(a^2 + 5)$

TEST 14

1. (a) 8   (b) 8   (c) 5
   (d) 10   (e) 4   (f) 4
   (g) 8   (h) 100
2. 7
3. 4.5 hours
4. (a) 4   (b) /   (c) 3
   (d) 9   (e) ⁻10   (f) ⁻6.8
   (g) 6   (h) 2   (i) ⁻12
   (j) 20
5. (a) 3.5   (b) 6.2   (c) 7
   (d) 3.5   (e) ⁻3.2   (f) ⁻0.1
   (g) ⁻0.5   (h) ⁻1.5
6. (a) 3   (b) 0.75   (c) ⁻2.5
   (d) 2   (e) 0.1   (f) 4.8
   (g) 14
7. (a) 16   (b) ⁻7.5   (c) ⁻36
   (d) 5   (e) 5.8   (f) 22.75
8. (a) $2(3x - 2) = 4(x + 5)$
   (b) $x = 12$, area $= 68$ cm²
9. (a) $6x + 30 = 360$ ∴ $x = 55°$
   (b) 150°

TEST 15

1. $2a + 3b$
2. $N = ax + by$
3. (a) $P = 2L + 2W - 8x$
   (b) $A = (L - 2x)(W - 2x)$
4. (a) 50   (b) 68   (c) 14
5. (a) 35   (b) 28
6. (a) 118   (b) 36
7. 1.47
8. (a) $x = {}^y/_5$ (b) $x = {}^{(y-2)}/_3$
   (c) $x = {}^{(y+3)}/_5$ (d) $x = {}^{(y-c)}/_a$
   (e) $x = {}^{(y-a)}/_3$ (f) $x = a(y - b)$
9. (a) $x = p^2y$ (b) $x = {}^y/_{p^2}$
   (c) $x = {}^5/_{p^2}$ (d) $x = p^2 - y$
10. (a) 3.6   (b) 8.29

11.(a) $z = {}^{(b + 3)}/_{(a - 1)}$

(b) $z = {}^{(b + d)}/_{(a - c)}$

(c) $z = {}^{(3a - b)}/_{(a - b)}$

(d) $z = {}^{y(x + 1)}/_{(x - 1)}$

(e) $z = {}^{(ay - b)}/_{(by - a)}$

(f) $z = {}^{a(y^2 + 1)}/_{(y^2 + 1)}$

TEST 16

1. (a) 29, 41 **(b)** 3, ⁻8

(c) 25, 52 **(d)** 3, 39

2. (a) $x - 2$ **(b)** $x + 6$

3. (a) 5, 8, 11, 14, 17 **(b)** ⁻9, ⁻5, ⁻1, 3, 7

(c) 1, ⁻2, 4, ⁻8, 16 **(d)** 0.25, 1, 4, 16, 64

4. (a) 4, 7, 10

(b) (i) 2, 7, 12 **(ii)** 3, 10, 17

(iii) 3, 8, 15 **(iv)** 2, 6, 12

(c) Not in $3n + 1$
(1 more than a multiple of 3 – 930 is a multiple of 3)
Not in $5n - 3$
(3 less than a multiple of 5 – 930 is a multiple of 5)
Not in $7n - 4$
(4 less than a multiple of 7 – 930 = 7 x 133 – 1, 1 less than a multiple of 7)
Not in $n^2 + 2n$
(29ᵗʰ term = 899 and 30ᵗʰ term = 960)
Yes in $n(n + 1)$ as 30ᵗʰ term = 30 x 31 = 930

5. (a) $2n + 1$ **(b)** $3n + 1$ **(c)** $4n - 3$

(d) $6n - 3$ **(e)** ${}^{(2n - 1)}/_{(4n - 1)}$

6. (a) n^2 **(b)** $n^2 + 2$

(c) $n^2 - 1$ **(d)** $2n^2$

7. (a) $2n + 4$

(b) 4 top squares remain the same
Vertical side squares increase by 2
from one pattern to the next

(c) 998

(d) 381 is odd, $2n + 4$ is even

TEST 17

1. (a)

x	⁻1	0	1	2	3
y	⁻7	⁻4	⁻1	2	5

(b)

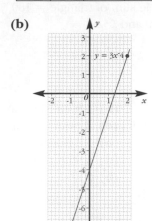

(c) $(0, ⁻4)$

2.

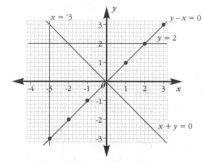

$x + y = 0$ has gradient ⁻1

3.

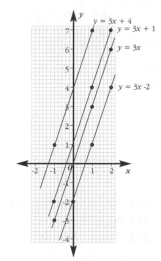

All lines are parallel

4.

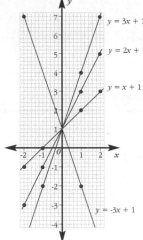

All lines have *y*-intercept 1

5. (a) (i) gradient 2, *y*-intercept 2
(ii) gradient 3, *y*-intercept ⁻1
(iii) gradient ⁻1, *y*-intercept 4
(iv) gradient ⁻2, *y*-intercept 4
(v) gradient ⁻1.5, *y*-intercept 6.5
(b)(i) $y = 2x + 2$ **(ii)** $y = 3x - 1$
(iii) $y = ⁻x + 4$ **(iv)** $y = ⁻2x + 4$
(v) $2y = ⁻3x + 13$

6. (a) $a = 2, b = 4$ **(b)** $a = ⁻8, b = 4$
(c) $a = 4, b = 6$ **(d)** $a = 2, b = 2.5$
(e) $a = ⁻6, b = 4$ **(f)** $a = 10, b = ⁻6$

7. (a) $y = ⁻^1/_2 x + 2$ **(b)** $y = 2x - 8$
(c) $y = ⁻^2/_3 x + 4$ **(d)** $y = ⁻^4/_5 x + 2$
(e) $y = 1^1/_2 x - 6$ **(f)** $y = 1^2/_3 x + 10$

8.

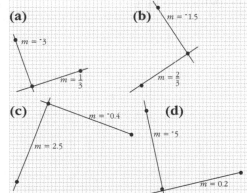

Each pair of lines is perpendicular.
Their gradients have a product of ⁻1.

9. $2y = 3 - x$ can be written as $y = ⁻^1/_2 x + 1^1/_2$
This line has gradient ⁻1/2.
$y - 2x = 7$ can be written as $y = 2x + 7$
This line has gradient 2.
$2 × ⁻^1/_2 = ⁻1$ so the lines are perpendicular.

10. $y = ⁻0.4x + 3$ (or $5y + 2x = 15$)

TEST 18

1.(a) 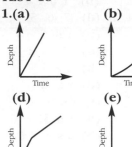   **(b)** 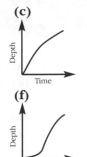   **(c)**

(d)   **(e)**   **(f)**

2.

3. (a) 0924
(b) 5km
(c) 36 minutes
(d) $4^2/_3$ (4.67) km/hour

4. (a)

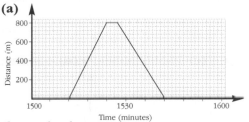

(b) 3.2 km/hour

5. (a) by 0.5 km/min
(b) *A* by 0.75 km/min²
(c) B by 0.5 km

TEST 19

1.

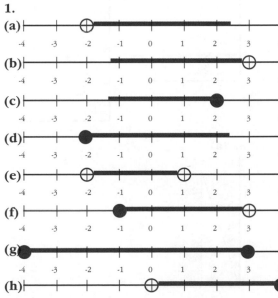

203

2. **(a)** 1, 0, 1   **(b)** ⁻1, 0, 1, 2
   (c) ⁻3, ⁻2, ⁻1, 0, 1, 2   **(d)** ⁻7, ⁻6, ⁻5, ⁻4, ⁻3

3. **(a)** $x > ^-2$ **(b)** $x \leq 3$
   (c) $^-3 \leq x < 2$ **(d)** $^-2 < x \leq 3$

4. **(a)** $x \leq 4$ **(b)** $x \geq 5$
   (c) $x < 4$ **(d)** $x \geq ^-2$
   (e) $x < ^-0.5$ **(f)** $x \leq 5$
   (g) $x \geq 2$ **(h)** $x \leq 5$

5. **(a)** $1 \leq x < 3$ **(b)** $2 \leq x < 6$
   (c) $2 < x \leq 6$ **(d)** $2 \leq x \leq 3$
   (e) $^-1 \leq x \leq 1$ **(f)** $^-2 \leq x < 3$

6. **(a)** 1, 2   **(b)** 2, 3, 4, 5
   (c) 3, 4, 5, 6   **(d)** 2, 3
   (e) ⁻1, 0, 1   **(f)** ⁻2, ⁻1, 0, 1, 2

7. **(a)**   **(b)**

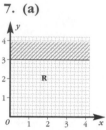 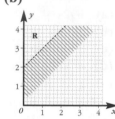

(c)   **(d)**

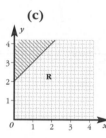 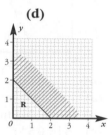

(e)   **(f)**

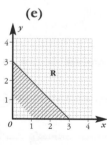 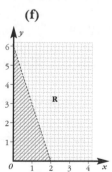

8. **(a)**

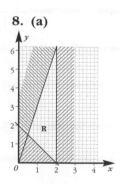

(b)   **(c)**

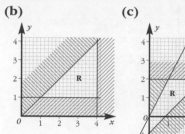

9. **(a)** $x \geq 1, y \geq 2, x + y \leq 6$
   (b) $x \leq 3, y \geq ^-2, y \leq x + 1$
   (c) $x \geq ^-3, x + y \leq 2, y \geq 2x$

TEST 20

1. **(a)** Cubic   **(b)** Linear
   (c) Quadratic   **(d)** Reciprocal

2. Reciprocal, Quadratic, Linear, Cubic, Quadratic

3. **(a)** $y = 5 - x^2$

x	⁻3	⁻2	⁻1	0	1	2	3
y	⁻4	1	4	5	4	1	⁻4

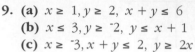
$y = x^2 - x + 3$

x	⁻2	⁻1	0	1	2	3
y	9	5	3	3	5	9

$y = x^2 + 3x - 1$

x	⁻4	⁻3	⁻2	⁻1	0	1
y	3	⁻1	⁻3	⁻3	⁻1	3

(b)

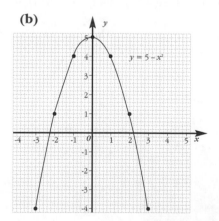

$y = 5 - x^2$

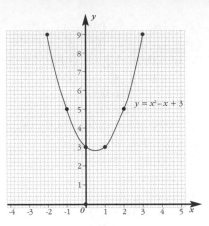

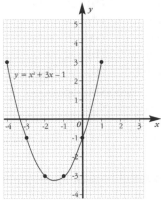

Answers to **(c)** and **(d)** are approximate
(c)(i) 2.2 and ⁻2.2 (ii) No solution
because it doesn't cross the *x*- axis.
(iii) 0.3 and ⁻3.3 (iv) 1.4 and ⁻1.4
(v) 2.6 and ⁻1.6 (vi) 0.8 and ⁻3.8
(d)(i) 1.8 and ⁻2.8 (ii) 1 and 2
(iii) 0.45 and ⁻4.45

4. (a)

x	⁻1	0	1	2	3	4	5
y	8	3	0	⁻1	0	3	8

(b)

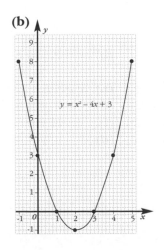

Answers to **(c)** are approximate
(c)(i) 1 and 3 (ii) 3.7 and 0.3
(iii) 4.8 and 0.2

5. (a) $x^2 = 1 - 3x$
Subtract 1 from both sides and
add $3x$ to both sides to give
$x^2 + 3x - 1 = 0$

(b) $x = 3 + \frac{1}{x}$
Multiply both sides by x.
$x^2 = 3x + 1$
Subtract $3x$ and 1 from both sides
and to give $x^2 - 3x - 1 = 0$

6. $y = 2x + 4$

7. (a)

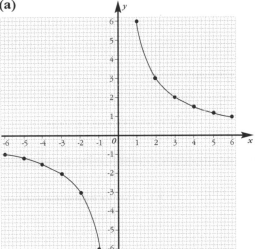

(b)

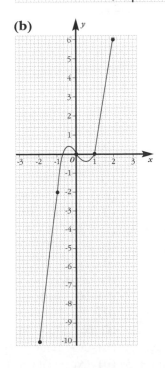

(c)

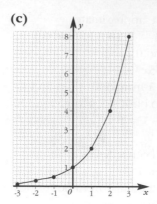

(d)

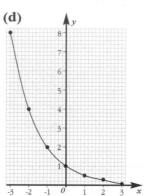

(e)

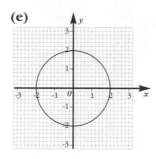

8. $x^2 + y^2 = 25$

TEST 21

1. (a) $2a + 6$ **(b)** $4x - 4$
   (c) $x^2 - x$ **(d)** $2x^2 + 2x$
   (e) $8x^2 + 2x$ **(f)** $15y^2 + 9y$

2. (a) $a^2 + 5a + 6$ **(b)** $x^2 + 7x + 10$
   (c) $2x^2 - x - 6$ **(d)** $y^2 - 7y + 10$
   (e) $2x^2 + 11x + 5$ **(f)** $5p^2 - 2p - 3$

3. (a) $x(x + 2)$ **(b)** $a(a + 1)$
   (c) $x(x - 6)$ **(d)** $2y(y - 2)$
   (e) $5x(2x - 3)$ **(f)** $2ax(ax + 2)$

4. (a) $(x + 1)(x + 2)$ **(b)** $(x + 6)(x + 1)$
   (c) $(x + 6)(x + 2)$ **(d)** $(x - 3)(x - 2)$
   (e) $(x - 7)(x + 2)$ **(f)** $(x - 5)(x - 4)$
   (g) $(x + 18)(x - 3)$ **(h)** $(x - 22)(x + 2)$

5. (a) $(2x + 1)(x + 3)$ **(b)** $(3x + 2)(x + 1)$

   (c) $(2x - 1)(x + 3)$ **(d)** $(4x - 1)(x + 3)$
   (e) $(4x - 1)(3x - 2)$ **(f)** $(3x + 2)(2x - 1)$

6. (a) $0, ^-2$ **(b)** $0, 1.5$ **(c)** $^-7, 4$
   (d) $^-8, 3$ **(e)** $2, 4$ **(f)** $10, ^-6$

7. (a) $1.5, ^-4$ **(b)** $0.5, ^-3$
   (c) $^4/_3, 1$ **(d)** $^-1, 0.75$

8. (a) $(x - 4)(x + 4)$
   (b) $(a - 10)(a + 10)$
   (c) $(2x - 3)(2x + 3)$
   (d) $(x - y)(x + y)$
   (e) $5(x - 2)(x + 2)$
   (f) $2(3x - 2y)(3x + 2y)$

9. (a) $(x + 8)^2$ **(b)** $(x - 8)^2$
   (c) $(x + 5)^2$ **(d)** $(x - 5)^2$
   (e) $(2x + 3)^2$ **(f)** $(3x - 4)^2$

10.(a) $(x + 8)^2 + 6$ **(b)** $(x - 8)^2 + 6$
   (c) $(x + 5)^2 - 5$ **(d)** $(x - 5)^2 - 30$
   (e) $(2x + 3)^2 - 2$ **(f)** $(3x - 4)^2 - 21$

11.(a) $^-4 \pm\sqrt{8}$, $^-1.17, ^-6.83$
   (b) $^-3 \pm\sqrt{13}, 0.61, ^-6.61$
   (c) $^-5 \pm\sqrt{27}, 0.20, ^-10.20$
   (d) $1 \pm\sqrt{6}, 3.45, ^-1.45$
   (e) $^{(^-1 \pm\sqrt{3})}/_2, 0.37, ^-1.37$
   (f) $^{(1 \pm\sqrt{3})}/_3, 0.91, ^-0.24$

12. See answers to questions 6, 7 and 11
The numbers beneath the square root sign
in questions 6 and 7 are all square numbers

13.(a) $4x + 3)(x - 2)$ **(b)** $^-0.75, 2$

14.(a) $x^2 + (x + 1)^2 = (x + 2)^2$
      $x^2 - 2x - 3 = 0$
   (b) $3, ^-1$
      Integers are 3, 4, 5 or $^-1, 0, 1$

15.   40.99 or 41.00 cm

16.(a) $2x^2 - 3x - 15 = 0$
   (b) $3.59, ^-2.09$
   (c) 3.64 cm

TEST 22

1. (a) $x = 2, y = 4$ **(b)** $x = 2, y = 6$
   (c) $x = 1, y = 5$

2. (a) $x = 3, y = ^-1^1/_4$ **(b)** $x = 5^1/_2, y = 1$
   (c) $x = 4, y = ^-2$ **(d)** $x = 1, y = 4^1/_2$
   (e) $x = ^-2, y = 2$ **(f)** $x = ^-1 y = 6$

3. (a) $x = ^-1, y = ^-2$ **(b)** $x = 1, y = 4$
   (c) $x = ^-2, y = ^-4$

4. (a) $x + 4y = 19; 3x + 2y = 22$
   (b) $x = 5, y = 3.5$

5. (a)

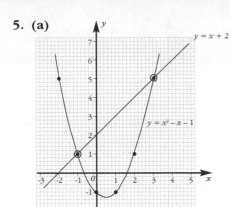
$y = x + 2$
$y = x^2 - x - 1$

(b) $x = {}^-1, y = 1$ and $x = 3, y = 5$

6. (a) $x = 1.61, y = 4.21$,
$\quad x = {}^-5.61, y = {}^-10.21$

(b) $x = 1.23, y = 2.23$,
$\quad x = {}^-1.90, y = {}^-0.90$

(c) $x = {}^-1.8, y = {}^-2.6$, $x = 1, y = 3$

(d) $x = {}^-1.43, y = 1.72$, $x = 2.23$,
$\quad y = {}^-0.12$

7. $(3.28, 2.28)$ and $({}^-2.28, {}^-3.28)$

TEST 23

1. (a) $x = 2.4$ **(b)** $x = 4.3$
   (c) $x = 3.2$ **(d)** $x = 2.6$

2. (a) ${}^-3(x + y)(x - y)$ **(b)** $2(x - 4)^2$
   (c) ${}^-33$ **(d)** $y(8x + 11y)$

4. (a) $^1/_2$ **(b)** $x - 1$
   (c) $^1/_3$ **(d)** $^1/_{(2x - 3y)}$
   (e) $x + 5$ **(f)** $^{(x - 4)}/_{(x - 1)}$
   (g) $^{(x + 1)}/_{(x + 2)}$ **(h)** $^{(x - 1)}/_{(x + 4)}$
   (i) $^{(2x + 5)}/_{3(x - 2)}$ **(j)** $^{(3x - 1)}/_{(x - 1)}$

5. (a) $^{2(x - 2)}/_{(x - 3)(x - 1)}$
   (b) $^{x^2 + 1}/_{x^2 - 1}$
   (c) $^{4x + 1}/_{(x + 1)(2x - 1)}$
   (d) $^{3 - 2x}/_{(3x + 2)(x^2 + 1)}$
   (e) $^{(x - 4)(x + 1)}/_{(x^2 + 2)(x - 1)}$

6. (a) $x = 8$ and 2.5
   (b) $x = {}^-0.51$ and 7.51
   (c) $x = ^1/_3$ and 3
   (d) $x = {}^-2.45$ and 0.20
   (e) $x = 1$ and 2.25

TEST 24

1. (a) f$(0) = {}^-2$, g$(0) = {}^-1$, h $(0) = 1$
   (b) f$(2) = 4$, g$(2) = 9$, h $(2) = 15$
   (c) f$({}^-2) = {}^-8$, g$({}^-2) = 15$, h$({}^-2) = {}^-5$

2. (a) (i) translation up 1
      (ii) translation 1 left
      (iii) stretch from x-axis, stretch factor $^1/_2$
      (iv) stretch from x-axis, stretch factor
            $^1/_2$ followed by reflection in x-axis

   (b) (i) $y = x^2 + 1$
      (ii) $y = (x + 1)^2$
      (iii) $y = ^1/_2 x^2$
      (iv) $y = {}^{-1}/_2 x^2$

3. (a)

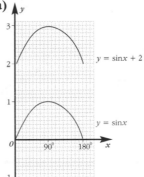
$y = \sin x + 2$
$y = \sin x$

(b)

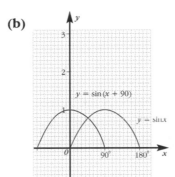
$y = \sin (x + 90)$
$y = \sin x$

(c)

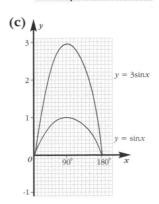
$y = 3\sin x$
$y = \sin x$

(d)

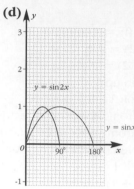

4. (a)

(i)

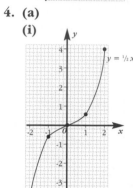

(ii)

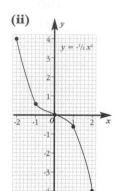

(iv)

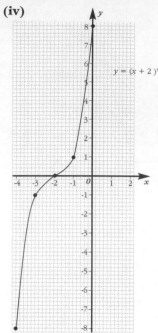

(iii)

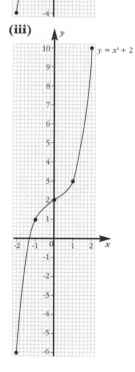

(v)

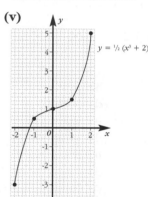

(vi)

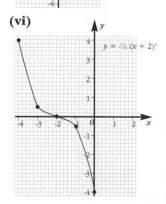

(b) (i) $(2, 4)$ (ii) $(2, ^-4)$
   (iii) $(2, 10)$ (iv) $(0, 8)$
    (v) $(2, 5)$ (vi) $(0, ^-4)$

5. (a) $y = \frac{1}{2} \cos x$
  (b) $y = \cos x + 1$

SHAPE, SPACE AND MEASURE

TEST 25

1. **(a)** 40° (supplementary angles)
   (b) 170° (sum of angles at a point = 360°)
   (c) 335° (sum of angles at a point = 360°)
2. **(a)** 110° (supplementary angles)
   (b) 65° (corresponding angles)
   (c) 120° (alternate angles)
3. **(a)** 75° (corresponding angles)
   (b) 40° (corresponding angles)
   (c) 65° (sum of angles in triangle is 180°)
   (d) 40° (sum of angles in triangle is 180°)
   (e) 65° (sum of angles in triangle is 180°)
   (f) 75° (supplementary angles)
   (g) 78° (sum of angles in triangle is 180°)
   (h) 27° (supplementary angles)
4. **(a)** 47° (sum of exterior angles − 360°)
   (b) 133° (supplementary angles)
   (c) 130° (supplementary angles)
   (d) 75° (angle sum of pentagon = 540°)
   (e) 145° (angle sum of hexagon = 720°)
5. **(a)** 72°   **(b)** 108°   **(c)** 72°
   (d) 108°   **(e)** 108°   **(f)** 108°
   (g) 160°   **(h)** 140°   **(i)** 22.5°
   (j) 67.5°   **(k)** 40°   **(l)** 85°
   (m) 24°   **(n)** 27°
6.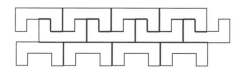

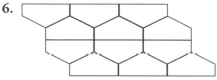

7. **(a) (i)** 040° **(ii)** 140° **(iii)** 225° **(iv)** 345°
   (b)

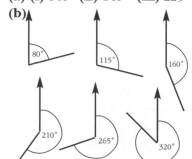

TEST 26

1. **(a)** 4 lines of symmetry
       Rotational symmetry order 4
   (b) Rotational symmetry order 2
   (c) 5 lines of symmetry
       Rotational symmetry order 5
   (d) Rotational symmetry order 4
   (e) 2 lines of symmetry
       Rotational symmetry order 2
2. **(a)**

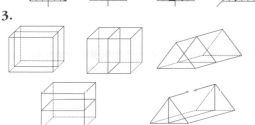

   (b)

   (c)

3.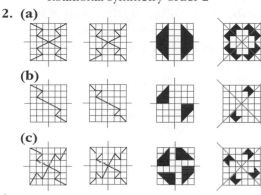

TEST 27

1. **(a)** 20°   **(b)** 40°   **(c)** 80°
   (d) 108°   **(e)** 80°   **(f)** 70°
   (g) 40°   **(h)** 72°   **(i)** 36°
   (j) 36°
4. **(a)** 105°   **(b)** 95°   **(c)** 110°
   (d) 50°   **(e)** 30°   **(f)** 30°
   (g) 150°   **(h)** 85°   **(i)** 85°
5. **(a)** Trapezium   **(b)** Rhombus
   (c) Parallelogram
6. The angles of a quadrilateral add up to 360°, so if a quadrilateral has 3 right angles then the 4ᵗʰ angle must also be a right angle because 360 − 3 x 90 = 90

TEST 28

1. **(a)** 60°   **(b)** 140°   **(c)** 55°
   (d) 110°   **(e)** 65°   **(f)** 95°
   (g) 70°   **(h)** 100°   **(i)** 110°
   (j) 30°   **(k)** 120°   **(l)** 60°
   (m) 60°   **(n)** 60°
2. **(a)** 85°   **(b)** 70°   **(c)** 30°

(d) 110°   (e) 55°   (f) 70°
(g) 145°   (h) 110°

TEST 29

1. (a) 16 cm²   (b) 20 cm²
   (c) 12 cm²   (d) 5 cm²
   (e) 16 cm²   (f) 32 cm²
   (g) 26 cm²

2. (a) Area = 33.14 cm², Perimeter = 26 cm
   (b) Area = 40.62 cm², Perimeter = 36.4 cm
   (c) Area = 52.3 cm², Perimeter = 33.4 cm

3. (a) Area = 25 x π, Circumference = 10 x π
   (b) Area = 36 x π, Circumference = 12 x π
   (c) Area = 4 x π, Circumference = 8 + 2 x π
   (d) Area = 32 x π, Circumference = 16 + 8 x π

4. (a) Length of perimeter = 405.7 m
   (b) 6857 m²

5. (a) 3.18 cm²   (b) 15.9 cm

6. 50 x π

7. (a) Area = 33.5, Perimeter = 24.4
   (b) Area = 104.7, Perimeter = 40.9
   (c) Area = 50.3, Perimeter = 32.4

8. (a) Area = 36 x π,
       Perimeter = 24 + 6 x π
   (b) Area = 5 x π, Perimeter = 8 + ⁸/₃ x π
   (c) Area = ⁹³/₄ x π,
       Perimeter = 12 + ¹⁹/₂ x π

TEST 30

1. (a) not a solid
   (b) a prism
   (c) a pyramid

2.
   (a) Plan 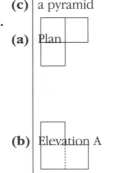   Plan

   (b) Elevation A 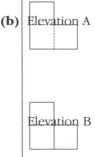   Elevation A

   Elevation B   Elevation B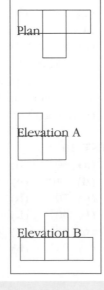

3. (a) The volume of both A and B is 90 cm³
   (b) A has the smaller surface area
       (A = 126 cm², B = 146 cm²)

4. 58 cm²

5. 57.6 cm³

6. (a) 2011 cm³   (b) 904.8 cm²

7. (a) 3.82 cm   (b) 3.09 cm

8. (a) 449.6 cm³   (b) 410 cm³
   (c) 8.38 m³   (d) 2525 cm³
   (e) 459.5 cm³

9. (a) 217.8 cm³   (b) 54.5 cm²

TEST 31

The following diagrams have been scaled down.

1.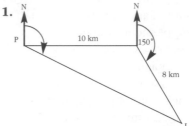

The distance of L to P is 15.6 km.
The bearing of L from P is 116°.

2.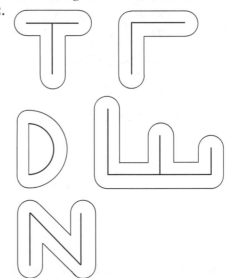

3. (a) Circle centre X radius 5 cm
   (b)

   A —5 cm— B
   3 cm
   P

   (c) Two circles both with centre X and radius 5 cm and 3 cm
   (d) Perpendicular bisector of AB.
   (e) Angle bisector of angle CAB.

4.

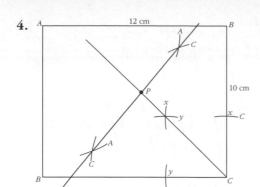

5.

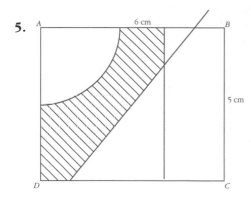

6. Check your answers with a protractor

7. Check your answers with a protractor

TEST 32

1.

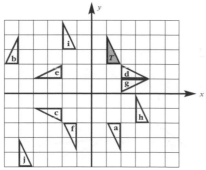

2. $T \rightarrow T_1$ by reflection in $x = -1$
$T \rightarrow T_2$ by reflection in $x = -y$
$T \rightarrow T_3$ by translation 3 right
$T \rightarrow T_4$ by translation 7 left, 2 up
$T \rightarrow T_5$ by rotation 180° about (1, 0)
$T \rightarrow T_6$ by rotation 90° anticlockwise
about (1, 1)
$T \rightarrow T_7$ by rotation 180° about (2.5, 0)
$T \rightarrow T_8$ by translation 6 left, 6 down
$T \rightarrow T_9$ by reflection in $x + y = 5$
$T \rightarrow T_{10}$ by rotation 90° anticlockwise
about (0, 1)

3. Trapezia with vertices at:
   (a) (4, 4), (4, 8), (6, 4), (6, 6)
   (b) (1, 1), (1, 2), (1.5, 1), (1.5, 1.5)
   (c) ((6, 6), (6, 12), (9, 6), (9, 9)
   (d) (⁻4, ⁻4), (⁻4, ⁻8), (⁻6, ⁻4), (⁻6, ⁻6)
   (e) (2, 8), (2, 4), (0, 8), (0, 6)
   (f) (3.5, 2), (3.5, 1), (3, 1.5), (3, 2)

4. (a) (i) eg *AHO*, *EFG*, *CID*, …
       (ii) eg *AOC*, *AEF*, *ABC*, …
       (iii) eg *OEF*, *OAF*, *OBC*, …
   (b)(i) eg *AFEGO*, *COABH*, …
      (ii) eg *EACO*, *ACEO*, …

5. $AB = AF$ (all sides of rhombus equal)
   $BC = EF$ (given)
   Angle *ABC* = angle *AFE* (opposite angles
   of rhombus) *SAS*

6. *AC* is common to both triangles
   $AB = AD$ (given)
   Angle *ABC* = angle *ADC* = 90° (angles in
   semi-circle) *RHS*

7. (a) $P = 3.75$, $Q = 4.4$
   (b) 105°

8. 675 cm³

9. (a) 12cm **(b)** 64 cm³

TEST 33

1. (a) 2 **(b)** 2.35 **(c)** 3
   (d) 3.23 **(e)** 0.734 **(f)** 0.07
   (g) 0.02 **(h)** 0.23 **(i)** 4000
   (j) 42 340

2. (a) 200 **(b)** 23 000 **(c)** 3 000 000
   (d) 230

3. (a) 0.2 **(b)** 3.562 **(c)** 0.03
   (d) 0.423 **(e)** 5 **(f)** 0.632

4. (a) 2000 **(b)** 0.346 **(c)** 3.478
   (d) 32 000 **(e)** 600 **(f)** 50

5. Clare by about 0.5 cm or 0.2 inches

6. (a) About 600 **(b)** About 4.8
   (c) About 5.7 **(d)** About 4.375
   (e) About 2.75

7. (a) 63.28 or 63.3
   (b) 9 stone 13 pounds

8. (a) 1.29 or 1.3
   (b) 1 290 000 or 1 300 000

9. (a) area **(b)** area **(c)** length
   (d) area **(e)** area **(f)** volume
   (g) volume

10.(a) length **(b)** area **(c)** volume
   (d) area **(e)** length **(f)** volume

TEST 34

1. (a) Length = 10 cm
   Area = 24 cm²
   Perimeter = 24 cm
   (b) Length = 12 cm
   Area = 30 cm²
   Perimeter = 30 cm
2. (a) ⁴/₅ **(b)** ³/₄ **(c)** ⁴/₅
   (d) ³/₅ **(e)** ⁴/₃
3. (a) 23.4 **(b)** 12.6 **(c)** 3.0
   (d) 46.6° **(e)** 9.4 **(f)** 3.2
   (g) 58.0° **(h)** 4.53
4. (a) 99.9 **(b)** 38.6°
5. (a) 20.6 **(b)** 234°
6. 25.5 m
7. $a = 37.0°$ $b = 96.8°$
   $c = 43.0°$ $d = 38.1°$
8. $w = 6.48$ $x = 8.05$
   $y = 4.78$ $z = 21.7$
9.

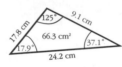 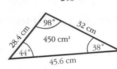

10. (a) 76.5 cm² **(b)** 61.4 cm²
11. 69.0°

TEST 35

1. (a)

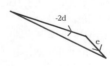

(b)

(c)

(d)

(e)

(f)

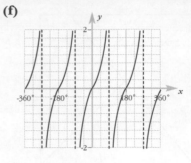

2. (a) ⁻342.5, ⁻197.5, 17.5, 162.5
   (b) ⁻162.5, ⁻17.5, 197.5, 342.5
   (c) ⁻216.9, ⁻143.1, 143.1, 216.9
   (d) ⁻338.2, ⁻158.2, 21.8, 201.8
   (e) ⁻290.5, ⁻69.5, 69.5, 290.5
   (f) ⁻196.7, ⁻16.7, 163.3, 343.3
3. e.g. ⁻287.5, ⁻72.5, 72.5, 287.5
4. e.g. ⁻30, ⁻150, 330
5. (a) 150
   (b) ⁻30, ⁻150, 210, 330
6. (a) 236.3
   (b) ⁻236.3, ⁻56.3, 123.7, 303.7

TEST 36

1. (a) $\mathbf{a} = \begin{pmatrix} 3 \\ 1 \end{pmatrix}$

   $\mathbf{b} = \begin{pmatrix} 2 \\ 3 \end{pmatrix}$

   $\mathbf{c} = \begin{pmatrix} ⁻2 \\ ⁻1 \end{pmatrix}$

   $\mathbf{d} = \begin{pmatrix} 3 \\ ⁻1 \end{pmatrix}$

   $\mathbf{e} = \begin{pmatrix} ⁻2 \\ ⁻2 \end{pmatrix}$

   (b)

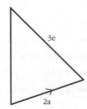

2. (a) 3a $\qquad$ **(b)** 2b

(c) a + b $\qquad$ **(d)** ⁻a + 3b

(e) ⁻4a – 2b $\qquad$ **(f)** 4a + 2b

(g) ⁻3a – 4b $\qquad$ **(h)** a – 4b

(i) a + 4b

3. (a) (i) ½ a + ½ b

(ii) ½ a + ½ b

(b) *M* and *N* are in the same position.
So the diagonals of a parallelogram
bisect each other.

4. (a) (i) 6a + 2b

(ii) 15a + 5b

(b) *PR* = 2.5*PQ*
So *PQ* and *PR* are parallel and have a
point, *P*, in common. So they must be
collinear.

(c) 2 : 3

5. $x = 1$ and $y = \frac{5}{3}$

6. (a) (i) b – a

(ii) a + 2b

(iii) ⅓a + ⅔b

(b) *OP* = ⅓*OC*
So *OP* and *OC* are parallel and have a
point, *O*, in common. So they must
be collinear.

(c) ⅓a

TEST 37

See 'Geometric Proofs' section.

DATA HANDLING

TEST 38

1.

Day	Tally	Frequency
Mon	⊞ I	6
Tue	III	3
Wed	II	2
Thu	II	2
Fri	II	2
Sat	III	3
Sun	II	2

2.

Height, *h*, cm	Tally	Frequency
$5 \le h < 10$	⊞ III	8
$10 \le h < 15$	⊞ ⊞	10
$15 \le h < 20$	⊞ II	7
$20 \le h < 25$	IIII	4
$25 \le h < 30$	I	1

3. For example

	Boys	Girls
1 packet		
2 packets		
3 packets		
4 packets		

4. For example
☐male ☐female $\qquad$ please tick
Please tick your age
☐11 ☐12 ☐13 ☐14 ☐15 ☐16
For what reasons did you read last week?
☐ For pleasure
☐ For information
☐ For homework
Which of these did you read yesterday?
☐ A novel
☐ A comic
☐ A magazine
☐ A newspaper
☐ A reference book
☐ A school textbook
☐ Other (please give details)

5. (a) Open question. A better question:
'Which of the following did you
watch on TV yesterday?'. Question
followed by a list of events with
options to tick against each event
such as: all, most, some, none.

(b) Question hard to answer and too
open.
Better question: 'Have you read a
comic in the last week?' with a Yes/No
response.

(c) Question too personal to guarantee
honest answers. Better to give a
choice of age ranges.
E.g. 15 – 20, 20 – 30, 30 – 40, … and
ask to tick a range.

(d) Leading and too open. Better question: Tick one of the following boxes
to give your opinion of R and B music.
Excellent, Good, OK, Don't like it
much, Hate it.

6. 25% (⁵⁄₂₀) of blue-eyed people surveyed are
blonde.
30% (³⁄₁₀) of green-eyed people surveyed
are blonde.
So the hypothesis is false.

7. People at work not included.
People who are not local are not included.
People who do not shop at the newsagent
are not included.

8. To make sure of a representative sample
choose a stratified random sample with
the proportions of each year group *and*
boys and girls equivalent to those in the
whole school.

9. 17, 20, 16, 22, 25

10. **(a)** 24 **(b)** 8

TEST 39

1. **(a)** *A* 15, *B* 10 **(b)** 20%
   (c) *A* scores 33 goals in 15 games
   B scores **23** goals in 10 games
   33 : 15 = 11 : 5 = **22** : 10,
   so hypothesis disproved.

2. Angles are: Bus 100°, Train 60°, Walk 200°

3. £20

4.
   ```
   2 | 8  9
   3 | 2  6  7  8
   4 | 0  2  3  4  5
   5 | 1
   ```
   | 3 | 8   means 3.8 kg |

5. Plant *B* has longer leaves and a wider
   spread of lengths.

6. **(a)**

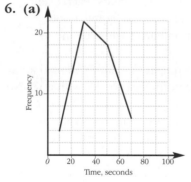

(b)

Time, t, seconds	$<$ 20	$<$ 40	$<$ 60	$<$ 80
Cumulative frequency	4	26	44	50

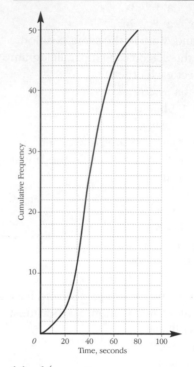

(c) 14

7. **(a)**

Time, t, minutes	$0 \leq t <$ 10	$10 \leq t <$ 15	$15 \leq t <$ 25	$25 \leq t <$ 50
Frequency density	0.8	2.8	1.8	0.4

(b)

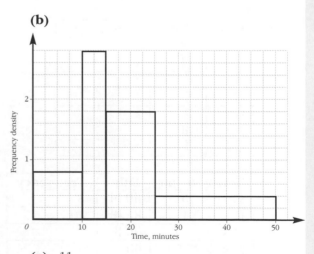

(c) 11

TEST 40

1. 3, 3, 4, 10, 20

2. (a) 27 cm

   (b) 145 cm

   (c) 143 cm

3. Mode = 2 rings

   Median = 2.5 rings

   Mean = 2.6 rings

   Range = 4 rings

4. (a)

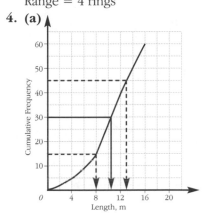

   (b) Median = 10.5 m, IQR = 5 m

   (c)

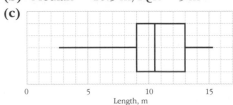

5. (a) £9.60

   (b)

Wage, w, £	< 5	< 10	< 15	< 20	< 25
Cumulative frequency	12	30	40	47	50

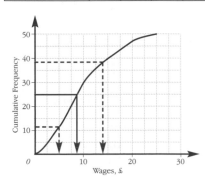

   (c) Median = £8

   IQR = £8.50

(d)

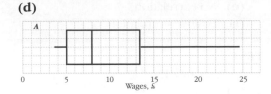

(e) Company *B* pays higher wages. Their spread of wages is also higher with the top 50% earning > £16 per hour whereas the top 50% for company *A* earn only £8 or more.

TEST 41

1. (a)

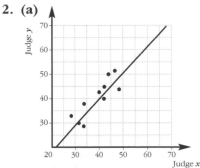

   (b) See diagram

   (c) Positive correlation. As the length increases so does the weight

   (d) 48 to 50 cm

2. (a)

   (b) See diagram

   (c) *Y*

   (d) About 60–65

      No. Previous marks not this high so no data on which to base estimate.

3. (a) Positive correlation

   (b) Negative correlation

   (c) No correlation

   (d) Negative correlation

(e) No correlation

(f) Positive correlation.

TEST 42

1. 18, 18.5 and 19

2. (a)

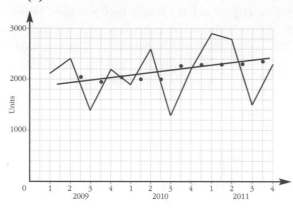

(b) 2025
1975
2025
2000
2000
2250
2300
2350
2375

(c) See diagram

(d) Steady use in 2009 then an increase of about 300 units a quarter from 2010 onwards.

TEST 43

1. (a) $^{50}/_{175}$ (b) $^{2}/_{175}$ (c) $^{1}/_{175}$

2. (a) $^{20}/_{80}$ (b) $^{12}/_{60}$

3. (a) $^{42}/_{600}$

(b) Dice is unlikely to be fair.
If it was you would expect closer to 100 sixes in 600 throws

4. (a)

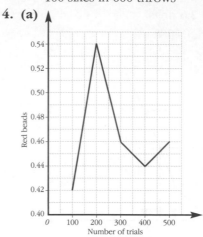

(b) 460

5. 0.45

6. Soup and Fish
Soup and Chicken
Soup and Pasta
Melon and Fish
Melon and Chicken
Melon and Pasta

7. (a) The addition rule can only be used when events are mutually exclusive. Left-handedness and wearing glasses are not mutually exclusive

(b) 0.24

8. (a)

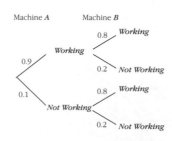

(b) 0.72 (c) 0.26

9. (a) $^{49}/_{100}$ (b) $^{42}/_{100}$

10. (a) $^{42}/_{90}$ (b) $^{42}/_{90}$

INDEX

INDEX

INDEX

INDEX

INDEX

INDEX

INDEX

INDEX